Employment Practice and Policies in Youth, Community and Play Work

(Second Edition)

In Pursuit of Fairness at Work

Doug Nicholls

General Secretary of the
Community and Youth Workers' Union
www.cywu.org.uk

Russell House Pu

D1332967

First published in 1995 with Second Edition in 2002 by:
Russell House Publishing Ltd.
4 St. George's House
Uplyme Road
Lyme Regis
Dorset DT7 3LS

Tel: 01297-443948
Fax: 01297-442722
e-mail: help@russellhouse.co.uk
www.russellhouse.co.uk

British Library Cataloguing-in-publication Data:
A catalogue record for this book is available from the British Library.

ISBN: 1-898924-63-5

Typeset by The Hallamshire Press Limited, Sheffield

Printed by Bell and Bain, Glasgow

Russell House Publishing

Is a group of social work, probation, education and youth and community work practitioners and academics working in collaboration with a professional publishing team. Our aim is to work closely with the field to produce innovative and valuable materials to help managers, trainers, practitioners and students. We are keen to receive feedback on publications and new ideas for future projects.

CONTENTS

Foreword

Alan Johnson MP, Minister of State for Employment Relations
and the Regions, DTI

Since the Government took office in 1997, we have placed a high priority on modernising employment law and fostering a partnership approach in the workplace. We have had two overriding objectives in doing so. First, to introduce decent, civilised standards at the workplace while ensuring that more and more people are able to gain access to that workplace. Second, to establish a lasting settlement in which basic employment rights are no longer party political issues but an accepted part of the employment landscape.

On the legislative front, we have introduced a number of new rights and strengthened others. For example, we now have a national minimum wage, a statutory procedure for trade union recognition, new protection against unfair dismissal for taking industrial action, working time regulations which give new rights to paid annual leave and protections against excessive working hours, new parental leave and improved maternity leave rights and new rights to time off for family emergencies. In addition we are protecting vulnerable groups through new measures to protect part-time and agency workers, whistleblowers and people on fixed term contracts.

At the same time, we are pursuing non-legislative means of developing partnerships in the workplace, which are essential to effective performance. Partnership applies to all organisations, private, public and voluntary. Within organisations it is important to involve everyone: managers, employees and employee representatives. Working together in partnership can have benefits for all parties: greater job satisfaction for the workforce; increased productivity for owners of the business and enhanced competitiveness for the economy as a whole. By jointly developing new working practices and supporting more flexible ways of working, employers can match the wishes and circumstances of their staff with the needs and demands of the organisation and of the people it serves.

I wish this edition of *Employment Practice and Policies in Youth, Community and Play Work* as much success as the first.

Author's Note

Youth, community and play workers are mainly employed by local authorities, but also by a bewildering variety of employers in the voluntary sector ranging from major national voluntary organisations, to small neighbourhood community projects. Local authority procedures and management can often be over-elaborate, bureaucratic, legalistic and daunting, while small scale voluntary sector employment practice can be frighteningly subjective, amateur and ill informed. The model procedures in this book have been written with both of these employment contexts in mind, but they may need modification according to the employer concerned.

A management committee comprised of unemployed local activists is very different from an employer with over ten professional personnel officers. Yet both can make the same mistakes when dealing with youth, community and play workers and their distinctive working patterns and methods. Given the diversity of employing backgrounds and the need to bring some rationale and harmonisation to them, the book concentrates in several places on matters of principle: what to look for in a procedure rather than the full procedure itself. Models of procedures which have become central through practice have been included. Naturally all models are presented here for local amendment. Please use them to improve things where you work or manage, but I refuse to be held liable for any misapplication!

Another fairly unusual aspect of youth, community and play work employment is that most workers are also managers. Nearly all full-time workers manage volunteers and paid staff. Increasingly part-time leaders in charge manage other part-time workers. It is vitally important therefore to develop user-friendly employment policies and procedures which can assist rather than block educational and potentially liberating practice. I believe it is also essential that more of the detail of employment procedures is taught on training courses. Indeed the last version of the *Guidelines to the Endorsement of Regional Accreditation and Moderation Schemes* (a document produced by the NYA, see Appendix 6) recognised this fact and strengthened the management section requirements.

You would perhaps expect me to say that the quality of employment practice in an organisation most reveals its values and ethos. Bullying, aggressive, trigger-happy, gung-ho management styles which do unfortunately exist, are incompatible both locally and nationally with youth, community and play work practice and the sooner they are eradicated the more young people and communities will benefit.

But worse, I have always thought, than either the Ghengis Khan or the ultra leftist approaches to managing employment relations, is the insipid 'let's all get on together nicely' approach. 'The work is about relationships so let's have nice working relationships, we are all one family.' Ultimately this leads to psychological stress because of the absence of established and workable, problem-solving procedures. Recognising differences of interest is surely an important first step in organisational development. At work youth, community and play workers are not part of a family: they are part of a professional team.

More and more employers in different sections are employing youth, community and play workers for their adaptable and informal approaches to education and to building groups and positive relationships. While appreciating their worker's skills, these new employers are often inexperienced in creating the employment environment that reflects and nourishes their distinctive professional development. Just as we have a specialist set of terms and conditions for youth, community and play work, the *JNC Report*, so we should now build up a set of practices for employment that enhance its work and culture.

My thumb aches from repeatedly typing 'youth, community and play workers'; really I should have written on each occasion 'youth workers, community workers, play workers and other informal education staff', which might have given me a full affliction of repetitive strain injury. Nevertheless I believe that much of this book will relate equally to the different groups across the sector, but can find no easy phrase to encompass them all.

I hope that this book will be equally relevant to all parts of Britain and that colleagues in other countries, can make something of it too. I have been particularly mindful of the developments currently taking place in America and South Africa to put youth work on a firmer footing and to consider the question of trade unionism and professional associations.

As this is a unique publication within the sector I would welcome any comment and suggestions for alteration and addition.

Finally, as Alan Johnson MP has indicated in his Introduction, the employment culture has changed. Fairness and partnership are now essential to the modern workplace, even more so in our sphere of activity where the treatment of individuals and groups is our primary concern. Since the last edition of this book over 26 new employment laws have been introduced, the Joint Negotiating Committee (JNC) has included part-time workers under a National Agreement and thereby encouraged the adoption of the principle of parity of treatment which the first edition of this book advocated and for which, CYWU had campaigned for fifteen years. New structures for youth, community and play work delivery are being created and many new employers, often through time expired short term schemes, have started to employ staff in these areas: frequently with disastrous results. New voluntary sector organisations are starting to adopt the youth work approach and employ JNC staff, and the voluntary sector as a whole is reviewing its infrastructure and employment practice.

CYWU itself has changed dramatically since 1994, particularly by providing more training and preventative work for individuals and organisations on employment practice and health and safety. New laws are affecting the recognition of trade unions and new principles of workplace relations have replaced the brutal regimes encouraged by the Tories. From the bleak and depressing days when the first edition of this book was written, youth, community and play workers are entering a new terrain in which decency and fairness at work can again start to be asserted on the basis of responsible and respected trade unionism. However it is too soon to relax. In August 2000 CYWU recorded one of its worst months on record for casework. August is usually quiet, but this year it received, on average, twenty serious casework referrals a week and there was real evidence of deteriorating workplace relations throughout the country. It is also pursuing its most tragic stress cases through the courts and 'burnout' has become endemic once again. These circumstances gave me impetus to republish this book and hope that it can be integrated with both CYWU's new projects designed to provide training and support for improved employment practice and staff development and the government's own initiatives in these areas. I also hope that perhaps this new edition can be on the bookshelf alongside two other publications which have been published since the last edition to encourage the development of improved workplace practice: *Health and Safety in Youth and Community Work* and *Managing Violence and Aggression in Youth and Community Work*.

Another great change since the last edition of this book has been the growth of the internet. Through its affiliation to various databases and research agencies CYWU can access the most up to date information available, and also has its own website where much employment related material can be found: www.cywu.org.uk. The websites of the Trades Union Congress and General Federation of Trade Unions will also be useful to you: www.tuc.org.uk and www.gftu.org.uk.

I have tried to take most of the recent government changes into account in this edition and while my acknowledgements to the previous edition remain valid I would also like to thank Dave Proctor, CYWU's National Caseworker and Negotiator for his comments and his provision of the new Model Partnership Agreement drafted by him and amended by a CYWU Staff Team meeting. In October 2000 the new Human Rights Act was introduced and I see the urgent need to improve employment practice in our sector as a very real and necessary part of attaining some basic human rights for highly skilled and important groups of workers. No person is an island. We all need each other in collective action at work so that services to children, young people and communities can be improved. Hence once again the return to trade unionism.

Doug Nicholls, November 2000

Part 1

The Joint Negotiating Committee Report

A brief guide

The full title of this important document is the *Report of the Joint Negotiating Committee for Youth and Community Workers*, but in this book it is generally referred to as the JNC Report. The Unions call it the Pink Book, while some employers have referred to it as the Fuchsia Book. Whatever the colour of the next issue, this is one document that should be available in every single workplace where youth, community and play workers are employed. It is available in an accessible format with a regular updating service from either the Employers' Side or from the Staff Side (see Appendix 4 for addresses). It is important when ordering the *JNC Report* to get a full copy of the Equal Opportunities Joint Advisory Booklet that is a separate document, but which is integral to the *JNC Report*. See Appendix 2 and Appendix 3 of this book for details of the matters dealt with by these documents.

Every year a JNC claim is submitted by the Staff Side. This itself can make interesting reading about the state of youth, community and play work, and copies of this are kept by CYWU (contact details see Appendix 4).

There is a separate book or *Report* for youth and community officers known as *Soulbury* or the *Soulbury Report*. Additionally, there is another book for clerical and administrative and ancillary staff known as the *Single Status Agreement* or *Green Book*. All workers within the youth, community and play work service should be covered by one of these reports. All youth, community and play workplaces are advised to have copies of these reports and the latest updates on their shelves.

The *JNC Report* says that where it is silent on a particular aspect of employment practice the conditions of the Single Status Agreement should apply or other appropriate local conditions. While the Staff Side of the JNC continues to try and make the *JNC Report* more detailed in its coverage, it is extremely advisable to ensure that everyone locally knows exactly what procedure applies to youth, community and play work staff. It is hoped that the checklist in the Model Agreement on Part-time Workers in Part 2 will help achieve this locally.

The JNC itself is a free standing, national, collective bargaining committee. This means that without any external interference the representative bodies of the employers and the workers within youth, community and play work come together on a regular basis to negotiate on aspects of pay terms and conditions for full and part-time youth, community and some play workers. On the Staff Side of the JNC, the CYWU is the majority union. The biggest organisation of the Employers' Side is naturally the Local Government Association, but the really good thing about the Employers' Side is that it includes representatives of the main voluntary sector umbrella bodies in community work and youth work, among them, *Community Matters* for the National Council for Voluntary Youth Services (NCVYS). In addition, employers in Wales are represented by the Welsh Joint

Education Committee and Council for Wales Voluntary Youth Services. Northern Ireland is discussing closer integration with the JNC. Scotland has its own separate arrangements. Perhaps one weakness of the Employers' Side is that it does not yet represent the smaller local authority employers like parish and district councils which are beginning to employ workers qualified to JNC standards, as are health authorities and new *Connexions* services.

Because of this Employers' Side composition, it is quite clear that the terms and conditions of the *JNC Report* should apply equally in the voluntary and local authority sectors. In fact, the *JNC Report* itself says that it has within its purview 'persons (qualified or otherwise) employed full-time or part-time as youth, community and play workers by voluntary organisations in receipt of a grant from local education authorities, or from the Department for Education.'

So, whatever the size of the employer, whether they are voluntary sector or local authorities, they are all signatories to the JNC by virtue of their position. This means that they must apply the conditions of the *JNC Report*. Both the Employers' Side and the Staff Side get together to intervene if any local employer is breaking the terms of the National Agreement.

Both sides of the JNC have their own secretaries. The Employers' Side Secretary is a member of staff at the Employers' Organisation, a national body which manages negotiations and industrial relations issues for local authorities as a whole. Meetings of the JNC are usually held in the offices of the Employers' Organisation or the National Union of Teachers. The Employees' Side Secretary is a member of staff of the National Union of Teachers (NUT), the trade union which has held this position since the inception of the JNC and which is a partner union of CYWU. Often the JNC Secretaries, as they are known, will meet and progress issues between full JNC meetings. Additionally, local employers contact the national Employers' Side Secretary with routine queries throughout the year, as do the Unions with their Secretary.

Both sides of the JNC will issue questionnaires and guidance notes to their constituencies throughout the year. Occasionally, the JNC will come to an agreement between negotiations and request that a Circular goes out to all employing organisations. These are known as Joint Education Services Circulars (JESCs). Within the local authorities these usually go to Chief Executives and Directors of Education and should get passed down to Principal Youth and Community Officers. It is less clear how the communication system works within the voluntary sector, though the Chief Executives of the larger organisations appear to be sent circulars. It is worth remembering that every employing organisation in our sector has access to the processes of JNC and the information that comes from it.

The JNC's main function is of course to agree salary levels and other conditions. But it is strengthened in doing this because its other main function is 'to recognise as conferring qualified status to youth, community and play workers qualifications which have been professionally endorsed or individually approved by the National Youth Agency and Wales Youth Agency' (Education and Training Standards Sub Committee). Thus in this book, a JNC worker means a worker who is qualified to the standards set by the JNC, and whose contract of employment is governed by the JNC terms and conditions set out in the *JNC Report*.

Until 1982, if a College wanted to put on a new course to qualify youth, community and play workers, they would send their submission to CYWU (or its predecessor unions). The Union would send representatives to the College to read the submission and make comment. Gradually this process developed and more people became involved in the endorsement of courses, particularly representatives from both sides of the JNC. Then in 1982, the Council for Education and Training in Youth and Community and Play Work (CETYCW) was established and this officially took on the role of 'professional endorsement'. In 1990, CETYCW's functions were transferred to the National Youth Agency which established a peer-led endorsement body known as ETS (Education and Training Standards). Throughout this process it is important to note that the JNC and the Government through the Department for Education signed a Memorandum of Understanding (see Appendix 6) which delegates the endorsement process to the NYA Advisory Council. An identical arrangements exists via the Wales Assembly, and the Wales Youth Agency (WYA).

If a University, or other institution, wants to put on a qualifying course, it seeks an NYA or WYA advisor from the ETS. It then puts together a written course submission. The ETS committee appoints a working party to read the submission and visit the institution. The working party assesses the submission and the responses to questions about it, according to nationally agreed *Guidelines to*

Endorsement of Initial Training. This process is becoming increasingly professionalised to the extent that *Guidelines* have been recently revised through a consultative exercise throughout the youth, community and play service. A pool of individuals is elected to form working parties which are inducted and trained. Importantly, the function of peer-led professional endorsement also extends to the newly formed *Regional Accreditation and Moderation Panels (RAMPs)* which, if they are approved, will then endorse local part-time worker training courses. It is hoped that a similar arrangement will be made for all future providers of training courses.

Because of this vital and close inter-relationship between the JNC and qualification, the JNC Secretaries are both members of the Executive Board of the NYA and representatives of both sides of JNC are elected to the ETS Committee and the NYA Advisory Council. In turn, as the majority union, the CYWU has representatives on University Boards, *RAMP* committees and an annual training event for students.

Another important connection, between the JNC and training, is that the JNC Grading Matrix, which sets out the ranges of duties undertaken by youth, community and play workers has frequently been used to give structure to training courses and curricula. Workers are trained according to the JNC work expectations. A great deal of the work to consider validating learning from experience has also referred to the *JNC Report* for outlines, as has recent work to define the distinctive elements of youth, community and play work training.

The JNC is, then, much more significant to the professional development of youth, community and play work than a simple fight over wages. Both the unions and the employers have a shared interest in ensuring that the highest standards of education and training are developed within the sector. It is also important to bear in mind that the new *Framework for Inspection of Youth Services*, published by Ofsted, maintains their long term commitment to quality by advocating the appointment of JNC qualified staff. It is interesting to note that those local authorities that tend to diminish the educational importance of youth, community and play work, have also tended to move workers away, from a qualification requirement and on to the, much worse, Single Status provisions. The JNC tendency is to make the requirement for youth, community and play qualification more specialist. Until 1988 for example, a teaching qualification was automatically considered as an entitlement to appointment on JNC terms and conditions, but this is no longer the case. Only those with a teaching qualification obtained prior to December 1988, will receive JNC pay and conditions, if working within the youth, community and play service. All those who qualified after, do not automatically get this status.

The JNC pay year runs from September 1st, so if a pay claim is not settled until October or later, the Award has to be backdated to September 1st. Employing organisations which are part of the JNC either in the voluntary or local authority sectors, must automatically pass on the Award made by JNC. If they do not, they are breaking the National Agreement and should be reported to the Joint Secretaries. Other agreements on Conditions of Service can be made throughout the year and reported back to the local employers through Circulars and updates to the *JNC Report*.

The key player obviously in formulating the JNC annual claim, is CYWU as the majority union, though often the concerns of the other unions, particularly the education unions NATFHE and NUT are fully incorporated into the claim. In any event, the draft claim prepared by the Staff Side Secretary is always subject to scrutiny by the constituent unions. CYWU formulates the outline of its pay claim at its national conference in April or May. Branches submit Motions. The Union also elects an eight-person National Negotiating Committee to sit on JNC known as the Salaries and Tenure Committee (S and T). Following conference S and T meets to put together the conference decisions. It then takes these points for debate to the meeting of the JNC unions, the Staff Side. The Staff Side debates the claim and puts it together for submission to the employers. The employers usually circulate this in full to local employing organisations who deal with it in various ways. Often, it is left to the Principal Youth Officer (PYO) or the Chief Executive to return some comments. The employers' side then digest these comments and a first full JNC meeting is held to begin negotiations on the claim. Meetings continue until there is a settlement for the year. From time to time the JNC will set up specialist working parties to consider aspects of claims: previous working parties have considered part-time workers (1994) and the grading matrix (1987). Such working parties can include 'experts' from outside the JNC for professional advice, but their reports must go back to the full JNC.

The JNC's position on part-time workers is detailed in Part 2 of this book. This section comments on some other important aspects of the *JNC Report* that are always a source of either 'negotiating interest' or ignorance, especially at local level. I have set out in Appendix 2 the full list of matters dealt with by the *JNC Report*, which takes into account the comprehensive revisions and updating made to the *Report* in 1999. The more comprehensive a National Agreement, the better it is for both management and workers, and each year new aspects are added to the *JNC Report*, so it really is worth subscribing.

Levels and scales

The *JNC Report* comprehends five different pay levels taken in ascending order of seniority, trainee, Level 1, Level 2, Level 3 and 'off scale points'. Off scale points are scales above the stated maxima, and awarded according to local discretion and negotiation to the largest and most senior posts which are covered by the *JNC Report*. These five levels are split across two categories of staff, JNC qualified staff working full or part-time, and staff with a local qualification working part-time.

Within Levels 2 and 3 there are incremental scales. Level 2 is an eleven point level with three scales of nine points within it. Posts within Level 2 could be graded therefore A, B or C. Level 3 is a seven point level with three scales of four points within it. Posts are therefore graded as both a level and a scale. There are additional increments on each level and scale for someone with a longer or higher training or qualification and of course for the various geographical weightings in the London area. In choosing scales within the levels the employers and unions are guided by some outline factors that have to be taken into account and which are set out in Paragraph 16 of the *JNC Report*. Every year a worker on *JNC Report* terms and conditions receives an annual increment and goes up one point on their scale. When they reach the top of the scale, unfortunately they stay there unless the grading of the post is reviewed. Annual increments are awarded on 1st April each year unless someone has transferred from teaching or *Soulbury Report* scales when their increment will be paid as of 1st September. Each year staff on *JNC Report* terms and conditions will receive a pay award negotiated by the unions within the JNC. Whenever this is agreed it takes effect as of 1st June. Workers temporarily acting up for more than four weeks into a more highly graded post than their own should receive the grading of that post for the period of their acting up.

Working time

What is a session? To ask the question is to threaten the professional deployment and flexibility required by professional judgement in the field. The *JNC Report* requires that 'work should be allocated fairly and reasonably according to the needs of the service locally and should not normally exceed ten sessions a week. There should be no more than eight evening sessions per fortnight.' This concept of a sessionally based week goes back to the origin of the *JNC Report* in 1961, when it was 11 sessions a week! The sessional requirement is a fundamental recognition of the professionalism of the service and the unpredictability and variety of work that is undertaken. By deliberately not specifying the number of hours of work that should be worked in a week, the *JNC Report* says that the deployment of time is best left to the professional worker and the local management structure. It recognises that a crisis session to counsel a young person may last five hours and that a piece of high quality group work may take a contemplative week to organise and two hours to deliver. Neither unions nor management have sought to change the sessional requirement in national negotiations. However, it was agreed in 1999, to add to the sessional requirement the following formulation on hours: 'The standard working week for full-time youth, community and play workers is 37 (36 in London).' This provides a safety limit to the excessive hours still expected by employers and worked by many staff for the good of the service. Similarly, eight evening sessions are not to be considered as minima. They are a safeguarding maximum.

However, in the drift towards new 'managerialism' and quasi industrial styles of management and mechanistic notions of accountability, employers at local level have begun to impose a variety of measures that undermine the professionalism of the sessional working week. Some have unilaterally introduced 37-hour-weeks into the contracts. Some, taking a more progressive line, have local agreements deciding on a 30 hour week. Many hours have been spent at the desktop publisher, producing timesheets, forecast sheets, numbers of child or adult counting sheets, computerised recording sheets for face to face work, and numerous other devices and reams of paper to compartmentalise time and generate statistics, often more akin to science fiction than a realist socialist novel, for bemused elected members troubled by 'gangs' of youths on their street corners. Workers are increasingly facing disciplinary action for failing to account properly for half an hour, or ten minute, units of time. The shattering of the sessional working week into ever smaller units has fragmented, in some employing organisations, the morale of workers used to deploying time in the best interests of the communities with whom they work and the effectiveness of their own contribution.

On the other hand, with so much of youth, community and play work originating in philanthropy, with so many of these workers deeply committed to what they do and enjoying it, there has been an equally dangerous trend amongst workers themselves to do nothing except work. The endless demands of a project, the endless needs of young people, children and hard pressed communities, the lack of administrative support, the frequent lack of effective management support, the competing demands of management committees, local authorities and users, all of these ingredients cause many youth, community and play workers to over-stretch themselves and work far too many hours. Every session worked beyond the agreed ten in a week is part of someone else's job. The amount of voluntary work performed by youth, community and play workers would be unthinkable in many other sectors, but equally, the 'knock off at five regardless of what's happening' attitude that can develop where management have imposed strict time-clock patterns, should not be encouraged in youth, community and play work.

While it is not professional for employers to continually nail workers down with tightly described hours of work, it is equally unprofessional for workers to overdo it and ultimately make themselves ineffective and diminish the service. The service is already chronically understaffed as it is. Isn't it better, if you have a lot to do, to campaign for another member of staff? Doesn't the community ultimately benefit from the provision of more workers? Is it really in the interests of workers, communities and employers to have workers working extra hours in order to cover for service cuts?

A session should be a professionally managed and deployed unit of time, mainly designed by the worker involved, but stemming from and approved through effective supervision. This is how the accountability should be shaped.

Because of the largely anti-social and fluctuating basis of youth, community and play workers' hours it is often tempting to work a three session day, or more than the maximum eight evening sessions a week, or worse still, not to take time off in lieu for residential and other work. The perpetual shifting-shift system is also not particularly good for your health unless there are clear restrictions and guidelines. Employers and unions must be clear on the local arrangements on these matters.

In terms of the duration of the working day and week, this is now covered by new laws and regulations. No one on JNC terms and conditions should work more than a three session day, and sessions involving residentials, international exchanges and trips should be sufficiently staffed to ensure that workers can have proper breaks. Furthermore in paragraph 5.1 the *JNC Report* has reiterated that the employers must abide by health and safety regulations and the new working time legislation, and they must compensate staff where hours vary from the normal pattern.

It is relevant to consider at this stage some of the legislation concerning working time. There are two especially important elements, as far as youth, community and play workers are concerned, Firstly, despite the JNC's professional and deliberate avoidance of an hourly definition to the working week, the *1993 Council of Ministers European Directive (93/104/EC 23rd November 1993)* on working time, prescribes in Article 6, a maximum working week of 48 hours, including overtime which is now incorporated into British law.

However, the maximum of 48 hours is not absolutely inflexible and a reference period of four months can apply to this.

There are other clauses that should be considered when constructing the Authorised Establishment for a post (see Grading of Posts below for a definition of Authorised Establishment). Article 3 of the Directive says: 'Member States shall take the measures necessary to ensure that every worker is entitled to a minimum daily rest period of 11 consecutive hours per 24 hour period.' Staffing arrangements on residentials should now be reviewed, to plan and pay for enough staff to cover adequately so that working time is spent fresh and productively.

Article 4 says the following: 'Member States shall take the measures necessary to ensure that, where the working day is longer than six hours, every worker is entitled to a rest break, the details of which, including duration and the terms on which it is granted, shall be laid down in collective agreements between the two sides of industry or, failing that, national legislation.'

Article 5 is also immediately relevant to the youth, community and play work sector and should be consciously regarded in supervision: 'Member States shall take the measures necessary to ensure that, per each seven-day period, every worker is entitled to a minimum uninterrupted rest period of 24 hours plus the 11 hours' daily rest referred to in Article 3.' Like Article 6, this can have a reference period applied to it, but in this case it shall not exceed 14 days.

Within the Directive there are certain permitted derogations from these principles where certain forms of work do not and cannot comply with such rulings. One such is referred to as 'family workers'. There is an overriding derogation that excludes, with due regard for the general principles of the protection of health and safety, those groups for whom the 'duration of the working time is not measured and/or predetermined, or can be determined by the workers themselves'. We should seek within youth, community and play work to use the Directive creatively, to become more conscious of quality use of time for educational purposes without undue stress. To apply the Directive mechanically will be as unhelpful as rejecting it as irrelevant. The Directive provides us rather with a constructive opportunity to assess again the implementation of the sessional working week.

Above all, youth, community and play workers themselves should recognise that every second worked beyond their contracted hours is part of somebody else's job, a second away from their own family and life, and a contributor to the stresses which may affect their ability to work effectively with those for whom they work. *Work smarter not longer.*

Sick pay

The *JNC Report* incorporates a long section on sick pay which is intended 'to supplement Statutory Sick Pay and Incapacity Benefit so as to maintain normal pay during defined periods of absence on account of sickness, disease, accident or assault.' Sick pay with various periods of full and half pay is allocated according to length of service, extending after five years to six months on full pay and six months on half pay.

Maternity scheme

A comprehensive maternity scheme is contained in the *JNC Report*. Importantly, this details the provisions concerning the right to return to work, and reporting procedures, and is clear and explicit.

In service training

The *JNC Report* has been increasingly concerned with in service training over the last few years and seeks to encourage paid continuous professional development for all staff. In service training should be viewed as a fundamental employment right.

Pensions

Workers with a teaching qualification have a right to join the Teachers' Superannuation Scheme. Others employed by local authorities have access to the Local Government Superannuation Scheme. For those in the voluntary sector, the first objective should be to ensure that a central condition of grant aid to the organisation is that enough money is available for the employer to pay a pension contribution for each worker, usually around 6.5 per cent of an employee's remuneration. All employers with over 5 employees must offer their staff an option to take out a stakeholder scheme.

The next is to explore all ways of establishing a pension scheme. In addition, new legislation has enabled employers to establish stakeholder pension schemes and at the time of writing CYWU is proposing one of these in the voluntary sector and the TUC has launched a new national scheme. Please note that the teachers' scheme can apply to qualified teachers employed as youth, community and play workers in voluntary projects grant aided by the local education authority. CYWU's financial services are designed to help particularly with this for individuals employed in small organisations.

Another difficulty for youth, community and play workers, is that their career can take them in and out of local authority and voluntary sector employers. Usefully a local authority scheme can apply for up to three years out of the direct employ of the authority which can help for temporary secondments. Where a career is projected involving a combination of different employment environments, staff are advised to contact their union.

Holidays

The entitlement is 30 days with under five years continuous service and 35 days with over five years service. Continuous service should be counted regardless of the nature of the employer or of any career breaks a worker may have had. In addition there should be the public holidays and any discretionary days agreed in local agreements with other local authority staff. Holidays should be taken with regard to the operational requirements of the service, but again, in general the professional needs of the worker for proper holiday leave and to develop an all year round provision, should enable most workers' requests to be agreed. Recognising the contribution of many Afro Caribbean and Asian workers to youth, community and play work, it is also essential to be sympathetic to requests for periods of extended leave.

Importantly the *JNC Report* in paragraph 10.2 reminds employers that 'Workers shall, irrespective of length of service, be entitled to a holiday with a normal day's pay for each of the statutory, general and public holidays as they occur.' This provision is still being abused by employers.

In addition the *JNC Report* grants paid leave of absence for jury service, serving on public bodies and undertaking public duties.

Strange as it may seem, taking groups abroad or on adventure holidays within Britain is not leave for those responsible for them! Such work should be properly compensated for, by time off in lieu (TOIL) arrangements. The *JNC Report* does not prescribe for these precisely but advocates a clear TOIL arrangement at local level. Obviously the Union's position is that this should be on an hour for hour basis. This has been backed up by recent European legislation.

Probation

It is no longer a requirement of the Department for Education and Skills for recently qualified youth, community and play workers to complete a probationary year before having their details concerning successful completion entered upon a register; there is no longer such a register. The section in the *JNC Report* is slightly antiquated therefore and needs updating, the persistence of ambiguous clauses about the probationary year in the *JNC Report* still causing confusion and encouraging some unscrupulous employers to hold a threatening axe over new entrants in their first post. This has led the Staff Side of JNC to claim that a new section should be written which stipulates that all new entrants into the service should be subject to comprehensive induction and management support.

To clarify the present position:

1. Once a student has successfully completed a course leading to an appropriate qualification they are fully qualified to undertake youth, community and play work. There is no requirement for a probationary period of work. When someone is in their first post they should expect management support which aids the transition from initial training to full-time work. They should be provided with relevant induction and in service training, non managerial

supervision, and agreed mechanisms for assessing work. They should be *supported* in their first year of work, not put further to the test.

2. When a newly qualified worker on JNC terms and conditions is appointed they will automatically be subject to an employment probation period. This is usually six months in duration. Details of what the employer is looking for during this time should be spelt out to the new employee as should the process for assessment and then the opportunity for appeal. Employment probation is about the basics, time keeping, adaptability and so on.

3. Any youth, community and play worker should receive full induction to a post, particularly if this is their first post. Induction should form part of a staff development policy endorsed by the National Youth Agency or Wales Youth Agency.

4. Staff development should include regular supervision and clear line management structures providing a regular mechanism for support and appraisal of work and the individual concerned.

5. Staff development should also provide a worker with an opportunity for non managerial supervision, arranged by the worker in their own interest, with a person of their choosing and facilitated by the employer.

6. In addition to their normal duties, a new entrant to youth, community and play work should expect the following regular meetings managed as separate processes:
   - induction
   - supervision
   - line management
   - employment probation
   - non managerial supervision
   - annual appraisal

Application of the *JNC Report* at interview

The exact application to the post of the terms and conditions set out in the *JNC Report* should be spelt out to every candidate at interview. Topics should include:
- incremental starting point
- salary level and scale
- any additional payment for high qualification
- additional payment for London and area allowances
- holiday entitlement
- pension arrangements

Although it is true that it is an employers' market, candidates should not feel the need to be reticent at interview about asking for more and better. This is particularly important in relation to the incremental starting point as employers will often advertise a post at the bottom of its scale. However, there is nothing to stop anyone starting work on a Monday and putting in for a regrading on the Tuesday, or requesting a negotiated change to the terms and conditions under which they are employed. 'Oaah, but you accepted this job on the terms on which it was offered,' says the ever so slightly worried employer, 'Yes, and the terms on which it was offered includes a right to regrading and a right to negotiate on my contract,' says the enlightened worker having joined CYWU.

The trainee scale

All employers should only appoint to post staff qualified to JNC standards. It is a flagrant abuse of the ethos of the JNC to appoint unqualified workers, pay them on the trainee scale and encourage them to undertake qualification training while simultaneously holding down a full-time Level 2 or 3 job. The trainee scale should apply to posts which have been created exclusively to provide training for the postholder. Such posts should be additional to the normal establishment: the best examples were the Education Support Grant Apprenticeship Schemes where apprenticeship places were created to provide young people with JNC qualification. With colleges having progressive equal opportunities policies applicable to their selection procedures with a proliferation of youth, community and play work students widening the range of origins, gender and ages, and with a geographical spread of qualification courses, there really are no grounds to justify the appointment of unqualified staff on the pretence of promoting equal opportunities locally.

Part-time workers

The *JNC Report* advocates the adoption of Grievance and Disciplinary Procedures at local level and draws employers attention to the all important ACAS Code on discipline at work.

Provision should be made to recompense workers temporarily undertaking additional duties or acting up to higher graded posts.

Grading of posts

The politics

For a worker, getting the right rate for the job is an integral part of job satisfaction. For the employer, it should be a desired feature of creating a motivated workforce with clear roles, and a balance of career opportunities and prospects within a service. Given the structure of the *JNC Report*, determining the right grade for a post is also essential for management budget planning. For every youth, community and play work post there needs to be an Authorised Establishment, a Job description, a Contract, and a format of regularly recorded supervision. Taken together, these assist in grading. In turn, grading assists budget planning, meeting needs of communities and establishing realistic staff ratios. Once this is done, a plan for resource allocation can be submitted to the elected members or the managing group.

The Authorised Establishment for posts is a much underestimated device within the service. The requirements of this are set out in the *JNC Report*. Basically it is a schedule linked to the Grading Matrix which says 'it is necessary for every employer to establish the volume of work in terms of full-time, part-time and voluntary sessions and the amount of equipment, plant, ancillary and other factors which are authorised to carry out the functions of any post'. This provides a very practical source of detailed information about real needs and potential ways of meeting them which can help build up a view of what is a sufficient service. When read in relation to the excellent National Advisory Council for the Youth Service report *Resourcing the Youth Service*, or *Planning for a Sufficient Youth Service*, or *From Rhetoric to Reality* this section of the *JNC Report* is actually the best performance indicator the youth service has and also provides a useful model for both play work and community work. It is fascinating that it has been so ignored in recent debates on quality management and accountability. Most employers have not yet constructed an Authorised Establishment for the posts for which they are responsible. Doing so could significantly contribute to their ability to defend the levels of, and extend where appropriate, the resources available to them.

The Authorised Establishment criteria, the Grading Matrix system and the pay levels were revised by the JNC in 1987 and 2000, and have since proved remarkably durable. The changes reflected the altered title from the *Report for Youth Leaders and Community Centre Wardens* to the *Report for Youth and Community Workers*. There was a recognition that the service had moved on substantially since its pioneering Albemarle origins and that youth, community and play work posts were more complex, often less based in buildings, and moving into separate areas of projects and specialist demands.

It was recognised too that the *JNC Report* is not just for youth workers. The qualification courses are about youth work, community work and increasingly more generic informal education themes and related occupation areas: health education, housing, play work, youth theatres, community arts. It was therefore necessary to ensure that this was properly reflected in the composition of the JNC as has always been the case, hence the involvement of community work and voluntary sector employers on the employers' side.

This meant that terms of reference were introduced into the grading criteria which specifically recognise qualitative dimensions of the work rather than just the head counting, key clanking quantitative elements of the pre-1987 *JNC Report*. Areas of specialist expertise, non building based work, workers operating at a sophisticated and senior level, but without staff to manage, inter-agency work and senior responsibilities across an area, or county, are all recognised for grading purposes.

The procedure

Grading a post: ten underlying principles

1. **It is a post not an individual that is graded.** The only elements of discretion that relate to the individual concern the incremental starting point which depend on an individual's age, qualification and experience, to some extent the choice of scales within the level, as there may be some specialist knowledge, or responsibility, and any higher qualification allowance awarded.

2. **No one factor determines the grading of a post alone.** Employers locked in the pre-1987 *JNC Report* and personnel officers used to grading administrative and clerical posts, tend to see isolated factors in a post, usually simple quantitative ones like the number of sessions supervised, or the number of user groups, as exclusive trigger points between levels or scales. They are not. The JNC itself made this clear in 1988 when it sent out guidance notes to employers on how to go about grading posts under the new *JNC Report*. From this it is evident that a balanced and inclusive approach is necessary for grading posts.

3. **According to JNC an individual can apply for regrading.** They can do this if they think that their post is wrongly graded, or if they think that the post has expanded since its last grading assessment. An individual can apply locally for any increase (a level, a scale, or an increment); if they lose locally, they can only appeal nationally to go up a level. Increases in increments and scales are excluded from National Grading Appeals as currently are appeals to achieve 'off scale' points above Level 3.

4. **There is a right to appeal against a rejected application for regrading locally.**

5. **There is a right to appeal against a lost local appeal** for regrading to the national *JNC Appeals Panel* on levels only.

6. **All workers count.** A session worked by another full-timer, or part-timer for whom the postholder has managerial responsibility is exactly equivalent to the session worked by a volunteer for the purposes of regrading. It is not in accordance with the *JNC Report* to downgrade the responsibility for volunteers. Volunteers count exactly the same as paid staff.

7. **All work counts.** Any work undertaken by a postholder counts towards regrading unless that work has been explicitly rejected or forbidden by the employer.

8. **Regrading is undertaken for individual posts.** The *JNC Report* talks of grading each post. Collective regradings are rare and can only be undertaken with the joint agreement of both the staff and management involved.

9. **What applies to one job does not necessarily apply to another.** All attempts to invent mathematically pure, point scoring systems to grade all jobs covered by the *JNC Report* across an authority have failed the service and lost staff morale.

10. **The level of responsibility counts.** Responsibility for staff often has two dimensions, or either one of them; management, that is, recruitment, line management, supervision, training, discipline, administering appointments etc..., or professional advice. Often full-time workers on contracts with JNC terms and conditions advise volunteers and part-time workers, and this advisory function is frequently more advanced than simply management and should be so regarded for grading purposes.

How to apply for a regrading

Regrading is not a legal procedure as such, but a voluntary one entered into by employers and their staff. The procedure should be conducted according to the laws of natural justice with rights to representation, the opportunity to present evidence and to cross examine anyone contradicting this evidence.

Having said this, employers are not over fond of regradings and procedures tend to be as open ended as possible, or as difficult as possible in order to dissuade workers from pursuing them to the bitter end. So, once the process starts, be prepared to see the whole thing through no matter how long it takes.

Step 1 Write a letter requesting regrading

There are only three important things that need to be included in the letter:

- Make sure the date is on your letter, as any award made to you will be backdated to the date of this letter even if the regrading finishes in two years time.
- Make clear that you are requesting regrading under the terms of the *JNC Report*.
- Request a copy of the employers' regrading procedure.

Many employers, particularly in the voluntary sector, do not have regrading procedures, so here is a list of the key factors in a regrading procedure under JNC, terms and conditions which should give a right to trade union representation, and set out clear time scales at all stages.

1. Application submitted.
2. Line manager must acknowledge the application within seven days.
3. Line manager must assess the application within 14 days.
4. Line manager must respond formally within 21 days from date of initial receipt of application.
5. If the response is negative the appellant must have a right to present their case to the next manager in line, usually the Head of Department. This should be a relatively informal meeting.
6. If the Head of Department rejects the application for regrading there should be a right of appeal to elected members, in the case of the local authority, or the appropriate management committee or sub committee in the voluntary sector.

This right of appeal should be exercised fairly and there should be a procedure for the conduct of appeals. Normally this would be fairly simple:

1. An Appeals Panel of three people with an independent notetaker.
2. Appellants and managements case circulated one week in advance to all parties.
3. Appellant presents case (no time constraint).
4. Management question appellant.
5. Panel question appellant.
6. Management present case.
7. Appellant questions management.
8. Panel questions management.
9. Management sums up case.
10. Appellant sums up case.
11. Both sides withdraw.
12. Panel makes decision on the day.

If the local appeal body rejects the regrading application, there is a right to national appeal, but national appeals can only be taken for cases requesting a higher *level*. You cannot take a national appeal to get a higher incremental point within a scale, or a higher scale within a level, the procedure for which is set out in a JNC guide available from the JNC. Requests for national appeal must be made within two months of losing the local appeal to the JNC Staff Side Secretary. A written case with supporting evidence then has to be submitted.

National appeal is held at the employers headquarters with an independent Chair and representatives of both the Employers' Side and Staff Side of the JNC hearing the case. If the two sides cannot agree on where the post should be graded the whole case falls, so there is a real incentive for compromise. The procedure can feel unnecessarily daunting and like a court room, but in the main, it is a rigorous and fair exercise.

There is no further appeal, after national appeal, unless some really unjust mistake, or problem has occurred and the Union feels ACAS should be approached or industrial action considered.

Step 2 Assess the case

For workers, this is best done by completing the CYWU Regrading Form available from its national office and printed here for the first time.

For employers, this is best done by considering all the information available on the Job Description, Authorised Establishment, supervision notes, work reports and what is known of the post and its history. Management are often impeded in their progress on this, by using the very reductivist criteria applied by some personnel departments to clerical and administrative grades. Forms used in *Single Status Agreement* regradings simply do not extract the relevant information for regrading under the *JNC Report*. Throughout the regrading procedure, it is best for management to involve both officers with a knowledge of the work and the post, and a representative from personnel. It is of course advisable for any individual seeking regrading to be represented by their CYWU representative. All applications for national regradings from CYWU members have to go through CYWU nationally in any event, and normally a national official would present the national case.

Bearing in mind that a successful regrading will take into account the post as a whole and balance the qualitative and quantitative aspects together with the complexity of duties performed, it is best to establish comprehensive descriptions of the post.

The three Levels in the JNC terms and conditions, are distinguished mainly by key words open to quite a bit of interpretation until the detail is considered. Basically, Level 1 workers assist others in doing the job, but there are very few Level 1 posts anywhere. Level 2 workers do the job mostly themselves, while Level 3 workers do the job at a 'senior' level. How workers work, is a complex amalgam of educational delivery and management, and it is not too difficult to devise a grid system for assessing at what level workers do each component duty and how the whole combination of duties, worked perhaps at various levels, generates a post at a certain level and scale, taking into account also, comparable jobs in the same employing organisation. To ascribe points, however and worse still weightings to different component parts, is fatal.

Step 3 Following the procedure

Following your application letter and your assessment of the post, work through the procedure, sticking to the timescales where possible, and agreeing to delay them slightly where mutually agreeable. Very rarely is the money due to a member of staff the personal property of their managers. In all cases, the more appropriately the worker is rewarded, the higher the eventual status of the project, because the most important and precious commodity in any organisation is the human resource. I have always found it a myth that community workers, for example, should work themselves out of a job. When they leave, a well paid post is representative of the value the community places on the job they did and their continuing initiative. A properly paid human resource is happier and more motivated than an underpaid one!

Model Regrading Form

Name . . . .

Address . . . .

. . . .

. . . .

Contact phone numbers . . . .

Title of post . . . .

Current salary scale (Please tick)

    JNC . . . .

    APT and C (Green Book, Single Status Agreement) . . . .

    Soulbury . . . .

    Teachers . . . .

    Specify other . . . .

    If mixed terms and conditions, please outline . . . .

Your annual salary . . . .

Salary point (e.g. JNC Level 2 Point 3). . . . .
For part-time workers it is also essential to include your hourly and sessional rates of pay.

When did you take up this post?   Month . . . .   Year . . . .

What was your starting salary as a point on a salary scale?

£ . . . . per annum

Scale . . . . Point . . . .

When was this post last regraded? Month . . . .   Year . . . .   Don't know . . .

In what month and year were the following agreed:

Your Contract of Employment	Month	Year . . . .
Your Job Description	Month	Year . . . .
The Grading of your post	Month	Year . . . .
The Authorised Establishment of your post?	Month	Year . . . .

(Each youth, community and play work post should have all of its dimensions, staffing establishment and gradings agreed by committee or the managing body before it is created. Try and find this out if you do not know about it.)

Checklist for enclosures

To give thorough analysis to your grading application both you, your employer and CYWU will require at least the following items in the first instance. Make sure they are enclosed. Further items may be requested as your claim continues.

Essential

Job description.
Written Statement of Particulars/Contract of Employment.
Details of budgets and equipment for which you are responsible.

Proof of your management responsibility for other staff.

Neighbourhood profile.

Desirable

Job descriptions of those you supervise and those who supervise you.
Project annual report.
Project staffing establishment and accountability diagram.
Diagram of the layout of the building/area for which you are responsible.
The *JNC Report* enables the grading of youth, community and play work posts, with or without buildings or staffing responsibilities. However, for many workers the most tangible grading criteria are associated with the numbers of staff and volunteers for whom they have responsibility. The *JNC Report* rewards your work in relation to other paid members of staff and volunteers, whether full-time, or part-time. You must also be recompensed for your work with clerical and other ancillary staff, as well as other informal education practitioners.

You may need to prove your level of responsibility for these other staff and demonstrate that you supervise and support them.

For the calculations below count a session as your normal allocation, usually three hours plus.

1. How many sessions of **paid part-time** work do you oversee each week?

    Youth work . . . .

    Community work . . . .

    Adult education . . . .

2. How many sessions of **voluntary work** do you oversee each week?

    Youth work . . . .

    Community work . . . .

    Adult education . . . .

3. For how many **full-time** Youth and Community workers are you responsible, i.e. number of individuals?
    . . . .

4. How many additional sessions of workers, students, volunteers, or others' time do you support/motivate/or relate to each week? (Specify on additional sheets of paper as necessary).

    . . . .

5. Please specify the number of **hours of paid ancillary and clerical staff** which you manage each week. Attach their job descriptions.

    Clerical . . . .

    Administrative . . . .

    Caretaking . . . .

    Cleaning . . . .

6. If there are any other sessions for which you are responsible for a **limited period of most years** only, please specify the nature of the posts and the total number of hours within the year.

    Post . . . .

    Hours per annum . . . .

    Post . . . .

    Hours per annum . . . .

7. How many **people use** the centre for which you are responsible in an average week?

    . . . .

8. How many **user groups use** your centre each week?   . . . .

9. How many **user groups come into contact** with your work?   . . . .

10. How many **people in the groups** for which you are responsible?   . . . .

11. What is the **total population** of the neighbourhood covered by your project?   . . . .

Quantities of work

You need in this section to describe further quantitative aspects of the work. These particularly include descriptions of your financial and administrative responsibilities, and the volume of activity you are responsible for. Obviously feel free to include additional paperwork describing this, but please fill in this section in any event.

1. What **specialist activities** function in your centre and how many times a month? (Ballroom dancing is not as specialist as trampolining in this meaning).

    Activities . . . .

    . . . .

    . . . .

    Frequency per month

    . . . .

    . . . .

    Describe some curriculum areas you generate

    . . . .

    . . . .

2. What **specialist groups/projects** are you responsible for overseeing and managing?

    . . . .

    . . . .

    . . . .

3. Is the **area** in which you work recognised as being one of social disadvantage?

    Please tick   Yes . . . . . .   No . . . . .

4. What **percentage** of the individuals and groups you work with, suffer identifiable and recognised social disadvantage?
    . . . .

5. Give the number of **user groups** with which you have a professional relationship and responsibility within your centre or project, and the total number of users in them all.

    Number of user groups . . . .

    Number of users in them . . . .

6. Give the number of **user groups** created by your work since you started. . . . .

7. List the **agencies** with which you regularly have professional contact. Contact needs to be more than casual. Describe the professional status of the staff with whom you usually have contact (e.g. head teacher, social services district manager, chief superintendent etc.).

    . . . .

    . . . .

8. How much **money** are you directly responsible for?

    Grants   £ . . . .

    Wages   £ . . . .

    Fund raising   £ . . . .

    Subscriptions   £ . . . .

    Canteen   £ . . . .

    Other   £ . . . .

    Trips   £ . . . .

    Maintenance   £ . . . .

    Cash   £ . . . .

    Total   £ . . . .

9. What **financial planning** and reporting are you responsible for and how much work does this involve? . . . .

    Do you prepare a **business plan**?   Yes . . . . .   No . . . . .

10. What is the **annual income and expenditure** of the project where you work?

    Income . . . .   Expenditure . . . .

11. How many **rooms** in the building where you work?   . . . .

12. How many **storeys** in the building where you work?   . . . .

13. What is the **square footage of the building** where you work?   . . . .

14. What **outdoor areas** are you responsible for?

    . . . .

15. What is the **square footage of the outdoor area**?   . . . .

16. What is the **minimum staffing requirement** each session?   . . . .

17. Describe the **equipment** you are responsible for and its total value?

     . . . .

     . . . .

     . . . .

     Total Value   £ . . . .

Quality of work

It is important that we are able to assess the seniority or the quality of your work and the educational and developmental responsibilities you have. It is also important for us to be able to get an idea of the scope of your job. The questions below relate to these areas and are important. How do you develop learning from action, how do you go about your social education work?

1. What **percentage of your time** do you spend on the following in an average week?

    Face to face work   . . . .

    Development of service provision   . . . .

    Finance and administration   . . . .

    Inter-agency work   . . . .

    Training others   . . . .

    Management and supervision of others   . . . .

    Health and safety responsibilities   . . . .

    Curriculum issues   . . . .

    Developing methods of work   . . . .

    Support for individuals   . . . .

    Support for groups   . . . .

2. Under each heading describe whether you **assist (A)** with the work, **manage it (M)** or **perform it directly (P)**. You may do all three, in which case put each role in order of main category.

    Face to face work   . . . .

    Development of service provision   . . . .
    (policy making reports etc.)

    Finance and administration   . . . .

    Inter-agency work   . . . .

    Training others   . . . .

    Management and supervision of others   . . . .

    Health and safety responsibilities   . . . .

    Curriculum issues   . . . .

    Developing methods of work   . . . .

3. If you **write reports** or make suggestions about future delivery, describe in order of frequency the bodies to whom your ideas are directed: line manager, management committee, local councillors, head of service, staff team, council committee, team of inter-agency staff, voluntary projects, national projects. Describe as appropriate.

    . . . .

    . . . .

    . . . .

4. By ticking beneath the appropriate letter do you **assist (A)**, **manage (M)** or actually directly **perform (P)** the following:

	A	M	P
Management of project(s)	. . . . .	. . . . .	. . . . .
Management of buildings	. . . . .	. . . . .	. . . . .
Detached work	. . . . .	. . . . .	. . . . .
Outreach work	. . . . .	. . . . .	. . . . .
Neighbourhood work	. . . . .	. . . . .	. . . . .
Area work	. . . . .	. . . . .	. . . . .
Regional work	. . . . .	. . . . .	. . . . .
County/City wide work	. . . . .	. . . . .	. . . . .
National work	. . . . .	. . . . .	. . . . .
Crime prevention work	. . . . .	. . . . .	. . . . .
Health education	. . . . .	. . . . .	. . . . .
Outdoor education	. . . . .	. . . . .	. . . . .
Project work	. . . . .	. . . . .	. . . . .
Representational work	. . . . .	. . . . .	. . . . .
Training others	. . . . .	. . . . .	. . . . .
Recruitment and selection of staff	. . . . .	. . . . .	. . . . .
Advising other agencies	. . . . .	. . . . .	. . . . .
Counselling	. . . . .	. . . . .	. . . . .
Reporting on work	. . . . .	. . . . .	. . . . .
Financial Management	. . . . .	. . . . .	. . . . .
Teaching	. . . . .	. . . . .	. . . . .
Employment related work	. . . . .	. . . . .	. . . . .
Welfare and advice work	. . . . .	. . . . .	. . . . .
Community development work	. . . . .	. . . . .	. . . . .
Work with other agencies	. . . . .	. . . . .	. . . . .
Responsibility for equipment	. . . . .	. . . . .	. . . . .
Work with the unwaged	. . . . .	. . . . .	. . . . .
Work with ethnic minorities	. . . . .	. . . . .	. . . . .
Work with disabled	. . . . .	. . . . .	. . . . .
Anti racist work	. . . . .	. . . . .	. . . . .
Anti sexist work	. . . . .	. . . . .	. . . . .

Personal advice work	. . . . .	. . . . .	. . . . .
Mentoring	. . . . .	. . . . .	. . . . .
Development of community groups	. . . . .	. . . . .	. . . . .
Work with Credit Unions	. . . . .	. . . . .	. . . . .
Skills learning	. . . . .	. . . . .	. . . . .
Vocational training	. . . . .	. . . . .	. . . . .
Non Vocational training	. . . . .	. . . . .	. . . . .
One to one counselling	. . . . .	. . . . .	. . . . .
Giving information	. . . . .	. . . . .	. . . . .
Organising play	. . . . .	. . . . .	. . . . .
Delivering play work	. . . . .	. . . . .	. . . . .
Educating adults	. . . . .	. . . . .	. . . . .
Advising committees	. . . . .	. . . . .	. . . . .

Please include further details to explain your role.

Other topics dealt with by the JNC Report

Written statement of particulars

In the current 2000 edition of the *JNC Report* the relevant extracts from the *Trade Union and Employment Rights 1993 Act* are quoted. Particular attention should be paid to the fact that this Appendix in the *JNC Report* includes emphasis on the right time off and facilities for trade union duties and activities.

Part-time workers

There is a new section of the *JNC Report* that brings together all of the agreements for part-time workers reached in 1995 and sets out the pay scales. All other provisions of *JNC Report* apply to them pro rata. Part 2 of this book deals with part time workers in more detail.

Qualifications

The *JNC Report* lists all of the relevant qualifications it has recognised since the 1940s. This is updated on a regular basis.

Notes on probation

The *JNC Report* has a section on this, but in this book, see pages 29–31 and 166–168 for more details.

Grievance procedure

The *JNC Report* incorporates a useful section on grievance procedures and offers the support of the Joint Secretaries in any local difficulties in establishing a procedure.

Guidance on application of the trainee scale

This guidance includes the significant wording: 'The nature and overall pattern of work for those on the trainee scale should reflect the training needs of the trainee and should include appropriate time within normal working hours to undertake formal elements of training.'

Pay rates

These are set out in the *JNC Report* and are updated every autumn through a circular.

Appeals against salary gradings

This section outlines the national procedure and gives advice on submissions.

Important JESC Circulars

After the 1995 settlement for part-time workers, the following Circulars were issued:
   No. 101: 15th December 1995
   No. 101A: 4th January 1996
   No. 102: 19th January 1996
A particularly important circular followed on 3rd April 1996 (number 104) which set out in greater detail the full implications of the part-time workers' settlement. Importantly, it confirmed the divisors for the calculation of part-time workers salary points: 36 hour week (London) 1562, and 37 hour week 1605.

Another important circular was No. 121, dated 15th September 1999, which emphasised the importance of in-service training and gave strong guidance on the need for payment for part-time workers undertaking it. It also gave guidance on working time arrangements, and following pressure from CYWU and increasing incidents of violence at work, it produced guidance on *Harassment, Bullying and Violence in the Youth and Community Work Sector.*

These circulars can be viewed on CYWU's website.

Further reading and reference

For a List of Useful Addresses and a Select Bibliography, see Appendices.

Working hours and the legal framework

Working Time, A Negotiator's Guide. Labour Research Department.

Superannuation

Your Pensions. National Union of Teachers.
Details of the Department for Education *Superannuation Scheme for Teachers* can be obtained directly from the DfEE. Details of the Local Government *Superannuation Scheme* can be obtained from your local authority Superannuation Department.

Probationary year

The First Year of Work After Qualifying. A CYWU Briefing Paper.

Regrading

National Appeals Procedure. JNC.

Part 2

Employing Youth, Community and Play Workers Well

Background: part-time or full-time worker?

All people at work should be entitled to equivalent treatment whether they are full-time, part-time, or temporary workers, self employed or working at home.

TUC's Negotiator's Handbook

The *Employment Relations Act 1999* introduced significant powers to ensure that part-time workers are treated 'no less favourably' than full-time workers. In reality, part-time youth, community and play workers are treated less favourably than their full-time colleagues and this fact indicates the poor health of these professions.

One of the biggest changes since the first edition of this book has been the incorporation of part-time workers into the national bargaining apparatus, the Joint Negotiating Committee for Youth and Community Workers (JNC). Following a very long campaign led by the Community and Youth Workers Union (CYWU), the system of casualisation of part-time workers and unfair treatment that lay at the heart of the profession was ended and it was agreed nationally that a proper professional structure of terms and conditions should be set down. This agreement was reached amicably with the employers and signed in 1995 following the intervention of the Arbitration, Conciliation and Advisory Services (ACAS), who produced a long report on the position of part-time workers. In this section, however, I take on the fact that this important National Agreement for Part-time Workers has not been fully embraced by many employers of part-time staff, and before giving details of the National Agreement there is a critique of those attitudes and illegal employment practices which persist and which the National Agreement was designed to eliminate. Local implementation of the National Agreement is still sadly essential and I believe that all employing organisations within the sector should begin their New Year's resolutions with a commitment to reviewing their agreements for part-time workers.

At the heart of youth, community and play work, lies inequality, injustice and disadvantage. Part-time youth, community and play workers, who are mainly women, are still often treated, as casual labour and lack the protection and employer support really necessary to maintain a quality education service. Despite the new National Agreement, the prolific equal opportunities statements that exist, the commitments of the Youth Service Statement of Purpose to opposing discrimination and disadvantage, and the definitions of community work which focus on opposition to social injustice, this is a service reliant in many parts, on unfairly treated workers. There is no other part of mainstream education so dependent on part-time workers; there are still eight part-time workers for every one full-time worker. Only adult education comes close to such a high ratio. In addition, it is clear that employers' increasing expectations of part-time workers are making jobs intensely pressured, and recruitment and retention problems, with some employing organisations having as much as a 25 per cent vacancy rate, are now a permanent feature of the employment scene. The National Agreement gave a perfect opportunity to change this.

Many part-time workers are still on short, fixed term contracts, or 46 week annually renewable contracts. There has been a trend in some parts to introduce three month contracts. Workers on these are the first to be sacked in re-organisations and cuts, and they are the first to have terms and conditions changed, usually unilaterally, when the going gets tough. This means that the majority of face to face work within youth, community and play work is viewed as temporary. The Community and Youth Workers' Union (CYWU) which has led the field in improving the employment situation for part-time workers has quite rightly said that so long as most youth, community and play workers are treated casually, the status and position of the service as a whole will be jeopardised. The Union says that the service is permanent, so the service workers should be on permanent contracts and employed as the professional staff they really are. With the increasing demands of face to face practice and foundation training, many employers have consolidated the part-time hours into posts of substantial hours requiring a full JNC qualification. Perhaps the day of a modern educational service relying on casual sessions of three or six hours a week may at last be numbered. Increasingly, a broad range of part-time staff with different specialisms, and drawn from the varied community groups that make up the sector, will be required.

Additionally, the wide diversity of employment conditions for part-time workers throughout the country reflects the localised and regionalised nature of the service, as opposed to its supposed national basis. This has created a deep 'postcode inequality' for children and young people and the more national standards are achieved in training and employment practice, the more rights and entitlements will be secured for young people. Just as the Audit of the Youth Service revealed uneven entitlements for young people to youth workers throughout the country, so it is perhaps not surprising to discover that part-time youth workers doing exactly the same job can be treated very differently in different parts of the country.

The national framework provided by the *JNC Report*, a manual of employment conditions and objectives in youth, community and play work (see Part 1) again gives an excellent foundation from which to build the idea of a national set of coherent provisions. There is now a national Statement of Purpose for the youth, community and play service, a national consensus on the nature of its delivery, a national qualification for part-time workers, national recognition under JNC, yet still an undermining diversity of local practice exists. The national certificate awarded to those part-time workers successfully completing a local qualification course endorsed by the *Regional Accreditation and Moderation Panels (RAMPs)* is transferable from one part of the country to another, although the whole contractual basis may vary in almost every clause in neighbouring authorities. The voluntary sector also has been given little guidance and support in its employment of part-time youth, community and play workers and huge variations of practice exist from project to project within often the same national voluntary organisation. It is hoped that this part of the book may help to encourage some commonality of purpose and practice.

Resources available to the local youth, community and play service have been the product mainly of ad hoc political history. There has been minimal work undertaken to establish needs related provision. Again, this is one particular advantage of the *JNC Report* which has an Authorised Establishment section enabling employing organisations to plan provision more scientifically. Resourcing has been hindered by the lack of statutory underpinning. Planning beyond the next budget round has been almost impossible. In making new arrangements to treat part-time workers fairly, many of the basic vulnerabilities of youth, community and play work will be confronted. It is therefore probably advisable to read this section in conjunction with *Planning a Sufficient Youth Service* (see further reading) which covers many aspects of resource allocation applicable to informal education groups. Related essential documents both produced by the UK Youth Work Alliance are *Agenda for a Generation* and *From Rhetoric to Reality* (see further reading). In order to deliver a modernised service which endorses equal opportunities and has part-timers professionally employed, the employing organisation will have to be able to plan a long term budget, allocate staff on the basis of realistic ratios, and incorporate into the budget allocations time off for professional training and trade union duties, payment for residential duties, pension contributions and so on.

The counter argument will run that this could lead to fewer employed part-time workers, to which there are many responses. Firstly, if we take the arguments of *Planning a Sufficient Youth Service* and *Agenda for a Generation* fully on board then it should be recognised that the effort to professionalise the employment of part-time staff increases political demand for more funding of a badly depleted service. It should be noted also that the brief of *PAULO* and *SPRITO* the newly formed National Training Organisations for this sector, has positive objectives in staff development and the qualification of part-time workers. Secondly, it enables a closer look at real need. Inevitably this will reveal some hidden dilemmas that require attention:

- At a time of such high unemployment should there be so many part-time workers who are in effect in second jobs?
- Should there not be more part-time workers working more sessions with higher levels of training and support?
- With the HMI *Ofsted Framework of Inspection* and its concentration on financial management issues, shouldn't the budget for part-time workers be expanded anyway?

National Charter for Part-time Workers

This Charter was adopted by the two main unions in the field, the National Association of Youth and Community Education Officers and the Community and Youth Workers Union. The Charter was agreed on 19th February 1990 and sets out some of the main principles upon which improvements for part-time workers were based in the JNC negotiations. These principles still need to be endorsed at local level:

Model Charter for Part-time Youth, Community and Play Workers

NAYCEO/CYWU

1. We believe that part-time working forms an essential component in the delivery of youth, community and play services and that the best possible terms and conditions for part-time workers and the best possible in-service and initial training opportunities should be made available to them.

2. We believe that the pay, terms and conditions of all part-time workers should be brought under the Joint Negotiating Committee Report for Youth, Community and Play Workers fully pro rata and believe that all part-time workers should be placed on permanent contracts.

3. We believe that in addition to permanency of contract and the provision of paid time off for training required by the employer, some important features of pro rata inclusion would entail:
   - job descriptions linked to the JNC Grading Matrix
   - access to grievance and disciplinary procedures
   - payment for residential work
   - access to car mileage allowances for work related duties
   - regular supervision and access to appropriate support structures
   - access to pension schemes
   - paid holiday and parental leave entitlement
   - full sick pay arrangements.

4. We recognise that the ultimate contractual responsibility for part-time employees lies with the employing organisation.

5. We urge all members to work jointly to raise the status of the service in a concerted attempt to de-casualise the part-time backbone of the service and encourage the widest trade union organisation membership.

6. Both organisations will work to obtain recognition of all existing part-time workers' contracts as permanent and work to consolidate and extend existing staffing.

The development of the Model Local Agreement for Part-time Workers

A brief history of the Union's long and successful campaign to incorporate part-time workers in the JNC, together with a bibliography of key articles from *Rapport*, CYWU's National Journal, is given in Appendix 1. A record and appreciation of this background is vital to good industrial relations in this sector and for those to whom this is all new, it would be useful to read it now as an aid to understanding what follows.

It is the intention of this chapter to show how good employment practice in this sector is only possible on the basis of fairly and properly employed part-time workers using the *JNC Report* as the essential tool. Set out below is a model Local Agreement between Employers and the Union on part-time workers, and a model Contract for the employment of part-time youth, community and play workers; these both incorporate notes on particularly important elements.

Then there are some chapters on the basic legal rights of part-time workers, on the importance of training and staff development and on the implications of some previous research into the part-time workforce. In conclusion, the main provisions of the *JNC Report* for part-time workers are described. These sections are prefaced by the wording of the National Charter between CYWU and the National Association of Youth and Community Education Officers (NAYCEO) which sets out the broad principles which underpin the detail and record of the various national agreements that follow. The suggestions made, based largely on personal negotiating experience, are not intended to disturb any preferable local agreements but to reflect as fully as possible the National Agreement of 1995 when the JNC incorporated part-time workers. The better we treat part-time workers the higher the value of the service as a whole. It is a simple principle that has proved very hard to put into practice.

Author's notes are given in italics.

Model Local Agreement between the Employers and CYWU for Part-time Youth, Community and Play Workers

Preamble

a) The purpose of this Agreement between the Local Authority ('the Authority'), grant aided, otherwise supported voluntary organisations ('the Voluntary Organisations'), and the Community and Youth Workers' Union ('CYWU') is to ensure that the part-time workforce in youth, community and play work is treated with full parity to full-time workers in youth, community and play work on the basis of the *JNC Report for Youth and Community Workers* (the '*JNC Report*'). This Agreement recognises that part-time workers within this sector are essential to providing a modern, professional and extensive service in youth, community and play work ('the Service') and should be subject to the same local and national collective agreements under the terms of the *JNC Report*, and any additional locally agreed terms and conditions and employment policies, as may be agreed through the Local Joint Negotiating Committee (LJNC).

b) This Agreement shall be subject to annual review through the local negotiating framework with CYWU and as and when required.

c) This Agreement and all of the model employment documents relating to part-time staff shall be deposited within every centre or project where part-time workers are employed ('the Workplace').

d) This Agreement shall apply to all part-time youth, community and play workers ('the Staff') employed by the Authority and to those paid by the Authority but seconded to the Voluntary Organisations.

e) The purposes of this Agreement are to ensure that all Staff are:
  - Employed as permanent salaried staff.
  - Trained, suitably qualified, supported in their work, provided with career opportunities and appropriately remunerated for all their work on behalf of the Authority or the Voluntary Organisations.

- Aware of their rights and responsibilities in employment and work and that they are aware of all the employment policies, opportunities and regulations that apply to them, which, unless otherwise agreed, will be those applying to full-time youth, community and play work Staff.

1. Contracts of employment and tenure

1.1 All Staff except those subject to Paragraph 2 of this Agreement, shall be placed with immediate effect on permanent contracts. All previous employment or work with this, or other related employers in youth, community and play work will be counted as continuous employment or work.

1.2 All subsequent variations to contractual terms shall be notified to individual employees and CYWU in advance and shall be subject to negotiation through the LJNC.
(See separate Model Statement of Particulars for Part-time Youth, Community and Play Workers.)

2. Temporary workers

2.1 It is recognised that there may from time to time be a need to employ Staff for specialist, or short term projects, or to cover for other Staff. Such employment shall be additional to the normal staffing establishment and its duration shall be subject to the approval of the LJNC

2.2 Recruitment and selection for temporary working shall be from the established 'pool' ('the Pool') of qualified and specialist part-time staff (see Paragraph 3.1 below), or where this is impossible, and by agreement with the LJNC, shall be subject to the agreed advertising, recruitment and selection policies and practice of the Authority.

2.3 Staff shall be designated in each Workplace to 'act up' in the absence of workers in charge or specialists. Acting up payment in accordance with JNC shall be paid.

3. Temporary and cover pool

3.1 A Pool of suitably qualified and specialist workers shall be registered which may be called on from time to time in accordance with Paragraph 2 above for employment by the Authority within the Service.
(This is a particularly useful agreement with regard to maternity and paternity cover and cover for part-time workers undertaking trade union duties.)

3.2 Holiday playscheme and specialist workers shall be employed on clearly defined contracts as agreed by the LJNC.

4. Employment policy

4.1 The creation of an establishment of part-time staffing should take into account the need for a diversity of professional skills based on a common qualification in youth, community and play work endorsed by the *Regional Accreditation and Moderation Panel* (RAMP) or other nationally recognised awarding body and employment should be based on the established equal opportunities policies of the Authority.

4.2 The part-time staffing establishment should create employment opportunities within the local community and with regard to Paragraph 4.1 above should seek to prioritise opportunities for those not otherwise fully employed.

5. The working year

5.1 It is recognised that there is a need for the Service to be provided throughout the year. It is therefore the intention of this Agreement to provide a 50 week Service and 52 week permanent contracts for the Staff.

5.2   The minimum number of sessions for which any member of the Staff (other than temporary appointments agreed according to Paragraph 3 above) shall be contracted is 60 sessions per annum (i.e. a minimum of 50 sessions for face to face work, plus 5 sessions for in service training, plus 5 sessions for supervision).

6. Employment policies and conditions

6.1   It is agreed as a matter of principle that the Staff should be employed on terms no less favourable pro rata than other full-time Staff on JNC terms and conditions within the Service with fully comparable rights and entitlements, and additional relevant conditions as agreed by the LJNC.

6.2   Every Workplace where the Staff are employed shall have available for reference all employment policies and conditions and amendments as agreed by the LJNC from time to time together with a copy of the National *JNC Report* and amendments to it as agreed from time to time.

   (This simple clause which really only necessitates photocopying would make an immeasurable difference to the delivery of the service and avoid all sorts of grievances and misunderstandings.)

6.3.   Among those procedures and policies that will be available in each Workplace are the following:
   Staff handbook
   JNC Report
   APT and C Report
   National Agreement on Part-time Workers'
   Staffing ratios policy
   Vulnerable situations policy
   Child abuse guidelines
   Staff contracts
   Job descriptions
   Staff development policy
   Pension scheme that applies
   Details of employers' insurance
   Equal opportunities policy
   Recruitment and selection procedures
   Re-deployment procedure
   Redundancy policy and procedure
   Staff pay rates
   Health and safety procedures, policies and structures
   Sexual harassment guidelines
   Job share policies
   Outdoor activity procedures and guidelines
   Hazardous activity guidelines
   Detached work policies
   Guidelines on taking responsibilities during work—(e.g. secretary of association,
      leaseholder)
   Parental leave procedures
   Carers' leave procedure
   Policies on violence at work
   Employer's welfare support structures
   Sick pay procedures and policies
   Financial management guidelines
   Disciplinary procedure
   Grievance procedure
   Collective disputes procedure
   Regrading procedure

Information and Communications Technology Procedures
Facilities agreement
Joint negotiating committee agreement
Time off in lieu arrangements
Residential pay arrangements
Travel and subsistence allowance schemes
Complaints procedure (how does the Authority respond if a member of the public complains
   about a member of the Staff?)
JNC regrading form and procedure
Compassionate leave scheme
Policy on writing references
Probationary year arrangements
Authorised establishment figures for JNC posts
Lists of all full and part-time JNC posts
Travel and subsistence guidelines
Security of employment agreement
Accident at work report forms
Official conduct guidelines. Important examples of official conduct guidelines are:
   Whole time service
   Interests of officers
   Information concerning officers
   Contact with the press

This is a non exhaustive list: for more comprehensive coverage see later Parts of this book.

6.4   The importance of reflecting in the composition of the Workforce the particular demographic composition of the communities and children and young people with whom the Service works shall be taken fully into account and it is recognised as being particularly important that black, disabled and other communities of interest that experience disadvantage or prejudice be accommodated within the staffing structures.

6.5   It shall not be the policy of this Authority to maintain any Workplace exclusively with Staff unsupervised by full-time colleagues.

6.6   It shall not be the policy of the Authority to issue more than one contract with stated sessions.

6.7   It shall not be the policy of the Authority to employ each part-time member of staff for more than four evening sessions per week.

7. Payment

7.1   Payment will reflect the professional nature of the work undertaken and be pro rata to the JNC Levels. JNC Pay awards will automatically be paid to Staff as will annual increments and increments for experience and training. To assist the payment of appropriate remuneration a grading form will be available in each workplace.

See the JNC Regrading Form in Part 1.

7.2   Payments will be made to all Staff on a monthly basis for twelve months of the year.

7.3   There will be five JNC based pay levels:
   1. **Trainee Scale.** Part-time staff yet to complete the locally recognised part-time worker training course. Ancillary assistants such as coffee bar or door assistants etc. will automatically be paid on this level.
   2. **Level One.** Assistant Service posts predominantly assisting other full and part-time staff with duties. It is recognised that this level would be a temporary entry grade and not the substantive grade for part-time workers.
   3. **Level Two.** General Service posts taking considerable independent initiative for activities and curriculum.

4. **Level Three.** Workers in charge or with specialist posts designated to lead and manage the Workplace teams and programmes. The main worker in a Workplace which does not have a full-time member of staff will automatically be paid on this level.

5. **Level Four.** Exceptional, substantial posts within the Service.

The placing of staff on these levels will reflect the National JNC criteria where the job description and the whole range of duties and responsibilities shall be taken into account.

7.4   Without prejudice to the ten session working week prescribed under JNC by full-time workers, part-time Staff shall be employed for a contractual number of sessions per annum and a session shall be defined as three hours. Incorporated within these three hours shall be a minimum of 15 minutes preparation and a minimum of 15 minutes clearing up and recording time. Training, residential, supervisory and other work related sessions shall be similarly defined. Sessional pay rates shall be in accordance with Paragraph 9 below and thereafter according to this Agreement.

Important note: the working year of 52 weeks is very much an ideal situation based on the provision of a 'Sufficient Service' being established, most services currently operate on the basis of a 44 or 46 week year.

8. Training

8.1   Initial and in service training is seen as essential for all part-time Staff. The particular emphasis of the JNC Agreement contained in Joint Education Services Circular No. 123 on Training and Development are to be considered. The specific reminder of Circular 123 on the legal requirements of employers to provide training to part-time workers is highlighted in terms of this agreement. No member of Staff shall be appointed to a post of Level one or above unless the local or regional training course has been completed. It is recognised that the initial training for a part-time member of Staff could amount to 260 hours. It shall be the intention of the Authority that all new entrants to the Service, and where possible all new in service arrangements shall be undertaken through courses endorsed by the *RAMP* which confers a National Youth Agency Certificate or other professionally recognised and endorsed certificate accepted by the JNC. In addition the Authority will seek to ensure that all local part-time worker training courses attract an academic validation and rating under the Credit Accumulation and Transfer Scheme. This Agreement takes into account the national JNC view that 'where a part-timer is required by the employer to attend a training course which coincides with his or her normal working session(s), every effort should be made to rearrange the session(s) to the mutual convenience of the employer and the worker. Where this is not possible, employers are advised that such a worker should nevertheless not be expected to forego his or her normal hourly/sessional pay.'

8.2   Assessment of work practice is recognised as an ongoing function of the Authority's management staff. Qualification and in service training shall be the product of separate schemes of learning and separate allocation of sessions. No less than ten percent of all part-time worker sessions shall be allocated to in service training per annum. Training shall be undertaken completely at the expense of the Authority.

8.3   The Authority shall establish a budget to enable part-time Staff to attend initial training courses for full JNC qualification. The Authority recognises the need to support a member of Staff's learning when on initial training and to allocate staff sessions, study time and work responsibilities accordingly.

8.4   Training can contain a high degree of on the job practice and should be particularly related to the strengths and capabilities of the individual.

9. Pay increments for development and training and other factors

9.1   Incremental credit is given for undertaking training approved by the Authority and other specialist training that benefits the Service.

9.2   Pay Increments may also be given for experience, and relevant experience and training are taken into account when establishing the incremental starting point for a new Member of Staff.

9.3   In taking into account the incremental position of any post, in addition to Paragraphs 9.1 and 9.2 above, the Authority will recognise factors particular to any post according to the *JNC Report*. These include:

Physical and social environment.

Nature of client groups.

Ratio of volunteers to paid staff.

Responsibility for equipment pool.

Fund raising responsibilities.

Relevant specialist skills.

Size and authorised establishment of the Workplace.

9.4   Award of increments

a) There are five pay levels subject to annual increment and an agreement on incremental starting points.

b) Transfer between levels will be reviewed after a year of achieving the top of the level.

c) A year runs from the 1st April to 31st March.

d) It is recognised that the JNC negotiating year runs from June 1st–May 31st.

e) It is the intention of the Authority to train and qualify all part-time Staff within two years of appointment. It is recognised that ancillary staff paid under the trainee scale will by agreement remain on the top of the level after two years.

f) Development and experience can be considered for incremental credit in terms of hours of work comparable to those contracted under the existing contract for any one year.

Please note that all calculations are based on the JNC Pay rates prevailing before 1st September 2000.

It is advisable while in the course of negotiations to agree jointly that in the interim at least the minimum JNC rates of the National Agreement will apply. Any abuse of this National Agreement minimum should be reported to the JNC Staff Side Secretary.

Rates quoted are hourly rates in order to provide some flexibility.

The method of payment to part-time Staff is significant. Twelve equal monthly instalments is the preferred form for most part-time workers. Where the Authority agree a definite pro rata holiday entitlement within the annual contract a 52 or 50 week divisor should be used; where they do not agree, a divisor based on the local working year should be used.

Part-time workers with a JNC qualification are entitled to the higher rate of pay.

Scale Rates	Part-time Locally Qualified 2001 Agreed Rates £	JNC Qualified 2001 Agreed Rates £
Trainee scale		
1	Not Applicable	12,552
2		13,140
3		13,746
Level one		
1	11,367	14,079
2	11,841	14,700
3	12,315	15,309
4	12,792	15,921
5	13,269	16,536
6	13,746	17,151
7	14,223	17,766
Level two		
1	11,670	16,548
2	12,315	17,250
3	12,969	17,955
4	13,635	18,654
5	14,331	19,362
6	15,048	20,061
7	15,786	20,766
8	16,530	21,468
9	17,301	22,179
10	18,075	22,875
11	18,873	23,589
Level three		
1	18,873	23,589
2	19,425	24,288
3	19,992	24,990
4	20,556	25,692
5	21,120	26,400
6	21,681	27,108
7	22,242	27,819
		28,530*
*Level 3: Discretionary scale extension. See paragraph 17(ii) of JNC's report.		29,238*

Longer training and/or higher qualification allowance		£813	
London area fringe allowance	Inner	£2,322	
	Outer	£1,527	
	Fringe	£594	

10. Job descriptions

10.1   All part-time Staff shall be issued with a Job Description. This agreement takes into account the advice of the JNC (Annex VIII, 1990) 'Local employers should issue written job descriptions to part-time hourly paid youth, community and play workers.'

10.2   Job descriptions shall be generic to the grade of post and subject to annual review through the LJNC.

11. Safeguarding

11.1   No member of Staff shall suffer detriment as a result of the implementation of this Agreement and protection of any previous conditions more favourable shall apply in all cases.

12. Appeals against grading

12.1   Part-time Staff shall have the right to appeal against the grading of their post according to the JNC grading appeal criteria. The Local Appeals Panel shall consist of two members of either side of the LJNC.

13. Other conditions and agreements

13.1   Other agreements reached by the national JNC or the LJNC from time to time concerning the employment practice of youth, community and play workers shall be automatically transferred to part-time Staff.

13.2   It is recognised that relocation and re-deployment are contractual matters and subject to individual and JNC agreement.

13.3   Travel and subsistence allowances shall be paid under the following scheme:

Note there are various nationally and locally negotiated schemes for travel and subsistence. Here the mileage allowances cited are those of the actual cost of motoring determined by the Automobile Association *and subsistence allowances are those commonly available to staff under* Single Status Agreement (Green Book). *For ease of reference only the maximum mileage brackets have been used. Note also that separate calculations are available for Diesel Car owners. A favourable mileage rate should be negotiated for the environmentally friendly use of bicycles and public transport.*

Mileage Allowance (2002 rates) Petrol Cars Engine Capacity (cc)					
	Up to 1100	1101– 1400	1401– 2000	2001– 3000	3001 4500
5,000 miles 10,000 miles	55p 35p	65p 45p	85p 55p	£1.35p 85p	£1.75p £1.10p
Mopeds, Motorcycles and Scooters Engine capacity (cc)					
	50	125	250	500	750 1000
5,000 miles	25p	45p	60p	80p	£1.00 £1.25

Subsistence	2002 Agreed Rates
Absence for less than 24 hours	£
Bed and Breakfast (outside London)	30.00
Bed and Breakfast (in London)	65.00
Breakfast	4.95
Lunch	5.95
Tea	2.00
Dinner	20.00
Absence for more than 24 hours	
Outside London	25.00
London	45.00

14. Trade union representation

14.1 It is recognised that in order to maintain this Agreement and develop a professional Service that part-time Staff should be encouraged to play an active part in CYWU and industrial relations with the Authority and the youth, community and play work field generally. To this end the Authority particularly welcomes the active participation of part-time Staff in the Staff Side of the LJNC and in the work of CYWU and makes arrangements for time off and cover as appropriate.

The development of the Model Contract and Statement of Particulars

1. It is both advisable, and a legal requirement, to have a written contract of employment, which should be as detailed, and specific and comprehensive as possible. A statement of Particulars setting out the particulars of the contract must be issued within eight weeks of the employee commencing their employment. The advisability stems from good practice and the need to know; the legality stems mainly from the Employment Relations Act 1999, and other acts cited at the opening of the Statement of Particulars, and details what should be set down in written Statements of Particulars. It requires:
    1. A brief description of the work for which the employee is employed.
    2. The period for which the employment is expected to continue where it is not permanent.
    3. The name and address of the employer and the normal workplace.
    4. Details of any collective agreements which directly affect the terms and conditions.
    5. Where the employee is required to work outside the UK for a period of more than one month, the period for which they are to work outside the UK, the currency in which remuneration is to be paid and any additional remuneration or benefits, and the terms and conditions of return to the UK.
2. The Statement of Particulars may refer to the provisions of some other document which the employee has reasonable opportunities of reading in the course of their employment or is made available in some other way, relating to incapacity and sick pay, pensions and pension schemes, and disciplinary and grievance procedures, but in relation to other matters it is no longer possible for employers to refer to some other document. The terms and conditions must be spelt out in full.
    It is good advice to incorporate everything relating to the employment of all staff whether full or part-time in the Principal Statement of Particulars which they must now receive within two months of beginning employment.
3. Leave, other than annual leave, is an interesting issue as far as part-time workers are concerned. The basic principle of the model Statement of Particulars and the model agreement is that part-time workers like their full-time colleagues should be fully entitled to paid leave in all circumstances. However, it is advisable to incorporate a voluntary facility for compensatory working. This is in recognition of the commitment of part-time staff and the need to maintain consistent levels of provision and relationships with young people. Within the overall terms of the contract it should be possible for a part-time worker to miss a session in week one of the year due to, let's say, a family bereavement, and make this up in week two if this suits them; equally if it does not suit them, they should be paid. Similarly with sick leave, there should be no penalty for being ill; the *JNC Report* requires sick pay to be paid to all part-time staff. In providing comprehensive non discriminatory leave arrangements employing organisations should plan their budgets and arrange a pool for cover. Annual leave of course should be sacrosanct as should clear arrangements for bank and other public holidays.
4. Grievance, disciplinary and employment rules etc., are the same as for full-time workers.
5. The contract is between the employee and employer. Managers, be they JNC full-time staff who supervise, or area officers who appoint, are not employers. An appreciation of this fact in practice would go a long way to improving the employment of part-time workers. It is in the interests of Staff on both *JNC Report* and *Soulbury Report* Contracts to improve the conditions and permanency of part-time workers. Both managers, full-time workers and part-time workers are usually employed under a similar basic contract, so if a manager does not uphold a disciplinary procedure fairly, they are jeopardising themselves as much as those they are attempting to 'discipline'.
6. A political implication of this model Contract is that there is a real need to employ more full-time staff and have more substantial part-time jobs. The continuity and quality of services, which rely predominantly on workers who work only one session a week is something that really should be examined, particularly perhaps in the light of the *HMI Framework of Inspection of the Youth Service*.

Model Contract and Statement of Particulars for Part-time Youth, Community and Play Workers

(Author's notes in italics)

At the base of all employment practice lies the written Statement of Particulars, the main part of the four component parts of a contract of employment. It is hoped that the use of this model will therefore be seen as particularly important in the development of good practice for all employed staff.

Principal Statement of Particulars, Terms and Conditions

This Statement, effective from January 2002, sets out particulars of the terms and conditions of employment, and grievance and disciplinary procedures, in accordance with the Employment Relations Act 1999 (and as subsequently amended) and related employment and trade union legislation, the Public Interest Disclosure Act 1998, the Data Protection Act 1998, the Children Act 1989, the Human Rights Act 2000. Throughout this statement, five working days equals one calendar week and a 'session' is three hours. Sections underlined are those you will need to adjust to meet your particular requirements.

1. Name and address of employing organisation.

   Local Authority of Karl Marx Street, Stalingrad, Kent 007 UR, hereinafter 'The Authority'.

2. Name of employee. Martin Jones, hereinafter 'You'.

3. Date of commencement of employment. 1st January 2001. This contract is regarded by the Authority as a permanent contract and all of your rights as an employee are effective as of this date. In addition the Authority will take into account for the purposes of redundancy or any other matter depending upon continuity of service, all that service undertaken as a youth, community and play worker, with the Authority and any other related employer of youth, community and play workers previously. Employment protection rights under this contract are equal to those of any full-time member of staff regardless of the length of service and hours worked per week.

4. Job title.

4.1 Part-time youth, community and play worker, general worker (e.g. for the purposes of this contract a general youth, community and play worker on level two).

4.2 Your principal duties will involve the social education of *young people (or, as appropriate, people or young children)*. This includes face to face informal education work, the development of the service through team meetings, some elements of financial administration and other administrative duties and liaison with other agencies to enhance the delivery of service.

4.3 You will be employed at Nelson Mandela Youth Centre/Project and other such locations as may be agreed with the Authority or as subject to the Authority's re-deployment or relocation procedures.

5. Remuneration.

5.1. Your salary will be paid under the levels agreed locally through the meetings of the LJNC and set out annually in 'The Agreement for part-time Workers'. This post is graded level two.

5.2 In respect of your one year's experience as a volunteer youth worker, your successful completion of the initial training course and your specialist knowledge of trampolining your starting point will be increment three.

5.3   This post is subject to annual increments as set out in 'The Agreement for part-time Workers' and pay increases as negotiated annually by the Joint Negotiating Committee for Youth, community and play workers (JNC). Annual increments take effect as of April 1st and annual pay awards take effect as of June 1st.

5.4.   Your salary will be paid monthly in arrears by the **28th** day of each month by bank transfer.

5.4.1 In the event of work at your normal place being unavailable you will be paid your normal salary.

5.5.   You will be paid for working **90** sessions a year. A session comprises three hours. In each working session at your identified place of work you will be allocated 15 minutes preparation time and 15 minutes clearing away and recording time. Travel to and from work time will not be included in a session. Sessions will be worked normally at the time specified below, but also by agreement with your line manager. Your **90** sessions a year include **9** sessions for personal in service training, and **9** sessions for supervision with your line manager and colleagues. Sessions throughout the year may include residential work or other work related duties as agreed with your line manager. Any sessions additional to **90** per annum will be separately negotiated between your line manager and the Authority. You will not be expected to work more than **four evening** sessions a week. You will not be expected to work more than two consecutive sessions in one 24 hour period, unless by prior agreement for residential duties etc.

5.6   You will be employed to work on **Tuesday and Thursday evenings**. Variation in this term will be by prior consultation and mutual agreement according to the relocation and re-deployment procedure.

5.7   Your grading and salary will be reviewed annually by the Authority and CYWU, in conjunction with you and, if desired, your representative.

5.8   You will not be expected to work three continuous sessions in any one day. It will be expected that your working time will be governed in strict adherence to the Working Time Directive and other relevant national and local agreements.

6.   Duties of the post.

6.1   The duties of the post are as set out in your job description and subject to any variation that is agreed between you (your Union representative) and the Authority.

6.2   Supervision meetings will be held with your line manager to a total of **nine** sessions per year to support the development of you in post and the post itself. You will be expected to participate in staff meetings and work evaluation.

7.   Time off in lieu and additional hours.

7.1   Residential and international exchange work are recognised as integral and important elements of education provision within the service and from time to time you may be required to assist in the organisation and participation in such work. Unless by separate arrangement under Paragraph 5.5 above, such additional duties will be from within the contractually allocated sessions per year. Every effort will be made to ensure that this work is resourced as additional to your contractual hours, but any such addition shall not be a contractual requirement. Work undertaken away from home on a residential basis shall be paid either as additional time or recompensed with full-time off in lieu. One day's residential duties shall be counted as four working sessions which shall be taken off normal duties as outlined in Paragraph 5.6 above. Time off in lieu shall be taken within one month of the extra duties being performed and shall be carried over only by joint agreement.

8.   Leave.

8.1   Your leave entitlement shall be pro rata to JNC (for someone who works ten sessions a week this is 30 days, with 35 days for five years or more continuous service). Thus of your **90** contractual sessions per year **5.5** will be taken as leave.

8.2 Should your normal sessional working fall upon a regular or other public holiday you will be entitled to leave on that day, but with the facility to rearrange your working session that week by agreement with your line manager.

8.3 All annual leave will be taken within the leave year and only in exceptional circumstances and with prior agreement shall leave be carried over. The leave year runs from April 1st to March 31st.

8.4 All employees joining after April 1st will be granted leave pro rata for the period worked in that leave year according to pro rata calculations of one twelfth of the annual entitlement for each month worked. If your employment terminates during a leave year you will be entitled to leave, or pay in lieu of leave, pro rata for the period worked in that leave year.

8.5 Special Leave without pay may be granted in exceptional circumstances by prior agreement with the line manager and LJNC.

8.6 Leave for examinations or training taken in connection with courses directly relevant to this post shall be granted with pay. Travel expenses and child caring expenses shall be paid for attending the initial part-time Worker Qualification course.

8.7 Other leave arrangements shall be in accordance with the terms and conditions set out in the JNC Report and 'The Local Agreement on part-time Workers'. This will include provisions for special leave to assist with family emergencies.

8.8 One month's notification of all leave under this section shall be given to your line manager.

9. Secondary employment.

9.1 Whilst in the employment of the Authority, you will not undertake any other employment that undermines and conflicts with your duty of fidelity to the Authority or conflicts with the professional interests of your work as a professional educator within the youth, community and play service.

10. Retirement.

10.1 You will normally retire from employment at the age of 60. This may be varied with the mutual consent of you and the Authority.

11. Confidentiality.

11.1 You may as an employee have access to or be entrusted with information that the Authority and the young people you work with have deemed confidential. You shall not at any time during or after the end of your employment disclose to any person, or make use of such confidential information.

11.2 In any case of doubt as to the status of information you should consult your line manager in the first instance.

11.3 Upon termination of your employment with the Authority you will deliver back to the Authority all documents, equipment or other materials or items belonging to the Authority.

11.4 You will be granted access to all records which name you. A minimum of two weeks' notice shall be given to consult your personnel records.

12. Job share.

12.1 Consideration will be given by the Authority to any request from an employee to job share, and attention will be paid to the Authority's equal opportunities policy.

13. Equal opportunities.

13.1 You are expected to be familiar with and implement the Authority's equal opportunities policy and any subsequent amendments thereto.

14. Health and safety.

14.1   The Authority undertakes to comply with the Offices, Shops and Railway Premises Act 1963, the Health and Safety at Work Act 1974, the Management of Health and Safety at Work Regulations 1992 and all regulations and codes of practice issued thereunder, and all subsequent amendments thereto, to provide and maintain a working environment for all employees that is safe, without risk to health, and with adequate arrangements for staff welfare.

14.2   You will be provided with all relevant guidelines and policies and these will be the subject of induction training and regular supervision.

14.3   Personal accidents occurring during youth, community and play work service activities must be notified in accordance with the procedures of the Authority.

14.4   It shall be the responsibility of the Authority to ensure that your workplace is supplied with the appropriate first aid and safety equipment and that you are trained in its use.

14.5   You will not be required to drive a mini bus with crew seats, or a mini bus without seat belts on all seats. Where you are required to drive a mini bus, the Authority will train and register you through the local scheme and ensure that you are not required to drive a mini bus on journeys over 150 miles, without another qualified driver being present.

15. Travelling and/or other appropriate expenses.

15.1   Travelling and/or other appropriate expenses and subsistence shall be paid to you at the rates agreed under 'The Local Agreement on part-time Workers'.

16. Training/study leave and pay.

16.1   You are encouraged to attend training courses relevant to your post in addition to the initial qualification.

16.2   If you wish to attend a training course you should inform your line manager, giving at least six week's notice. This request will then be considered in relation to the Authority's overall training strategies.

16.3   While undertaking agreed training courses you will receive your normal salary.

16.4   Travelling and other appropriate expenses, including course fees, while on an agreed training course, will be paid by the Authority.

17. Statutory and public duties.

17.1   Time off with full pay, less deductions for payments received in this connection, for public duties shall be allowed, as specified in the Employment Protection (Consolidation) Act 1978, as amended.

17.2   The Authority will pay for time spent on these activities, but payments will be reduced by the amount of any allowances the employee is entitled to claim.

17.3   If you are standing as a candidate for election to a Local Authority Council, or for Parliament, reasonable time off with full pay will be allowed to you following full consultation with your line manager.

18. Trade union membership.

18.1   You are encouraged to belong to the Community and Youth Workers' Union which is recognised by the Authority for the purposes of negotiation.

18.2   Reasonable time off for you to attend trade union meetings or training, will be granted following prior notification to and agreement with the Authority.

18.3   The Authority and the Community and Youth Workers' Union are equally concerned to enable part-time workers to participate fully in industrial relations and time off and cover arrangements will be made for those part-time workers elected as accredited representatives for local, regional or national negotiations.

19. Jury service

19.1 If you are summoned to undertake jury service, you will be granted leave of absence, unless exemption is secured.

19.2 If you serve as a juror, you must claim the allowance for loss of earnings to which you are entitled under the juror's allowances currently in force. An amount equivalent to the allowance will be deducted from your pay.

20. Maternity leave and pay.

20.1 Female employees are entitled to the maternity leave and pay provisions set out in the Appendix attached to this contract. *(You will need to devise a local scheme, building on national minima. Consult the JNC Report and Labour Research Department Publications).*

21. Parental leave.

21.1 If you have parental/carer's responsibility for a newly born or adopted child and its mother, you are entitled to paid leave to be taken within two months of the date of the birth or adoption. This will equate to two sessions. *(You will of course need to negotiate an acceptable local formula.)*

22. Adoption leave.

22.1 You are entitled to reasonable time off with pay to attend court hearings and attend essential meetings prior to and including the court decision to grant an adoption order where such hearings or meetings take place within your normal contracted period of employment.

23. Compassionate leave.

23.1 In the following cases of urgent domestic distress or upheaval:
– bereavement following the loss of a partner or close relative
– breakdown of committed relationship
– caring for a sick relative
– fire, flood etc.
– you may be granted leave of up to two weeks.
By mutual arrangement with your line manager the sessions which you would normally have worked in those two weeks could be worked at other times within two months of the event.

23.2 You may take reasonable time off work, without loss of pay, to receive medical and dental and optical treatment and ante natal care where this coincides with your normal sessional hours worked.

23.3 You will be entitled to all public holiday leave.

24. Sick leave.

24.1 If you are prevented from reporting for duty due to illness, you shall notify your line manager as soon as possible giving the reason for your absence and the likely date of your return to work.

24.2 In the event of the illness lasting not less than four and not more than seven calendar days which coincide with your normal or rearranged sessional working hours, on the first day of returning to work you must complete and submit a self certification form SC2.

24.3 After an absence of seven calendar days which coincide with your normal sessional working hours a medical certificate signed by your doctor is required to cover the eighth and subsequent days of illness.

24.4 In the case of frequent or persistent illness, if the Authority, after consultation with you, is concerned about the absences, or is not satisfied with the reasons given, the Authority may require you to produce a medical certificate when you are next absent from work, or may, in the case of a prolonged absence from work, seek a report from your GP and/or a second medical opinion as to the cause of the incapacity and prognosis. The Authority will meet all costs incurred, and no such steps will be taken without reasonable cause and prior consultation with you.

25. Sick pay.

25.1   You will not be financially penalised for sickness from work. Under normal circumstances you will receive your regular payment for your sessions, even though you were absent through sickness, but in recognition of your commitment to your project and the Authority's needs for the service, you will be entitled to work your sessions at other times by mutual agreement with your line manager. This will not however, be a requirement but is a facility within this contract.

25.2   After six months employment, if you are absent from work owing to illness (including injury or other disability) you shall be entitled to receive an allowance of 26 weeks at full pay, 26 weeks at half pay. After completing four years of service, for each year over four years continuous service you will be entitled to an extra week on full pay for each completed year, and one week less on half pay for each completed year, up to a maximum of 52 weeks full pay (no half pay).

25.3   This sick pay shall be inclusive of Statutory Sick Pay (at whatever rate paid). SSP is subject to PAYE and National Insurance, and these deductions shall be made accordingly.

25.4   The Authority has the discretion to extend the application of the above scale in exceptional cases, and will review your position at an early opportunity and before your entitlement to paid sick leave expires.

26. Termination of employment.

26.1   The period of notice required to terminate your employment shall be as follows:

Continuous Service	Period of Notice
One month or more but less than two years Two years or more but less than 12 years	1 month +1 week for each year of continuous employment
12 years or more	Not less than 12 weeks

26.2   Redundancy payment will be made on a pro rata basis in accordance with the local scheme arranged for all full-time employees of the authority. This is calculated on the basis of length of service, age, and earnings.

27. Pension.

27.1   Occupational pension schemes have thresholds of the minimum number of hours that have to be worked before there is access to the scheme. Where such thresholds are met the Authority intends that you should have the facility of joining the scheme. Where such thresholds are not met the Authority and CYWU will work together to offer you the appropriate alternative through their own arrangements and professional advice.

28. Employment probation.

28.1   In addition to your regular supervision meetings with your line manager, there will be a full assessment of your performance in post measured against the job description and requirements and contractual obligations. This will take place after your first six months of employment.

29. Induction.

29.1 All new employees will receive a minimum of three sessions of induction and you will be provided with copies of all employment procedures relating to this post, rules and guidelines and local Authority policies.

30. Serving notices.

30.1 Any notice served under the provisions of this contract shall be duly served on you if handed to you personally, or left at, or posted to, your last known address. Any notice served by you under the provisions of this contract shall be duly served on the Authority if handed by you to your line manager or posted to the Authority's address.

31. Disciplinary procedure.

31.1 The disciplinary procedure that applies to this post shall be as set out in the Appendix A attached.

32. Grievance procedure.

32.1 The grievance procedure that applies to this post shall be as set out in the Appendix B attached.

33. Employment rules.

33.1 The employment rules that apply to this post shall be as set out in the Appendix C attached. *(You will need to attach your standard documents relating to the above three clauses.)*

34. Staff handbook.

34.1 You will be provided with a staff handbook and any mutually agreed updates. You will be expected to maintain and create personal access to this handbook.

35. Job description.

35.1 You will be provided with a Job Description which will be subject to annual review and amendment through consultation.

36. Supervision reports and notes.

36.1 You will provide a written report for supervision and in turn be provided with a written record of the supervision meetings which you will file for personal access.

37. Information concerning you.

37.1 Information concerning your private life that may be known to the Authority through normal management procedures will not be disseminated within the Authority or externally unless your consent has first been obtained. Information you may be aware of concerning the private life of the Authority members or officers will be subject to your contractual obligations of confidentiality.

38. Professional conduct.

38.1 The Authority recognises you as a professional educator involved with the informal social education of young people, adults and children and will endeavour to ensure that you are supported and guided in all aspects of your work and provide you with written details of the appropriate policies and procedures to invoke in various circumstances.

38.2   You are not expected to work in unsafe or unhealthy situations and in situations where normal staffing ratios have been exceeded or in situations where you would be unnecessarily vulnerable.

38.3   You are expected to sign the Code of Professional Conduct. *(See later section, but ensure that this is incorporated as a separate appendix alongside this written Statement of Particulars.)*

39.   Any other matters.

39.1   Any other matters not provided for in this Contract and determined by the published agreements of the JNC Report or other local agreements shall be deemed included in this contract.

39.2   The Authority shall insure you at work against injury as a result of the Authority's negligence, loss or damage to property while at work and shall seek to provide you with legal protection and support in cases of unjustifiable complaint from the public or Press. Where a complaint is made against you by a member of the public, or young person or parent the attached procedure shall be applied.

39.3   Where you are concerned that an act of commission or omission by another colleague or superior is endangering or otherwise harming the effective service provided by the Authority you will raise this matter in the first instance using the grievance procedure within the organisation.

40.   Acknowledgement.

40.1   This Statement comprises your contract of employment. It should be signed by you and dated and signed and dated by your line manager. You should retain a copy in your possession as should the Authority.

Signature of Employee

Date   2002

Signature of Employer

Date   2002

Changing the contract

The Contract of Employment cannot legally be changed without the agreement of the part-time worker concerned. If changes are proposed, proper periods of notice must be given with time for representation and discussion, and if the employee agrees, a new Contract which incorporates the changes must be issued within a month of the changes taking place.

  If an employer gives notice of changing a contract they are in effect giving notice to terminate the contract and offering a new one on altered terms. This is always a difficult situation. Individuals are scared into accepting variations to their contract under threat of losing their job.

  On the other hand, an employer who threatens a united workforce with the same change of contract, will be forced to think twice and negotiate, when that workforce all say no at the same time.

  If the employer fails to consult about a change to a contract, the employee has a right to claim breach of contract in the civil court. They will have to demonstrate that the change was fundamental, and if the court agrees it has the power to restore the contract to its original form. There are many cases of precedent within this area of legislation.

Rights of part-time workers

It seems unthinkable that until recently, employees themselves deprived of basic employment rights have been expected to intervene so much to assist young people and communities in obtaining their rights. Employers in this sector, as in most others, have been less than magnanimous in their information to part-time workers concerning their rights and entitlements. Indeed many youth, community and play work officers have deliberately employed part-time workers in such a way as to deprive them of the minimal rights that existed under law until 1994. It is worth commenting that the parity agreement which the British unions have long sought for part-time workers, is law in Belgium, Denmark, France, Germany, Greece, Italy, Luxembourg, Holland, Portugal and Spain, where part-time workers' rights to pay and conditions are the same as full-time employees. At last it is law here too, though most employers of part-time workers in the youth, community and play work sector are ignorant of the fact.

Under pressure from the European Court of justice, the British Trade Union Movement and the Equal Opportunities Commission together successfully challenged Britain's unjust legislation and employment practices which have now by and large changed. The Staff Side of the JNC particularly pressed to end discriminatory practice within the sector and were instrumental in agreeing a full schedule of parity within the *JNC Report* in 1995. It is therefore important to consider some of the central rights that exist, and with several of the most common abuses in youth, community and play work in mind, to look at some case law.

In a landmark decision on 3rd March 1994, the House of Lords decided in *R. v. Secretary of State for Employment ex parte Equal Opportunities Commission* (EOC) that the UK was in breach of its obligations under European legislation in the way it differentiated between full-time and part-time employees. The EOC had challenged the continuous service requirement in UK law whereby those employed for under 16 but at least eight hours per week had to wait five years to obtain comparable rights with those working at least 16 hours per week for the following:

- The right not to be unfairly dismissed.
- The right to unfair dismissal compensation.
- The right to redundancy payment.

The House of Lords decided that the maintenance of disparate treatment was against Article 119 of the Treaty of Rome, and the Equal Pay Directive. Indeed in a recent case (*Warren v Wylie and Wylie*, Southampton Tribunal, IRLR 316) a Tribunal interpreted the House of Lords' judgement that employment thresholds were discriminatory, as applying to the eight hour threshold as well, and they permitted a complainant to bring her case for unfair dismissal to the tribunal, regardless of the fact that the employee worked less than 16 hours per week and, at times, less than eight hours a week. The two year employment threshold for employees, before they could enforce most of their rights, was also reduced to one year, and in many cases, as appears below, an employee need only be in work three months before they can exercise their right to complain at tribunal. From 1999 onwards, many rights came into effect. The trade union movement largely supports the notion that it should in fact be only one day at work that qualifies an employee for all rights.

These days, it is more accurate to talk of *workers* rights, rather than the rights of full- or part-time workers. Workers rights, as detailed below, can be asserted through the Employment Tribunals after certain qualifying periods of service. One element of compensation which has been significantly enhanced is the maximum award for unfair dismissal, which at the time of writing in November 2000 stands at £50,000.

Having rights is one thing. Asserting them is another. Invoking them when things go wrong is another still. Workplace rights are important, but how much advice about them are youth, community and play workers given? The emphasis so far in this series has been to use the Labour governments positive workplace legislation to both enshrine human and employment rights at work and establish employment policies and contracts of employment that incorporate these rights. This both seeks to show that attention to good contracts, managed by effective supervision and health and safety assessments and monitored where necessary by a proper use of discipline creates a healthy problem solving environment.

Life isn't always so nice, especially in the caring and sharing professions! On average ten serious workplace problems are referred to CYWU's national office every week. Countless more are dealt with at branch level. Many of the problems arise because of the ignorance of staff and employers about employment rights and indeed the increasingly high penalties that face bad employers. A court's finding of unfair dismissal could now cost an employer £50,000, enough to bankrupt some small voluntary organisations. In asserting these rights employers and employees need to exercise the principles of natural justice in getting a fair hearing and examining all the evidence.

To improve work, we need to make the most important cultural shifts. Firstly, the grievance procedure to which all workers have a right, needs to be seen as a positive thing. A grievance procedure permits you to complain about a problem and get an answer within a timescale. It is a problem solving mechanism professionally introduced so that irritations do not fester untreated. You are not a trouble maker in taking out a grievance. You are acting professionally in trying to sort something that is inhibiting performance and that no other discussions have solved. Good supervision helps avoid grievances.

Secondly, particularly in youth, community and play work, there is often an exaggerated sense of 'us and them' in relation to officers and managers. While both parties can be at fault and may not get on personally, both have an interest in upholding high standards of employment practice. Within a youth work hierarchy the Principal Youth Officers, Area Officers, full-time staff and part-time workers all have the same basic contracts of employment giving them the same access to discipline, grievance, and other employment procedure. They all share, of course, the same employment rights in law. If a superior misuses a procedure with a junior, or flouts a right, they are in effect misusing and endangering their own contract of employment. There should be a shared interest between management and staff in getting procedures and rights at work correct. This is why both grievance and disciplinary procedures should be seen as positive components of a professional workplace. It is not the nasty boss who should use discipline, nor the stroppy worker who should take out a grievance. Professionals should use these procedures to resolve intractable workplace problems in a dignified and constructive way.

Where something goes wrong in terms of the implementation of a procedure that an individual has a right to, for instance where there has been no regular risk assessment of an individual's stress levels, then all other individuals with the same contractual right to that procedure are threatened, that is, the individual's stress levels impact on those of their colleagues. This is where the collective grievance can come in. A group of one or more staff aggrieved about an issue has a right to have their collective grievance properly and fairly heard. This should solve rather than store up problems.

But what if things really deteriorate at work ? In what circumstances can an employer act so badly that employees have legal redress ? Very often workers mistake terrible employment practice and unfairness for illegality. While there is a growing list of illegal employment acts, it is worth bearing in mind the actual circumstances which the courts can cover. The Employment Tribunals can only deal with certain situations as set out in the major laws of employment. These laws are shaped by the political pressures of employers and unions at national level. A government biased towards employers shapes them one way, a government more interested in partnership shapes them another.

You cannot just go to an Employment Tribunal and complain that you are being treated badly. You have to have a case which could involve an illegality. But it is not even this simple. To have your case heard on some matters, you must have had a certain length of service with your employer. In many circumstances, particularly, of course, unfair dismissal, you actually have to be out of work before you can claim. The tribunal can then rule that you should be reinstated or re-engaged or compensated. In other words, to complain to a Tribunal, you have to qualify by virtue of your length of service and the nature of your complaint. The Employment Tribunals consider cases involving:

- dismissal
- redundancy and business transfers
- maternity rights
- discrimination (on the grounds only of race, sex or disability, discrimination on the basis of sexual orientation is not in itself illegal)

- victimisation of trade union members
- rights concerning time off work
- working time regulations
- matters relating to the application of the National Minimum Wage
- contractual and payment claims. While the Tribunals are less formal than any other court setting, they are nevertheless legal proceedings and you are always advised to seek advice and representation before taking a claim to Tribunal to pursue your rights.

To illustrate. Employees now have rights to a set minimum of annual leave, and to daily and weekly rest periods. If your employer denies these rights you can complain to an Employment Tribunal after three months of service. However, from day one of your employment, you have rights to a range of other entitlements. For example you can claim unpaid time off for public duties, paid time for ante natal care, paid time off for being a union representative or safety representative, or, if you are a young person, time off for study or training. Nor do you need any qualifying service to complain to a Tribunal against sexual, racial or disability discrimination at work.

Rights to redundancy pay, and to claim unfair dismissal and compensation are important, very important in a lot of cases, but they are not exactly the most positive rights. Of course, where a Statement of Particulars seeks, as in the model above, to improve on this position explicitly, then the Contract would override the limited protection in law. Here is a summary of the current position with respect to those rights you can assert through Tribunal and the time in work needed to assert them. (*Note: EDT=Effective Date of Termination of employment*)

Workers' rights

Right	Qualifying period	Time limit for ET complaint
Unfair Dismissal		
Written reasons for dismissal	one year	three months starting with EDT
Unfair dismissal complaint	one year	three months
Unfair dismissal connected with medical suspension	one year	three months starting with EDT
Unfair dismissal connected with industrial action	one year	six months starting with EDT
Unfair dismissal connected with business transfer	one year	three months starting with EDT
Unfair Dismissal for being a health and safety representative or for a health and safety reason	none	three months starting with EDT
Unfair dismissal for a reason connected with the working time regulations	none	three months starting with EDT
Unfair dismissal for performing functions as an employee representative or standing for election as such	none	three months starting with EDT
Unfair dismissal for making a protected disclosure	none	three months starting with EDT
Unfair dismissal for asserting an individual statutory right	none	three months starting with EDT
Unfair dismissal for a reason connected with the National Minimum Wage	none	three months starting with EDT
Unfair dismissal for being or refusing to be a member of an independent trade union or taking part in union activities or recognition ballots	none	three months starting with EDT

Unfair dismissal for a reason related to tax credits	none	three months starting with EDT
Unfair dismissal for seeking to exercise right to be accompanied at disciplinary hearing or accompanying a worker at such a hearing	none	three months starting with EDT
Unfair dismissal for taking part in protected industrial action	none	three months starting with EDT
Dismissal for redundancy but reason for selection one for which no qualifying period required	none	three months starting with EDT
Interim relief pending a complaint under some sections of the ER Act	none	seven days immediately following EDT

Redundancy and Business Transfer

Redundancy payments	two years	six months starting with relevant date
Claims for protective award because of failure to consult with appropriate representatives over proposed redundancies	n/a	either before dismissal or three months starting with date on which dismissal takes effect
Failure to pay remuneration under protective award	none	three months starting with last day in respect of which complaint is made
Consultation with appropriate representatives over a business transfer	n/a	three months starting with date of completion of transfer
Failure to comply with a compensation order made under Reg. 11	n/a	three months starting with date of tribunal's order

Family Rights

Unfair dismissal and the right not to suffer a detriment for family reasons (Maternity and Parental Regs)	none	three months starting with EDT
Right to be offered alternative work before maternity suspension	none	three months starting with first day of suspension.
Right to be paid during maternity suspension	none	three months starting with EDT
Right to time off for parental leave	one year	three months beginning with the date of the matter complained of
Right to time off for a dependent	none	three months beginning with the date of the matter complained of

Discrimination

Sex discrimination claim	none	three months starting with date of act complained of
Race discrimination claim	none	three months starting with date of act complained of
Disability discrimination claim	none	three months starting with date of act complained of
Appeals against non discrimination notices issued by the CRE, EOC and DRC	n/a	six weeks after notice

Equal pay/value claim	none	six months starting with termination of employment
Preliminary complaint by EOC/CRE	n/a	six months starting with date of act complained of
Application by EOC/CRE in connection with discriminatory advertising or pressure to discriminate	n/a	six months starting when act to which application relates was committed
Trade Unions and Union Members		
Action short of dismissal for trade union membership or activities or recognition Ballots	none	three months starting with date of last act complained of
Unlawful exclusion/expulsion from union	none	six months starting with date of exclusion/expulsion.
Failure of an employer to consult with a recognised union over training	n/a	three months beginning with date of alleged failure
Failure to comply with a compensation order	n/a	three months beginning with the alleged failure
Unjustifiable discipline by union	none	three months from the union's decision
Application for compensation for above	none	not before four weeks and not after 6 months from date of ET's decision
Unauthorised deduction of union subscriptions	none	three months starting with date of payment
Refusal of employment on grounds related to union membership	n/a	three months starting with date of conduct complained of
Time Off (Other than for family reasons)		
Right to unpaid time off for public duties	none	three months from date of failure to give time off
Right to paid time off to look for work where notice of dismissal by reason of redundancy has been given	1 year	three months starting from the day time off should have been allowed
Right to paid time off for ante natal care	none	three months starting with date of appointment
Right to paid time off for pension scheme trustees	none	three months starting with date when the failure occurred
Right to paid time off for employee representative	none	three months starting with date when the failure occurred
Right to paid time off for employee safety representatives and for candidates standing for election as such	none	three months starting with date when the failure occurred
Right to paid time off for safety representatives	none	three months starting with date when the failure occurred
Right to paid time off for Union duties	none	three months starting with date when the failure occurred
Right to unpaid time off for union activities	none	three months starting with date when the failure occurred
Right of young person to time off for study or training	none	three months starting the day time off taken or on which time off should have been allowed

Working Time Regulations

Right to daily rest	none	three months from date when right should have been permitted
Right to rest breaks	none	three months from date when right should have been permitted
Right to compensatory rest in cases where the above regulations are modified or excluded	none	three months from date when right should have been permitted
Right to annual leave	none	three months from date when right should have been permitted or if leave extended over more than one day, date when right should have been permitted to begin
Right to payment in lieu of holiday on termination of employment	none	three months from date payment should have been made
Right to pay during annual leave	none	three months from date payment should have been made

National Minimum Wage

Worker paid less than minimum wage	none	three months from starting date of underpayment
Appeal by employer against enforcement notice	n/a	four weeks from date of service of the notice
Appeal by employer against penalty	n/a	four weeks from the date of service of the notice
Failure to permit employee access to pay records	n/a	three months from the expiration of 14 days following service of the production notice

Miscellaneous

Guarantee pay	one month	three months starting with day for which payment claimed
Rights on insolvency of employer	none	three months starting with communication of Secretary of State's decision
Right to itemised pay statement	none	three months starting with date on which employment ceased
Right to written particulars of employment	one month	three months starting with date on which employment ceased
Medical suspension pay	one month	three months starting with first day of suspension
Unlawful deduction from wages	none	three months from date of (last) deduction or (last) payment to employee
Right not to suffer detriment in relation to health and safety, Sunday working. and working time, etc.	none	three months starting with date of (last) act or failure to act
Contract claim by employee	none	three months from EDT or last day on which the employee worked

Contract claim by employer	n/a	six weeks from receipt of employee's claim
Appeals against health and safety prohibition and improvement notices	n/a	21 days from service of notice
Appeals against assessments to training levy	n/a	one month from the date of service of assessment notice
Right to be accompanied at a disciplinary hearing	none	three months beginning with the date of the act complained about
Application by the Secretary of State for an order prohibiting a person from carrying on business as an employment agency	n/a	none

EC Council Directive and part-time workers

It is important that youth, community and play work employment practice is consistent with the progressive thinking on which the work is based. Many proposals have been made within Europe concerning favourable legislation for part-time, temporary and casual workers. Their emphasis has been to increase rights and move towards full parity with full-time workers. The Council of the European Communities has proposed a directive be agreed, the full text of which is given below. A further interesting concept enshrined within the Council's proposal is the notion that part-time workers' representative bodies will be informed of developments that affect them. One could say that the European Judges are in advance of part-time youth, community and play workers and their employers in encouraging trade unionism! It is also important to note that several previous drafts of this proposal were more radical in their suggestions and that the British Government was particularly vehement in opposition to them.

EC Council Directive on Non-standard Work

The Council of the European Communities having regard to the:
- treaty establishing the European Economic Community, and in particular Article 100 thereof
- proposal from the Commission
- opinion of the European Parliament
- opinion of the Economic and Social Committee

has adopted this Directive.

Article 1
Scope

1. This Directive applies to:
   a) Part-time employment carried out by a worker whose normal working hours are shorter than the normal working hours of full-time workers in a comparable situation.
   b) Employment governed by a fixed term contract concluded directly between the employer and the worker, where the end of the contract is established by objective conditions such as, reaching a specific date, completing a specific task or the occurrence of a specific event.

c) Temporary employment relationships between a temporary employment agency, which is the employer, and the worker, where the latter is available to work for and under the control of a user undertaking and/or establishment.

2. This Directive shall apply to workers in private and public undertakings working under one of the arrangements referred to in Paragraph 1.

Article 2
Minimum remuneration

The basic remuneration for workers covered by this Directive may not be lower than the basic remuneration for full-time workers, solely on the grounds that they are working part-time, on a fixed term contract or under a temporary employment relationship, and where appropriate it should be calculated pro rata of full-time workers and/or workers on open ended contracts in a comparable situation.

Article 3
Annual leave and public holidays

Member States shall take the necessary steps to ensure that the workers covered by this Directive enjoy conditions equivalent to those of full-time workers and/or workers employed on open ended contracts in respect of annual leave and public holidays.

Article 4
Statutory social security schemes

1. Member States shall take the necessary measures to ensure that the workers covered by this Directive are not excluded from the statutory social security schemes associated with the exercise of a professional activity and enjoy conditions equivalent to those of full-time workers employed on open ended contracts.
   Where appropriate, these conditions may be determined by reference to the duration of the work or to contributions or benefits.
2. However, Member States may exclude from statutory social security schemes, except for those providing services relating to accidents at work and occupational diseases, workers covered by this Directive whose remuneration or duration of work is less than a given threshold.
3. This threshold should be sufficiently low so as not to exclude an unduly high proportion of the workers covered by this Directive.

Article 5
Constitution of workers' representative bodies.

Member States shall take the necessary measures to ensure that the workers covered by this Directive are not excluded from the calculation of the threshold above which the constitution of workers' representative bodies within the undertaking is required by national provisions.

Article 6
Briefing workers' representatives

Member States shall take the necessary steps to ensure that the employer supplies to the workers' representative bodies within the undertaking a periodic statement of the type of work covered by the Directive in terms of the development of the workforce as a whole.

Article 7

More favourable provisions

This Directive shall not affect the rights of Member States to apply or introduce laws, regulations or administrative provisions more favourable to the workers covered by the Directive.

Workers' rights in relation to their service

As mentioned before, having rights is one thing, winning something meaningful back if they are abused is quite another matter. The minefield of legal interpretation and the daunting prospect of taking a case through Industrial Tribunals or Courts is often a deterrent to exercising rights. If legal rights have been abused or denied, within employment legislation the remedies are often extremely weak. Very rarely does an unfairly dismissed worker, or one who has been made redundant with no regard for the law, get their job back.

Whether rights appear relatively strong, or weak, whether they are written down directly in statute, or implied in case law, you will always have to organise to enforce them. Hence the most important right that part-time workers have is to belong to a trade union. Once in the trade union, the right to attend all Branch meetings and influence the negotiations locally and nationally on part-time workers' issues is an essential responsibility. The right to join a trade union goes alongside the responsibility to play a part in its democracy.

There really is no substitute for collective organisation in improving terms and conditions, or establishing and defending rights.

This is why so much emphasis is placed here on the importance of centrally agreed documents such as the Model Local Agreement on Part-time Workers, the Statement of Particulars, Job Descriptions and Employment Policies. part-time workers must join together to mandate negotiators to improve these on their behalf. It should naturally be a condition of grant aid to voluntary sector projects that the same conditions and management support were provided there. Nevertheless, some description of the current position may be helpful.

Rights requiring one year's continuous service

Unfair dismissal

This is a complex, and ever changing, aspect of case law. Basically, for a dismissal to be fair, the employer has to prove that it was made according to the five admissible reasons for dismissal contained in the *Employment Relations Act 1999* and that fair procedures were used in the dismissal.

The five admissible reasons for dismissal under the Act are:

1. Related to the capability or qualifications of the employee for performing work of the kind he was employed by the employer to do.
2. Related to the conduct of the employee.
3. That the employee was redundant.
4. That the employee could not continue to work in the same position which he held, without contravention (either on his part or on that of his employer) of a duty or a restriction imposed by or under an enactment.
5. That it was for some other substantial reason of a kind such as to justify the dismissal of an employee holding the position which that employee held.

If someone does not have continuous service for a year they can be dismissed with impunity for any reason.

Written reasons for dismissal

An employer must give written reasons for dismissal following a request to do so from an ex employee. This right is automatic for those dismissed while on maternity leave.

Redundancy payments

The whole period (not just that worked after the two year qualifying period) has to be added up for the purpose of redundancy payment. Service before the age of eighteen is ignored and calculations are made on the basis of earnings, length of service and age. It is important to ensure that this is spelt out clearly in the Statement of Particulars.

Time off prior to redundancy

Following a notice of redundancy, an employee is entitled to reasonable time off with pay to look for work, or arrange re-training.

Maternity provisions

A female employee has the right not to be unreasonably refused time off with pay for ante natal care, to return to work after the birth of the baby, and to statutory maternity pay (dependent on pay level and qualifying service). Note also that since 16th October 1994 there has been an entitlement to 14 weeks maternity leave for all pregnant workers regardless of their length of service or hours of work. The right to return to work after 29 weeks post natal leave is conditional upon the worker having completed a qualifying period of two years service. This is assessed on the basis of the beginning of the eleventh week before the expected confinement proved by the certification of form Mat B1 by the pregnant worker's doctor. The return to work must be to the job in which the worker was employed under the original contract and there must be no detriment to terms and conditions. If the job has been made redundant during the period of absence the employer must offer a suitable alternative.

Rights requiring one month's employment

Guarantee payments

It is particularly important to negotiate contracts that are permanent and guarantee a monthly wage.

Notice of termination

This right ensures that there is minimum paid notice of termination which increases in length with length of service. Workers are entitled to one week's notice after one month's employment. This goes up to two weeks after two years and then by one week every year to a maximum of twelve. Unless otherwise specified in the contract the worker's period of notice to the employer is one week regardless of length of service.

Medical suspension payment.

This is rarely invoked in youth, community and play work, but gives a right to pay if suspended from work in designated health and safety cases as a preventative measure.

Statement of particulars of employment.

All youth, community and play workers, regardless of the hours they work should receive a statement within two months of taking up employment, but the right in law is to have one in all cases. Additionally, there are legal requirements on what must be included in the contract, *see the section on the Model Statement of Particulars above.*

Rights taking immediate effect upon employment

Time off for trade union and public duties

Historically within the youth, community and play work service, part-time workers have been discriminated against in this regard. Rights to trade union involvement are enshrined in Paragraphs 168–70 of the *Trade Union and Labour Relations (Consolidation) Act 1992* in relation to trade union duties and Paragraph 29 of the *Employment Protection (Consolidation) Act 1978* in relation to public duties. The basic rights are to:

- Time off with pay to carry out trade union duties.
- Time off without pay for trade union activities.
- Time off without pay for public duties.

There is a growing tendency, particularly in Europe and again through the European Court of Justice (ECJ) to see the refusal of appropriate trade union facilities for part-time workers as discriminatory. In an important case (*Arbeiterzwolfahrt der Stadt Berlin e VV. Botel, 1992, IRLR 423, ECJ*) the ECJ argued that a trade union training course in connection with trade union duties, which required the presence of part-time workers outside of their normal working time, could involve indirect sex discrimination if the time spent were to be with pay for the full-time colleagues. In such circumstances the employer would have to show objective justification for the difference in treatment. There are stronger legal rights to time off with pay for health and safety representatives.

It is clear that part-time workers will have to spend more time involved in CYWU activities, negotiations and training. Indeed, it has always surprised me that employers have not been more magnanimous in allowing time off for either trade union or public duties among youth, community and play workers, because it is surely to the advantage of the whole service to have trade union and civic leaders originating from our sector. On top of any rights there should be a proactive policy of encouragement.

Itemised pay statements

The components of pay and deductions must be set out.

Equal pay

This is a question in law between the sexes, not between full and part-time workers. However, where most part-time workers can be demonstrated to be women (as is almost invariably the case) and it can be argued that they are doing like work, work rated as equivalent under a job evaluation study, or work of equal value, (this is determined by a tribunal, following the report of an expert independent person who compares the woman's job with a comparable man's job) then a case can be fought. An individual woman has to fight the case. This of course, is very often the deterrent. The relevant legislation, the *Equal Pay Act 1970*, does not prohibit differential treatment between full and part-time workers per se.

Health and safety

This is a much underestimated area of entitlement within youth, community and play work. *The Health and Safety at Work Act 1974*, the complex host of regulations and codes of practice which have followed, and the obligations that have flowed from the new legal framework laid out in the *European Framework Directive 1993*, provide a range of useful rights which have immediate effect upon taking up employment. The legislation does not distinguish between full and part-time workers.

For many youth, community and play workers, dangers relate to traditional issues affecting many groups of workers like unsafe buildings, but they also relate to the more difficult occupation-specific issues like staffing ratios, working alone, working at night, driving vehicles, outdoor pursuits and hazardous activities.

Negotiations to establish minimum staffing levels, distribution of mobile phones, emergency lines, alarms etc., should all be considered in the sector as integral to health and safety protection. The provisions of the *Personal Protective Equipment at Work Regulations 1992* require employers to provide protective equipment to anyone exposed to risks.

The Health and Safety (Display Screen Equipment) Regulations 1992 will be particularly of interest to part-time staff employed in resource centres etc. who have to use computers. These regulations cover a range of important details including break times, eyesight testing and employers' responsibilities etc.

Many youth, community and play workers work in dilapidated, cramped buildings and offices. *The Workplace (Health, Safety and Welfare) Regulations 1992* set standards for the physical environment. Since 1st January 1993 all new workplaces must comply immediately with the regulations, while existing workplaces had until 1st January 1996 to comply. This is why it is so important that there is a national health and safety and suitability audit of all youth, community and play work premises. *The Approved Code of Practice* on the Regulations says among many other things that:

- each worker should have 11 cubic metres of space available to them
- there must be sufficient sanitary and washing facilities, dependent on the maximum number using the premises at any one time
- there must be sufficient accommodation for clothing.

In the *Management of Health and Safety at Work Regulations 1992*, Regulation 7, employers are required to establish procedures to cope with circumstances of serious and imminent danger to those at work. This is usefully supported by Paragraph 57a of the *Employment Protection (Consolidation) Act 1978* which allows employees to leave their workplace in circumstances of serious and imminent danger without being subject to employer's action against them.

Apart from the right to withdraw from an unsafe, or imminently unsafe environment, the right to be protected, and the right to time off as a trade union health and safety representative, perhaps the most important rights are those that require the employer to inform you of the health and safety environment and to be trained in health and safety measures and awareness. There should really be at least one training session each year for all youth, community and play workers on health and safety issues.

Regulation 11 of the *Management of Health and Safety at Work Regulations 1992* means that employers must provide their workers with adequate health and safety training when they are recruited and then when they become exposed to new risks. This should be held within normal working hours, or if outside these hours be regarded as an extension of working time.

Regulation 8 of the *Management Regulations* imposes a duty on the employers to provide workers with comprehensible and relevant information on the risks to their health and safety which have been identified, relevant preventative and protective measures, evacuation procedures and how to handle them together with those authorised to be in charge etc.

A basic checklist of health and safety issues is contained in Part 7 on Health and Safety Issues.

Training and qualification for part-time workers

From the Bessey programmes of the 1960s through *Starting From Strengths* in 1985 to the development of *RAMPs* in 1990 and now the retrogressive introduction of various off-the-shelf schemes based on functional analysis (Open Learning, RSA, City and Guilds, NVQs, Occupational Standards), part-time workers' training has been subject to continual and lively debate within the field; see Appendix 7 for some of the main publications in this area.

A recognised qualification has become a requirement for all workers. Basic initial training is supplemented by in service modular approaches, where sufficient training officers and resources remain. While advocating above that access to, and participation in, training should be at no detriment to the worker and within the terms of the contract, this section highlights three elements of training that will need to be appreciated if the employment practice is to be right:

1. The core features of training.
2. The professionalism of part-time workers qualification.
3. The level of part-time workers qualification and rights within training.

The core features of training

This has been a matter of periodic analysis both locally and nationally; Appendix 7 has some examples of reviews. What constitutes the core elements of training is also a theoretical and historical construction. The favoured learning models of trainers, the political perspectives of different youth, community and play work services, and funders' objectives, have all influenced the nature of what part-time workers are expected to develop through learning and extend through professional practice. With competences and performance indicators currently all the rage it is salutary to remind ourselves that these words too have different meanings, applications and effects on practice. The drive towards competency assessment, though partly a result of lack of definition arising from *Starting from Strengths*, is driven at heart by right wing behaviourist models of performance assessment and product analysis, that derive from private industry management in the United States.

Despite this, there is a general consensus on distinctive elements of training and, regardless of different words sometimes spoken, a very similar language of expectations is being talked throughout the profession. Much of the consensus remains enshrined within the National Youth Agency *Guidelines to the Endorsement* of both *Initial Training Courses* and *RAMPs*. Significantly, *Endorsement Guidelines* recognises the need to train staff who have a capacity for bringing experience to bear on work, learning from experience, reflecting creatively on continuing practice, and holding a number of different dimensions of educational practice together simultaneously.

This was an aspect of the professionalism of youth, community and play work firmly noted by the *Report of the Working Group*, '…to define the distinctive elements that form the core of all youth, community and play work' (NYA, 1993). In this, five elements were seen as being critical to the educational purpose and outcomes of both community work and youth work and indicative of the essential value base of the work which should inform every level and aspect of practice, another concept denied in the NVQ model. These were:

1. informal education process
2. collective action
3. autonomy of individuals and groups
4. change and development
5. justice and equality

Such elements included earlier commitments in training and learning outcomes to:

- interaction with individuals and groups
- management and administration
- use of self analysis
- communication
- education
- learning, planning and evaluation

In turn, these aspects would be developed broadly speaking in the range of duties identified by the *JNC Report* which are:

- face to face work
- development of service provision
- finance and administration
- work with other agencies

If education through informal methods is the purpose of the work, then anyone practising the work must be able to:

- facilitate the learning of young people and adults
- respond to the expressed learning needs of individuals and groups
- identify the learning needs of individuals and groups
- engage in dialogue and problem posing with individuals and groups
- devise learning strategies to seek to meet needs of individuals and groups

One of the most significant points advocated by the Core Elements Working Party was that the core of the work was felt to be less about the separation of all the functional strands of the work and more about their fusion together with the appropriate values into action. The core focus of youth, community and play work training was seen as equipping workers to make such a synthesis, and this complex amalgam applied to part-time workers equally. The core of the work is distinctive, said the working party, '…because of its holistic nature and the degree of professional judgement and responsibility workers need to exercise in balancing sometimes conflicting forces' (p19).

Analyses of part-time worker training courses reveal components designed to achieve the understanding of values, education techniques and work management implied by the above statement. Expectations are simply much higher now than they were at the outset of organised training following the Bessey Report. Components of courses picked at random include:

- understanding the aims, objectives and history of the youth service
- understanding social education techniques, equal opportunities and anti discriminatory practice
- adolescent behaviour and growth
- health and safety
- general legislation
- employers' procedures
- administrative procedures
- youth and community and play work setting
- cultural diversity
- curriculum development
- relationship between theory and practice
- counselling
- awareness of self and others
- personal management techniques
- effective communication methods
- sports opportunities
- health risks
- artistic, cultural and spiritual opportunities
- wider social and political context
- evaluation techniques

Indeed, the *HMI summary report on part-time worker training* (1992) reviewed the complex composite training requirements and quoted from the eight core areas identified in North Yorkshire:

1. The ability to demonstrate a knowledge and understanding of the needs of young people and to respond effectively to those needs within specific settings.
2. Competence in relation to the formation, maintenance and development of relationships with young people and adults through a recognition of their own self awareness.
3. The ability to communicate effectively with young people and adults.
4. The ability to demonstrate an understanding of the group process through working as part of a team and making interventions within groups as appropriate.
5. Competence with regard to planning and organising work through the setting of objectives and the effective use of resources.
6. The ability to evaluate their work in order to develop future strategies and objectives.
7. Competence in relationship to the acknowledgement of the equality of all regardless of race, gender, creed or physical or intellectual abilities, and the ability to develop strategies within the work setting which support this basic premise.
8. Competence in relationship to the involvement of young people in the organisation or community to which they belong.

It is hardly surprising that the Core Elements Working Party developed an important theme introduced at the *In Crisis of Confidence Conference* of 1992 which took stock of the position in training. This was to reassert a positive, non elitist conception of professionalism to apply to all workers in the field. The work undertaken in this period has not been surpassed since, despite the creation of sets of national occupational standards for youth work, play work and community work. While the lists, of elements of work that these staff may do, created by working groups and national training organisations may be interesting lists, they float free of the embedded culture of collective professional development and pitch the level of qualification too low.

Since the nineties an elaborate structure of National Occupational Standards have been developed which detail hundreds of component parts of even the simplest youth work and play work and community work interventions. Various modular and portfolio approaches to part-time workers' training and assessment have developed and private awarding bodies have moved into the field to accredit qualifications. The effect in general has often been to alienate staff from the educational process and create the feeling of having to conform to highly prescribed educational attainment criteria. Some would argue that this has taken a lot of the life out of youth work and social education processes.

Professionalism and the level of part-time workers qualification

Drawing on work undertaken by Professor Richard Winter at the Anglia Polytechnic, assessment criteria can be drawn up for establishing concepts of professionalism. Importantly, the criteria incorporate ideas of moral and ethical based judgement so alien to the 'competences tick box' approach now favoured within functional analysis models (City and Guilds, NVQ etc.). Winter lists seven core criteria:

1. commitment to professional values
2. continuous professional learning
3. interpersonal effectiveness
4. effective communication
5. executive effectiveness
6. effective synthesis of a wide range of knowledge
7. intellectual flexibility

Professionalism has a higher productive value, therefore its qualification level is high and the remuneration for it should be high. The *Core Elements Working Party* concluded that if NVQ parallels were to be drawn, part-time workers' qualification would be at least Level Three, but really they need to be seen in their own terms independent of a national framework created for other purposes.

On achieving the necessary paid release for training, it is important that part-time workers are rewarded with:

- a certificate from their own local qualifying scheme
- an increment for completing their training
- a certificate from the National Youth Agency (now nationally transferable) and
- a parallel academically validated certificate which will be recognised within higher education either as contributing points towards various courses of higher education, or contributing significantly to the entry requirements to a full JNC endorsed course.

Regrettably, some would wish to replace this proposed system of professional and academic validation and qualification for part-time workers, which gives, where it operates, three recognised qualifications, with another which gives only one qualification: a meagre NVQ (should it ever be established). It is now likely that new awarding bodies and schemes for part-time workers' training will emerge and these should be integrated with the JNC approval system.

Rights within training

With the development of *RAMPs* part-time workers training became more rigorous and objective, but youth, community and play work services are small and there will always be an element of subjectivity involved with local trainers, assessors and moderators. To help ease this, all *RAMPs* are expected to scrutinise the appeals mechanisms within the local courses they endorse. part-time workers should be given ample opportunity to complain about access and structural features of courses and challenge any decision made against them. Selection for training opportunities and assessment of students in training should be fair and equitable and subject to objective analysis. Once again, this will be a difficult right to maintain under NVQ-led systems, but it should be remembered that the JNC has asserted the right of all part-timers to in service training.

Union and employer negotiators should:

1. Establish fair recruitment and selection procedures for training.
2. Establish the rights and entitlements outlined in the model agreement above.
3. Establish clear and quick rights of appeal, incorporating clear timescales, rights to representation etc., against any decision not to select someone for training, or any decision while on training that may affect the learning environment or outcome. The right should be established that the trainee can invoke the appeals procedure at any stage should they feel that their performance is likely to suffer as the result of some negligence or problem not of their making.
4. Establish the right to consultation on all curriculum issues and requests to employ additional training staff.

One of the most important recent developments within the lifelong learning agenda has been the creation by government of a Trade Union Learning Fund. This has established resources for trade unions, often in partnership with others to provide training. As a beneficiary of this fund CYWU has in fact become the largest provider of training in the youth, community and play work sector. The government's interest in trade unions as transmission belts of quality training has led them to legislate for the creation of trade union learning representatives. These will have the same entitlements to time off and facilities as health and safety representatives. It is hope that our sector will make great use of this new opportunity.

The job description

All too often part-time staff are shoved into a post with no induction, no training and no clear statement of expected role. The job description is an essential requirement and both sides of the JNC have advocated that part-time workers receive one. Some of the main causes of stress in youth, community and play work are a lack of clarity about role, and mixed messages of expectation. A good Contract and Job Description, coupled with regular supervision can significantly contribute to a good working environment, free from stress and full of reward.

The main functions of a job description are to:

- Outline main duties and responsibilities.
- Establish lines of accountability and management.
- Clarify expectations.
- Provide a baseline for assessing performance and work.
- Set parameters.
- Focus work in times of conflicting demands.

Under the Model Local Agreement five separate job descriptions for part-time youth, community and play workers have been promulgated for use by employers. All staff in a service should be equally aware of the main elements of all other worker's job descriptions. Often this is communicated in the first section of Staff Handbooks which outline everyone's role. By way of illustration the following model is a job description for a general youth worker, Level 2. Paragraph 3 will be a controversial one. It is suggested because it recognises the automatically conflictual nature of political education. Paragraph 4 may also raise some eyebrows. This is incorporated to try and minimise the growth of unsubstantiated complaint and gossip that has caused so much casework in recent years. There are four general principles that should be borne in mind:

1. Job descriptions should be negotiated at the point of origin through the LJNC.
2. Job descriptions should be subject to regular review and amendment with the post holder.
3. Job descriptions should be taken into account as only one part of the grading equation.
4. Assessment of work should be undertaken with the job description as a basis.

A clear job description will be structured around:

a) The job title.
b) Clear statement of *to whom* the postholder is responsible.
c) Clear statement of *for whom* the postholder is responsible.
d) The job purpose.
e) The main duties of the post.

Model Job Description

Name of employer:

Name of department:

Title of post:

General Youth Worker.

Responsible to:

The Director of Education.

Responsible for:

Overseeing the work of one coffee bar assistant.

Your line manager is:

The Area Youth Worker.

The date of this job description:

1st January 2001.

Hours of duty:

Two three hour sessions per week.

Qualifications required:

The local basic training course as endorsed by the Regional Accreditation and Moderation Panel conferring a National Youth Agency Certificate or equivalent approved by the Joint Negotiating Committee for Youth and Community workers.

Purpose of the post:

a) To assist young people in becoming more socially, individually and politically and culturally, aware through a process of education.

b) To assist with the development of the youth work programme at the centre, by working face to face with young people, attending staff meetings, building effective relationships with young people and colleagues and developing an educational programme.

c) To work with other agencies and individuals as required to maximise the opportunities for social education for young people.

Key tasks and responsibilities.

1. To develop the social education curriculum at the centre in conjunction with the staff team, and build close, and trusting relationships with young people so that the above purposes may be fulfilled.

2. To identify and respond to young people's needs and encourage their participation in the centre, the wider community and relevant social institutions.

3. To be familiar with the relevant youth service, civic, community, administrative, and wider political structures in order to create opportunity for young people and assist them and the wider community in countering disadvantage, abuses, misuses and unjust power.

4. To participate with colleagues in centre staff meetings and staff development opportunities, and in service training and to monitor and evaluate work professionally through regular supervision and in accordance with the Authority's procedures for dealing with grievances, complaints and discipline as appropriate and to make your concern about performance or events involving others immediately known to your line manager.
5. To be aware and make use of the community facilities, agencies, social structure, demography and opportunities for young people within the area.
6. To attend regular supervision meetings according to the Staff Development Policy and to prepare reports for them.
7. To work in such a way that continually challenges personal assumptions and those of others which discriminate, prevent participation and foster disadvantage.
8. To undertake the preparation and administration that may be necessary to undertake the duties of the post together with any financial and other responsibilities that may be devolved.
9. To participate in activities outside the centre as required, so that opportunities for residential and international experience may be developed.
10. To assist with the team approach to monitoring and evaluation of work.
11. To provide information, counselling and advice to young people.
12. To take into account the emerging issues which affect and inform the practices of youth work.
13. To assist in ensuring that the centre is run in accordance with the policies of the Authority, the centre itself and those devised from time to time by young people.

Supervision

Good supervision is the single most important factor in improving employment practice and policy.   D. Nicholls

Many potential problems can be prevented if:
- The quality of supervision is high.
- The manager, workers and staff team are open and honest.
- Sufficient time is dedicated to supervision.
- The agenda is sufficiently comprehensive.

Supervision should be available to all part-time workers, all full-time workers and all officers and senior management within the service. The climate of self survival and personal self reliance and heroism, is simply inimical to professional development in youth, community and play work. No one should be made to sink, or swim in their role, however senior it may be. Everyone should be supported and supervised.

The ten per cent of work time of a part-time worker that should be dedicated to supervision is a minimum and should follow on from the completion of the initial training course which can be of anything from 60–100 hours in duration. Supervision should be diaried on an annual basis, and sufficient time and appropriate venues should be arranged. Agreed notes of the meetings should be kept by both parties and the meetings should be based on similar guidelines to those set out below. Strategic problems and tensions should be dealt with openly and honestly and mutually identified weaknesses should be dealt with through in service training.

It is very often the case that part-time workers who are in other full or part-time employment are unused to the kind of supervision practice frequently found at its best within the youth, community and play service. So, it is recommended that an integral part of induction is discussion of the nature of the supervision entailed in the job. Perhaps an outline statement as appears at the end of this section, would be a helpful inclusion in the induction packs.

Of course, regular, main supervision meetings do not preclude day to day management, team discussion, meetings and problem solving. In fact team meetings, regular contact with the line manager and recording work in the project's day book or the employer's recording sheets are an essential part of ensuring that when the supervision is held it is based on actual working situations and difficulties. Supervision is no substitute for team meetings, but is a necessary complement to them.

Above all, supervision can help to alleviate stress and it does this by ensuring that unresolved problems are at least regularly looked at rather than left to fester. It does it too by making it clear to everyone concerned that problems are the stuff of youth, community and play work practice, and that there is no such thing as a smooth and easy relationship or a perfect educational curriculum. Stress sets in with individuals when problems are seen to pile up without any hope of solving them and when they are seen as a result of weak individuals rather than systems and structures. Sometimes, stress sets in when people don't know how to get something done in a big bureaucracy and feel too afraid to ask.

Regular supervision also helps to ensure that everyone is aware of the correct procedures that need to be used to deal with various different things. No worker can be expected to know everything and supervision provides the perfect opportunity to identify future training needs and to clarify what is the best approach to a new difficulty that has arisen, perhaps in a young person's behaviour, or a new aspect of the law that has arisen.

Getting lines of communication right is always important in 'people' work, and to establish a system which can help to minimise gossip and channel concerns through one professional route, is always advisable. A good supervisor will be glad if you are frank, even if there is a terrible personality clash.

Model Statement on Supervision

1. Supervision is designed to support you in your work and your career as a part-time youth, community and play worker; it is distinct from day to day line management and employer directive.
2. Supervision is about making your work more enjoyable, creative, planned, and effective, and identifying and solving any problems that may be perceived.
3. To be successful, supervision will need to be:
   a) held at regular intervals to fulfil the contractual obligation to that 10 per cent of your working time should be spent in prepared supervision
   b) undertaken with a commitment to openness
4. Dates for supervision meetings will be planned six months in advance and will not be altered except in cases of extreme emergency.
5. In supervision meetings it is expected that anything and everything related to your work can be expressed.
6. For the supervision meetings you will be expected to produce a brief written report. This report will cover anything that you want it to cover, but should include:
   - report on work undertaken since previous supervision
   - plans for the next period of work
   - requests for leave
   - identification of training requirements
   - special requests of your line manager or employer
   - details of any concerns, problems and suggested solutions
   - perceived positive and negative progress
7. Your meetings will be held in a mutually agreeable venue with your line manager who will take notes of the meetings for your subsequent approval at the following meeting. These notes will be kept on file.
8. Supervision meetings are separate from disciplinary and grievance procedures.
9. Health and safety matters including risk assessment, stress management and other concerns will be addressed.

A Code of Conduct

Another particularly advantageous procedure resulting from CYWU membership is the Union's Professional Code of Conduct within the Union. This recognises the management responsibilities that many full-time JNC Staff have for part-time workers and the need to hold together a membership of officers, JNC full-time workers and part-time workers. In this way the procedure seeks to maintain unity of all those contracted by an employer in their dealings with the employer, rather than each worker competing with the other or mismanaging each other. In short, no member of staff should complain about a colleague to management, prior to telling their colleague about it directly in the first instance.

It is regrettably the case sometimes, that a member of staff will become aware of a really serious misdemeanour by a colleague. CYWU does not defend bad practice or practices such as discrimination or harassment which are outside its own policies, but all bad practice must be dealt with fairly by management. CYWU members accused of behaving contrary to the anti discriminatory practices of the Union can be subject to the Union's own disciplinary procedures as well.

In most instances though, members of staff teams, particularly in the interaction between part-time and full-time staff, have gripes and grievances with each other. These should be dealt with in regular supervision which should be based on open and frank exchanges. If they cannot be, then either through third parties within the Union branch or directly with the colleague in the Union, a member of staff should take the problem for resolution within the Union before it goes to formal grievance.

If the Union is unable to resolve the problem, then the matter can go to grievance. Remember a grievance procedure is a positive thing and only rarely and in the most serious of instances, is anyone who has disciplined, been subject to a grievance themselves. The following code was adopted at the National Conference in 1993 and remains unamended since.

Model Code of Union Conduct

CYWU Code of Professional Conduct of Members

This Code of Conduct shall have effect subject to Section 3 of the *Employment Act 1988*, or any statutory provision which may amend, or be submitted to this section.

This Code of Professional Conduct should be valid for all youth, community and play workers within the Community and Youth Workers' Union and applies to workers at all levels within the organisation for which they work.

Actions which are alleged to be in breach of CYWU's Code of Professional Conduct can be dealt with under the Disciplinary Procedure, Section 15 of the National Constitution.

1. All workers should observe confidentiality in respect of any discussions with other individual workers about their professional problems and difficulties, except where there is an overriding concern and responsibility for the clients or the organisation.

2. If a worker experiences any concern or dissatisfaction regarding a colleague's work or standards of work, the worker should, wherever possible, discuss the matter informally and in confidence with the colleague concerned. Should the issue not be resolved informally, the worker should take no further action without informing the colleague, and in the first instance this further action should be in the form of taking the matter to the Union rather than to the Employers. In cases of harassment, or where the member has a reason to believe they may be at personal or professional risk, they may refer directly to the Union.

3. Workers should not denigrate colleagues in the presence of third parties, nor should workers adversely criticise a colleague in the presence of others save in the context of appropriate procedures.

4. Workers should not take appointments from which, in the judgement of CYWU's National Executive Committee (NEC) a member has been unjustly dismissed.
5. Workers should not impose on another worker an excessive and unreasonable amount of work of any kind.
6. Workers should not harass, discriminate against or oppress any group, or individual by reference to their gender, race, sexual orientation, disability, class, or on any other ground. Workers should uphold and promote CYWU Equal Opportunities Policies to ensure anti discriminatory and anti oppressive practice in their workplace.
7. Workers should not seek to undermine outside constitutional procedures, or agreed CYWU policy, nor work against the interests of CYWU, nor seek to bring CYWU, its Officers, or its members, into disrepute.

A code of professional ethics for all those working with children, young people and adults

As well as an internal Code of Professional Conduct, CYWU, along with the National Association of Youth and Community Education Officers (NAYCEO) and the Association of Principal Youth and Community Officers (APYCO) advocates that all those working with young people are subject to a professional Code of Ethics. The demand for the adoption of such a code has been highlighted in recent consultation on the issue and in discussions about the development of *Connexions*, *Youth Offender Teams* and new Services to young people throughout the voluntary sector and other providing organisations. Given the importance of the concept and the need to adopt a code, some background to the issue is given.

Explanation of terms used

Arguably, a Code of Ethics would be identical for all professions, in the same way as the value base for youth, community and play work, an adjustable set of liberal of values is in no significant way at odds with that in social work, teaching or other areas of public service. I therefore refer to a Code of Professional Ethics meaning something specifically applicable within the field of youth work. It would appear that most other occupations refer to various Professional Codes of Conduct. This has the advantage of applying an abstract ethical framework to real and developing situations; a Professional Code of Conduct embeds principles in regulated practice. Professional Guidelines can be considered as more detailed sub-sets of Codes of Conduct. The youth, community and play work service needs to develop more of all three.

Youth, community and play work requires an agreed Code of Professional Ethics, and an Ethics and Conduct Committee to uphold this and to advise on the production of various Codes of Professional Conduct and Guidelines.

Scope

Youth work practice is an aspect of informal education provision. In this sense it is indistinguishable from community work practice, play work practice and adult education practice (Endorsement of Informal Education Interim Officers group (EIEIO) 1996). All are based on voluntary client relationships and combine welfare and education in a more freely negotiated curriculum where subjective questions of power can easily be wrongly expressed or perceived.

1. Background to the development of a code of professional ethics

There have been previous discussions about establishing a written code of professional ethics within youth, community and play work. Most of these have been held within the conferences of the Community and Youth Workers' Union (CYWU) and its predecessor associations and in academic institutions (Barnett, 1977; Casemore, 1982).The National Youth Bureau (NYB, now NYA) published on the subject (NYB, 1983). CYWU returned to this issue again in 1996, 1997 and 1998 and through detailed debate with workers adopted a Code substantially in the format below. The Union also worked closely with child care and social work colleagues on the development of an adopted Code in this sector also. This work was given further priority in 1999 and 2000 and with some minor revisions CYWU worked with NAYCEO and the APYCO to adopt a Code. The UK Youth Work Alliance agreed that all countries should consult on this draft Code between 1998 and 2000. The Education and Training Standards Committee (ETS) of the National Youth Agency (NYA) commissioned a paper and a draft on the subject in 1998, subsequently published on the subject of ethical behaviours, and through consultation, recognised in 2000 that the field was in favour of the adoption of a national Code of Ethics. However, as a result of these discussions there is currently no nationally agreed Code but a renewed sense that such a Code is urgently required. Previous work on the subject has led to ethical concerns being incorporated into training modules and to some local authority employers adopting practice guidelines.

Wide and extensive consultation on this Code of Ethics in Wales throughout 2000/2001 also led to a greater recognition that this work was crucial to the professionalisation and development of the service. The realisation of many new monitoring projects and Connexions partnerships also led more employers in these areas to see the sense of adopting a clear national code.

There is therefore renewed academic, employer and trade union interest in developing a Code of Professional Ethics. At the end of 1996 in particular, two youth and community work academics promoted further work on the subject for discussion (Banks, 1996, 1997; Fairbairn, 1997). At its Conference in April 1997, the Community and Youth Workers' Union agreed to consult its membership with a view to accepting a Professional Code of Ethics which would be enforceable through the Union's internal disciplinary procedures (CYWU, 1996). Some Local Authorities, most notably Cornwall, adopted guidelines for ethical practice (Cornwall County Council, 1995). The newly formed Institute of Child Care and Social Education has also established an Ethical Committee and produced a draft set of Guidelines for consultation (Lane, 1996). These have drawn on some youth work experience, particularly Cornwall's Code.

A number of negative pressures have underpinned the renewed interest in a Code of Professional Ethics. These include:

- The marginalisation of youth, community and play work expressed by the lack of statutory provision and the consequently huge service cuts.
- The expansion of Higher Education and loosening of entry criteria onto youth and community courses.
- The lowering of the exit age from training courses.
- The prevalence of abuse in child care and youth related services.
- The decline of specific training officer posts and the parallel decline in service training.
- The failure of some employers to insist on staff being qualified to JNC standards.

To these we must add the relative lack of guidelines within youth, community and play work in relation to employment practices, and health and safety (Nicholls, 1995, 1996, 1997). Regrettably, we cannot ignore the high profile given by the media to the persistence in related spheres of work of 'professionals' being involved in criminal activities against young people. Finally, the emotional and social stresses that have multiplied (Rutter, 1995) over the last twenty years have meant that client groups are more vulnerable and volatile than previously, and qualified staff have not been able to rely so heavily on their reputation and relationship skills for protection. The relationship between client and worker has altered considerably to the extent that youth work no longer rejects the concept of 'client'. Similarly professional autonomy has been diminished with the introduction of highly mechanistic work-time recording devices based on the JNC hourly working week and within the culture of new managerialism (Millar, 1995; Bloxham, 1994).

These are all positive motives for the current return to the discussions on a Code of Professional Ethics. Wherever you take your starting point, whether it be the formation of the first professional association in 1938 (Nicholls, 1996a), the 1944 Education Act (Holmes, 1996), the Seebohm Report

(Thomas, 1983), the Alexander Report 1975, (McConnell, 1996) the Albemarle Report and JNC of 1961 (Smith, 1996) or CETYCW's formation in 1982, youth, community and play work is a recently codified occupation and profession, and the formulation of a Code of Professional Ethics represents a positive, and logical crystallisation of its professional status, and social and educational importance.

This also recognises that the public at large, through the state and public funds, is becoming more committed to supporting and funding youth, community and play work and ensuring its effectiveness and accountability. This in turn necessitates the development of a more recognisable and codified set of standards. Society's commitment to youth, community and play work, evidenced by the Labour government's education legislation, which will be implemented by individual staff whose practice must reflect the best elements of the state's non sectarian, non discriminatory and largely agnostic, purpose. A Code of Professional Ethics could become an occupational alternative to legislation, expressed in more philosophical and general terms. It would express a new national consensus around the social and educational expectations of the individual within the youth, community and play work public service.

This prompts very fundamental ethical considerations about the public nature of education:

> *No one can doubt that it is the legislator's very special duty to regulate the education of youth, otherwise the constitution of the state will suffer harm…Since the whole state has a single end, it is clear that education must be one and the same for all, and that it must be in public rather than, as today, in private hands, when every father has authority to provide for the instruction of his children just as he thinks fit. No, the training in matters which are of public concern must be carried out by the state. It is indeed quite false to imagine that any citizen belongs to himself. The correct view is that all belong to the state because each is a part thereof; and care of the whole follows inevitably from that of the parts.*
>
> Aristotle, *Politics, Book VIII Youth Training*, around 322 BC

In more recent times also, local education authorities, social services departments, and youth, community and play work departments have begun to develop written Codes of Conduct clearly delineating likely professional boundaries in relation to a variety of occupational dilemmas. In addition, the casework files of CYWU expanded to an extent that in 1998 over a half of the national membership requested national casework support and in many of these cases a lack of clarity and policy within employing organisations was the cause of the problem (CYWU, 1996a). Throughout 1996, youth workers in particular, sought to establish national guidelines specific to the youth service culture concerning the processing of disclosures of child abuse (CYWU, 1995). There was a strong feeling in this regard that the professional integrity of the youth workers' relationship with young people had been weakened by the adoption of often inappropriate social services guidelines (DfEE, 1995).

Higher professional expectations are now being made by employers with regard to full-time, professionally qualified staff, part-time and volunteer staff. An employer only has to demonstrate reasonable grounds for the belief that an employee was guilty of a misdemeanour in order to dismiss them fairly. A volunteer is in many senses of course more vulnerable to complaint and allegation, but a youth, community and play worker's career in their chosen profession can be ruined and their name entered onto the Department for Education and Employment's (DfEE) List 99 on the basis of an unproven allegation, which nevertheless led to dismissal. An employer can also chose to permit an obviously guilty member of staff to resign rather than be dismissed and have their name entered on the List. Similarly, the DfEE can reject an employer's request to include a dismissed worker on the list.

Neither training courses nor employing organisations provide a consistent set of benchmarks in relation to some basic conduct related issues. The *Endorsement Guidelines* do not assist in this respect either (NYA, 1997). For example Local Authority X, though it has no written policy to back its position, will automatically dismiss a youth worker who establishes a sexual relationship with any young person within the Local Authority area under the age of 25. Local Authority Y will dismiss a youth worker who gives a lift to a lone young person in their car at any stage. Local Authority Z will expect youth workers as a matter of routine to transport young people, lone, or otherwise, in their own transport, though they may not reimburse or insure them for this. Local Authority W may say that the youth worker who took the young homeless person back to their house for a bed for the night because they were seen in the early hours wandering the village when the nearest homeless hostel was 20 miles away, is guilty of gross professional misconduct.

A Code of Professional Ethics represents a highly concentrated form of regulation, standard setting and public commitment. It does not however exist above, beyond or in isolation from all of those other elements of occupational development that combine to give a sense of purpose, consolidation, identity and professionalism.

A Code of Professional Ethics does not float free as an ideal model from the social and occupational context which it is designed to assist. We cannot design a code without examining the current context of social and occupational developments.

2. The occupation: full-time, part-time, volunteer

Youth, community and play work originated in philanthropy and the voluntary sector (Nicholls, 1997; Smith, 1997; Davies, 1999). So, for that matter, did teaching and medicine. But unlike other professions, youth, community and play work has retained a preponderance of volunteers in association with children and young people. With the advance of the post Second World War social consensus, more state funded provision emerged due in no small part of the lobbying of the voluntary sector itself. The voluntary sector instigated the development, primarily through the formation of CYWU, then known as the Club Leaders' Association (CLA), of professional training for full and part-time staff, the notion of special qualification related terms and conditions, and the need to create publicly funded, local authority controlled Youth Services. This inter-related set of proposals culminated in the 1960 Albemarle Report which established the JNC, accelerated the development of specialist training and consolidated local authority based services in partnership with expanding voluntary sector provision. The consequences of this history are two fold.

Firstly the local authorities, despite all of the depletion of their resources in recent years remain by far the largest provider of Youth Services. They also have the majority stake in the main national agencies that support youth work. They are the main funders of the voluntary sector along with the government. Youth work in general is not the same as the Youth Service in particular. The former does not exist properly without the latter. With the changes to *Individual Recognition* criteria under the JNC as of September 1998, the youth, community and play work service became a profession allowing paid staff entry with qualification. With new legislative developments in the year 2000, particularly the formation of *Learning and Skills Councils* and the development of a new *Youth Support Service* at arms length from local authorities and known as *Connexions*, to be staffed by new categories of professionals, the need to consolidate national standards of approach to young people is all that much greater.

Secondly, professional practice, while historically emanating from the voluntary sector in the thirties and forties, has, since 1960 at least, been based on the *JNC Grading Matrix and Authorised Establishment Criteria* for full-time workers' posts. As already discussed, the *JNC Report* has since 1995 been extended to include part-time workers, and the Matrix in turn provides the foundation for the *Guidelines for the Endorsement of Initial Training Courses*, which in turn provide the base line for the endorsement of *Regional Accreditation and Moderation Panels* (*RAMPs*) for part-time and volunteer training and assessment. When we consider mechanisms such as *Validating Learning From Experience* (VLFE) or *Accreditation of Prior Experience and Learning* (APEL), the emphasis is decidedly on the concept of **learning** from the experience. The development of National Occupation Standards within 2000, further demonstrates the desire to consolidate a set of professional practices within a common moral ethos.

Despite this origin and development, there are at least half a million adults working voluntarily with young people. The number multiplies many times over if we consider community work and adult education. To their voluntary contribution we add the voluntary effort undertaken by every part-time worker over and above their allotted hours and the voluntary time given over and above their contractual hours by every full-time worker.

With the Labour government's commitment to a learning society and its current profiling of youth, community and play work, an opportunity is afforded to raise the standards of performance and self regulation within the whole sector. The development of a Code of Professional Ethics is a consistent and necessary development enabling us to lift the morale, value and cohesion of all those working with young people whether voluntary, part-time or full-time.

3. The partnership

The unique configuration of the youth, community and play work sector as described above also involves a unique set of alliances. Local authorities are required to secure provision both with regard to the voluntary sector and in partnership locally with voluntary organisations, whilst the Government also makes some central funds available for voluntary organisations. At an operational level staff may be seconded by a local authority to a voluntary sector organisation.

Unfortunately, the partnership between paid staff and volunteers and the individual secondments is not always based on shared values.

A worker's role in youth and community work is often to develop their voluntary organisation employers and to organise opposition to the plans their local authority employers may have for the community they serve. Alternatively, with the advent of the Local Government Act and neighbourhood renewal schemes, youth workers are often in key positions of power between client groups and controlling political structures seeking to come closer to those groups. A straightforward primary ethical commitment to the patient or client as in medicine is therefore impossible in this sector. An ethical code needs to encompass complex boundaries.

Another valid consideration when considering this Code is its scope. Should it perhaps also apply to lecturers, placement supervisors, or management committee members?

4. Training and qualification

There is an increasing concern to provide better training for all those involved in youth, community and play work from volunteer to Principal Youth Officer.

There is no requirement to train and qualify *part-time* workers, though with the 1995 JNC Part-time Workers Agreement this has changed and will change further with the adoption of National Occupational Standards. CYWU has encouraged compulsory *RAMPs* qualification for part-time workers.

There is no legal requirement to train and qualify *full-time* youth, community and play workers. The link between professional qualification, and employment terms and conditions is made voluntarily by the local authorities and the voluntary sector through the JNC which currently mainly applies to full-time youth workers in England and Wales. With new employers developing 'youth work' in the field, often through temporary projects funded in the short term only, there is increasing need to spread good practice. In addition, there is no specific qualification requirement for Youth and Community Service Officers or Principal Youth Officers.

5. Youth work and upbringing

Youth work has indeed a unique role in the support of the transition from childhood to adulthood. However, it does not have an exclusive role. Other occupations are now socially essential to the fulfilment of the transition. Children and young people relate to a variety of professional staff. With the development of *Connexions* this is likely to increase. Below are a list of occupations where workers have contact with young people. As at 2000, italicised entries indicate where closer working relationships are likely in the future. Asterisks indicate a group with an established Code of Ethics. A double asterisk indicates a group with a mechanism of regulation and discipline relating to a Code. A simplified list may include:

parents	*playgroup staff*
nursery teachers	infant teachers
sports officers	trade union stewards
special needs teachers	welfare officers
advice workers	sports officers
leisure service personnel	trade union service personnel
senior education personnel	personal advisers
academic examiners	college lecturers
university lecturers	opticians

primary teachers	*church leaders*
community leaders/elders	employers
careers officers	health educators (many JNC qualified)
health visitors*	mentors
nursery nurses*	childminders*
*education psychologists**	advice and counselling staff*
welfare officers*	*residential care workers**
*probation officers**	*police**
	*prison officers**
nurses**	doctors**
learning mentors**	*social workers***
*lawyers***	dentists**

Given the increasing requirement of inter-agency collaboration, it will be essential to familiarise other occupation areas with our new Code, and indeed if we are to retain our value base in the shifting sands of policy provision, we should consider asking others to adopt our Code.

6. Parties to the code

The Code of Professional Ethics is primarily designed to enhance, secure and gain credibility for the nature of the face to face work undertaken with young people by volunteers and paid staff. However, that work is produced and driven by a variety of partner agencies and individuals who should all be seen to adopt the highest professional standards of practice. The sanctions that can be applied in terms of the license to practice in each related occupation should be the same, which will necessitate the agreement of at least:

- the Department for Education and Skills
- the Local Government Associations
- Ofsted
- NAYCEO
- Principle Officers' Groups
- the Training Agencies' Group (TAG)
- the Committee of Vice Chancellors
- the JNC.

Principal officers, managers and workers

The interface between the main providers at each level is a critical one for sustaining professional practice. Specific training for officers and managers within the culture of youth, community and play work practice, voluntary organisations and local government structures is only just beginning. Membership of Principal Officers' groups is neither compulsory, nor voluntary, as Principal Officers lack any binding code of ethics. Membership of NAYCEO or its equivalents is voluntary, but members are not bound by any prevailing ethical code, and nor are Principal Youth and Community Officers. Membership of the main organisation for paid staff CYWU is voluntary though members are currently subject to a professional Code of Conduct which can be enforced by a disciplinary procedure. A procedure also exists for opposing the membership of an individual at the point of application, though it should be borne in mind that trade union legislation can complicate the enforcement of such disciplinary codes. The CYWU Code leans, as you would expect, towards the collectivist morality of the trade union movement of which it is part, more than towards questions of professional practice.

Model Code of Professional Ethics

1. Professional intervention

a) Staff who work with children and young people in the informal education context have a personal responsibility concerning themselves and the nature of their intervention in the lives of those people. They should plan and reflect on all aspects of their intervention and organise their work continually to do so. They need at all times to be aware of their role in different contexts, the likely dilemmas in each situation, the purpose of their intervention, the limitations of their role and power and the latest ideas concerning good practice in the area of intervention concerned. They should at all times be aware of the policies, procedures, and guidance available to them to support work with children and young people in a safe, legal and productively educational environment. The repertoire of curricular approaches and activities should be continually updated so that the practitioner is able to offer a wide range of educational experiences to the children and young people with whom they work.

b) There are particular responsibilities to:
   - Develop and utilise skills, knowledge and experience, as fully as possible.
   - Undertake in service training and professional development in order to remain up to date on professional issues and relevant curricular and legal issues.
   - Regularly re-examine attitudes and methods of intervention in order to renew motivation, and manage dilemmas at work.
   - Maintain high personal standards of professional conduct and avoid acts which may bring the profession or service into disrepute, or which may diminish the trust and confidence of the public.
   - Foster good interpersonal relationships with all those involved with the service.
   - Behave and act reliably and consistently.
   - Manage conflict and boundaries objectively, and in the interests of the delivery to children and young people of educational and support programmes.
   - Acknowledge personal limitations in knowledge and competence, and to decline duties or responsibilities if unable to perform them in a safe and skilled manner.
   - Seek advice as necessary.
   - Ensure that professional practice is not influenced by commercial, or private considerations.
   - Continuously evaluate outcomes and dilemmas encountered in the course of professional duties, and to reflect on them in an organised manner with colleagues.
   - Be aware of personal, physical and mental fitness at the level required to meet service users' needs.
   - Refuse to use illegal drugs, or alcohol, prior to or during work.
   - Ensure the safety of service users at all times and to ensure the use of appropriate equipment, clothing, insurances and procedures etc.
   - Avoid the personalisation of issues with service users and colleagues at work.
   - Act in a way that encourages equal opportunities, opposes discriminatory action or policy, and harassing, intimidating or bullying behaviour.

c) It is recognised that staff working with children and young people have a particular responsibility to maintain and enhance the physical, emotional and educational well being of the children and young people with whom they work and to provide them with honest descriptions of roles and responsibilities and opportunities. It is therefore important to have contemporary knowledge of:
   - health and safety legislation and good practice
   - the law as it affects young people, families and citizen's rights
   - anti-discriminatory practice and legislation
   - employment law, practice and policies
   - employers' expectations
   - good practice in advice and counselling
   - effective communication skills
   - the needs and aspirations of children and young people
   - educational, welfare and other support opportunities available to children and young people

2. Responsibility for children and young people

a) Staff working with children and young people have a responsibility to:

- Promote the policies and practice that enhance the self determination, self esteem, collective responsibility and active citizenship of children and young people.
- Promote the rights of children and young people and their parents and guardians.
- Advise, befriend and counsel children and young people for the purpose of extending and developing the interests, awareness and responsibility of children and young people themselves.
- Assist children and young people in the transition to adulthood by respecting and understanding their needs, and the opportunities available to them.
- Respecting the privacy and confidences shared by children and young people, while upholding those professionally established protection and employment guidelines developed to support and protect children and young people and ensuring that the welfare and personal safety of the child or young person is at all times primary.
- Involve children and young people in the development of the service.
- Create and ensure the maintenance of safe and healthy settings that foster the physical, intellectual, social, emotional, moral and spiritual development of children and young people.
- Avoid participation in, and inform appropriate authorities of practices which are disrespectful, degrading, dangerous, exploitative, intimidating, psychologically damaging or physically harmful to children or young people.
- Protect children and young people from abuse and neglect.
- Report abuse and neglect so that action can be taken.
- Avoid commissioning or assisting an infringement of the law.
- Avoid active collusion with children or young people in evasion of the consequences of illegal acts, where laws seek to protect children, young people and the wider community from harm.

b) Staff should recognise that their work is primarily concerned with the creation of informal learning opportunities for the purpose of social education, and they need to ensure clear boundaries at all times between professional and personal relationships. In particular they must:

- Ensure that the children and young people themselves understand the boundaries between professional and personal relationships.
- Avoid relationships with children and young people which involve emotional dependency.
- Avoid sexual intimacy with children and young people, both inside and outside work.
- Be sensitive to the use of inappropriate words and language.
- Respect the physical and emotional privacy of children and young people.
- Focus on the needs of young people as being primary.
- Develop professional relationships **with** children and young people and not in order to achieve power **over** them for personal interest, gain or fulfilment.
- Ensure that educational needs within the service are paramount and not those of commercial or other interests.

c) Staff working with children and young people work with a variety of individuals and agencies to secure provision and meet the needs of children and young people. This work should have as its prime focus the meeting of the needs of those children and young people and the encouragement of collaborative partnerships which enable communities and children and young people to further their interests and create new and more varied learning opportunities by being more involved in decision making processes. Those working with children and young people will need to assure parents, and other agencies, that their planned intervention and processes are transparent and comprehensible, and that all staff working with children and young people are appropriately trained and supported.

3. Responsibility to colleagues

Staff have responsibilities to their immediate colleagues and to staff and volunteers in other agencies seeking to collaborate with the service to benefit children and young people. Consequently, there are professional responsibilities to:

- Foster professional working relationships which continually aim at excellence in practice.
- Belong to the appropriate professional association or organisation and respect its Codes of Conduct and policies.
- Treat colleagues with respect, courtesy, fairness and good faith.
- Recognise colleagues' professional achievements.
- Maintain professional relationships of trust and co-operation.
- Ensure that volunteers are appropriately managed and supported on the basis of clear expectations and boundaries and are recruited using the approved clearance procedures and regularly supported in their efforts.
- Act as a member of a team, sharing information, concerns and opportunities, and ensuring effective communications, prompt responses and mutual support.
- Support, train, supervise and manage colleagues according to policies and procedures which have been professionally agreed and properly negotiated and understood and according to continuous professional development approaches.
- Observe confidentiality in respect of discussions with colleagues about their professional problems and difficulties.
- Draw bad practice and shortfalls in professional practice to the attention of colleagues or to the appropriate organisations for action.
- Assist in the design and implementation of agreed mechanisms for monitoring and appraisal.
- Seek to resolve differences and difficulties openly, swiftly and within the recognised professional channels of communication.
- Uphold health and safety legislation and ensure that all potential risks and dangers are appropriately notified.
- Promote equality of access to opportunities for in service training.

4. Staff responsibility to employers

a) Youth workers and other staff working with children and young people are employed in a variety of organisations with various degrees of experience in play and youth work delivery and employment practice. A worker will contribute, depending upon the level of development of the employing organisation, to the creation of a clear and comprehensive set of employment policies and practices that make explicit the contractual terms of the employment of workers. There is a responsibility to fulfil and develop contractual obligations and duties in the interests of the service, and the profession.

b) In addition there are responsibilities to:
- Uphold health and safety standards.
- Maintain agreed employment rules and contractual obligations.
- Work according to the agreements of the relevant national committees governing the professions.
- Participate in the professional associations recognised by the employer for the purposes of bargaining and agreeing employment policies and practices.
- Uphold the employers' interests.
- Record transactions honestly on behalf of the employer.
- Ensure the employer, rather than the employee, is signatory to key legal documents, such as insurances, leases, hiring agreements, etc.
- Remain accountable to the employer for all work undertaken on their behalf and to report regularly to the employer on this work.

5. Responsibility of employers

a) Employing organisations will ensure that their responsible persons are:
- Implementing this Code of Professional Ethics which has been accepted by staff.
- Implementing agreed employment, and health and safety legislation.
- Prepared to accept the guidance and policies of the Youth and Community Work Ethical Committee.
- Acting in accordance with the *JNC Report for Youth and Community Workers* and the *Soulbury Committee* and other relevant professional committees.

- Fully recognising the member trade unions of the JNC and Soulbury committees for the purposes of local negotiations and discussions.
- Aware of the services and support materials available to them through the principal support agencies in their field of activity.
- Participants in the appropriate local, regional and national professional bodies.
- Encouraging part-time staff to undertake endorsed qualifications.
- Operating a fully recognised staff development policy by NYA, WYA, CLS and NTO.
- Involving children and young people in their service delivery planning.
- Operating agreed systems of performance appraisal, and monitoring and evaluation of delivery.
- Committed to co-operating with requests for information from and the participation of the recognised youth work support agencies and other appropriate local and national government agencies.
- Promoting this Code and policies as from time to time adopted by the Youth and Community Work Ethical Committee.
- Aware of the different interests, conflicts, dilemmas and conflicts between the various parties to the delivery of effective play work and youth work and the roles and responsibilities of staff and participants in the service.
- Operating clear systems of child protection and other supportive procedures for children, young people and staff.

6. Responsibilities of employers and employees

In addition to contractual, health and safety and other legislative responsibilities, the employing organisation and its staff have a particular responsibility to establish, through organised discussion with recognised professional associations, clear agreements about working conditions and practice. Management responsibilities are arranged between officers and full-time staff, full-time staff and part-time workers, and between full or part-time staff and volunteers. In this context, the creation of agreements between the employers' and the staff's representative organisations provides the clearest basis for the fulfilment of different management functions. The extent and nature of delegated powers and responsibilities, in every employing organisation, should be spelt out and available to all staff and responsible employers. Private and personal arrangements between the employer and individual staff should be discouraged in favour of open, transparent, agreed and collective arrangements.

7. Responsibility to volunteers and voluntary organisations

a) Youth workers and other staff working with children and young people have a responsibility to ensure that volunteers are engaged appropriately in order to assist in meeting the needs of children and young people, organisational interests and the aims of the service as a whole, and that in this contribution they are clear of their role, supported in it, provided with training and not exploited as alternative forms of support to professional or other paid staff.

b) Youth workers and other staff working with children and young people have a responsibility to ensure that voluntary organisations are supported and promoted, and that personnel within them are appropriately trained and made aware of the policies of child and youth services as a whole, so that they can work in effective partnership with all other providing agencies.

8. Responsibility to the profession

a) Youth workers and other staff working with children and young people are accountable to their professions and have responsibilities to:

- Belong to and play an active part in the appropriate professional associations and to abide by the rules and regulations set by those bodies.
- Ensure professional quality assurance of work.
- Share developments in theory and practice through the mechanisms within the profession.
- Uphold Codes of Practice established by the Ethics and Conduct Committee.
- Support the implementation of this Code of Professional Ethics.
- Discuss professional disagreements and concerns and potential breaches of the Code openly and honestly with the colleagues concerned.
- Undertake in service training, identify training needs and assist where appropriate with the supervision, support, training and placement supervision of other colleagues and students.

Union benefits and services

While expecting the best possible employment practice to be negotiated with the employers, it is essential that a trade union for part-time youth, community and play workers also makes a special effort to be relevant and effective. CYWU has done this. It has a high involvement rate amongst part-time workers, indeed four out of eight of its national negotiators are part-time workers and the Union has specialist committees dealing with these issues. Many of the Union's benefits and services are geared towards part-time workers and its subscription system is banded.

All CYWU benefits and services are available equally to all full members of the Union including part-time workers. Its benefits and services are designed to save part-time workers money and to be convenient.

Part-time workers can save their subscriptions several times over by using the Union's various discount schemes and other benefits.

A brief outline of some union benefits

- National journal. A free copy of *Rapport*
- Discount travel. Inland and abroad, and package holidays.
- Discount shopping comes automatically with your membership each year. You will get a Countdown Card and a brochure of participating shops in your area.
- Financial services. Arrangements available from CYWU are exceptional, you can save a great deal on life and home insurance, car insurance, personal investments and get free, and sound financial advice either in your home or at a branch meeting, individually or collectively. The pension schemes are good for people without an occupational pension in the voluntary sector.
- Personal, car and property insurance. The CYWU scheme seeks to indemnify you so that you do not lose your No Claims Bonus and will give you £100 or so. If you have your property or car damaged or stolen at work, ring NUT and ask for an insurance claim form. Remember to ask about discount car recovery service and maintenance either from NUT or CYWU.
- Hospitalisation benefit. If you are hospitalised as a result of an injury at work, in addition to legal support, the Union will give you over £100 per week. Ring NUT and ask for a hospitalisation claim form.
- Casework support. This is accessed through the branch. If the branch or National Casework Committee consider it necessary, it will be referred for legal support.
- Legal advice. You have access to one free interview with a Union solicitor on any issue.
- Stoke Rochford Hall. This is a beautiful residential centre in Lincolnshire. Members are entitled to discounts for visits or group bookings. Phone the manager direct.
- Hardship financial support. In certain circumstances CYWU may be able to assist. This help is accessed through your local NUT association as are requests to use convalescent homes.
- Trade Union training. This is provided free of charge (with all expenses paid including travel and accommodation) by CYWU, locally, regionally and nationally. Also members can attend GFTU courses free of charge. Obtain an application form from your branch.
- Car/Minibus leasing scheme. CYWU has linked up with a lease scheme provider, who is an expert and health and safety conscious, to make low cost, high quality minibuses available to projects where members work.
- Professional indemnity insurance. These days you need to ensure comprehensive personal protection against any mishap or allegation at work.
- Free student membership to students. Available if they are earning less than £2,000 a year from youth and community work.
- Access to education bursaries.
- Access to International Federation of Youth Workers.

Conclusion

The issue of equal treatment for all workers, is not just one of improving terms and conditions, or of creating equality of employment which is consistent within the European Union with the aims and objectives of youth, community and play work. It is also about creating a respected, permanent, sufficiently resourced, professional and modern Education Service. To treat part-time workers properly along the lines in the Model Agreement and Statement of Particulars suggested here, as the JNC itself has advocated, and as all services ultimately will have to, will mean planning, accountability and a higher level of personnel and resource management than the youth, community and play work services have been accustomed to. To treat part-time workers properly will be part of the creation of quality curriculum delivery.

It will be essential to ensure that all part-time workers are trained through nationally endorsed courses and that a nationally recognised academic equivalent is obtained for the NYA *RAMP* certificate when this is superseded at the end of 2002. Competence based assessment through NVQs or other 'tick box' assessment schemes, and the management selection for qualification opportunities that goes with it, will prove to be a major irrelevance and an obviously deprofessionalising hindrance. Training and qualification to at least the equivalent of Level Three must be the minimum license to practice and to ensure that staff are trained in the proper art of youth, community and play work.

Further reading and reference

For addresses of various bodies, and Select Bibliography see Appendices.

There is a vast literature now on all aspects of employment legislation, and part-time workers. However, two particularly affordable and accessible publications remain the best and most suitable for purchase within youth, community and play work, *The Law At Work* and *Part-time Workers, a Negotiator's Guide*. Both are published by the Labour Research Department and can be obtained from their publications office. The former currently costs £3.25 and the latter £1.50. CYWU has also produced the first ever *Handbook to support Part-time Youth Workers*. It is hoped that all part-time workers will have a copy of this. There is a companion publication, free to all students, known as the *Student Handbook*. Together these are probably the best investment any youth, community and play work service or project could make. All youth, community and play projects could do a lot worse than take out an annual subscription to *Labour Research*. This provides a monthly update on important precedent cases, the state of the economy and a host of other issues affecting workers. The Trades Union Congress publishes a useful lay person's guide: *Your Rights at Work, a TUC Guide*, available from the TUC.

All youth, community and play work centres and services should possess up to date copies of the *JNC Report for Youth and Community workers*. Copies are obtainable with an updating service either from the Secretary of the Staff Side JNC, or the Secretary of the Employers' Side.

For CYWU Members, the Union has a useful general guide, *The Branch Support Pack* obtainable from CYWU National Office.

On the question of supervision, so central to all youth, community and play work practice, an early publication remains one of the finest books: *Supervision in Youth Work* by Joan Tash.

I have never come across a better document on discipline, than the excellent pamphlet published by ACAS, *Discipline at Work*, available from your nearest ACAS Office. This is another small document that should be in every youth, community and play work workplace.

Planning for a Sufficient Youth Service. Available from CYWU.

Agenda for a Generation and *From Rhetoric to Reality* available from the National Youth Agency. The following works on supervision are useful:

Christian C. and Kitto, J. (1987). *The Theory and Practice of Supervision*. YMCA George Williams College.

Brown, A. and Bourne, I. (1996). *The Social Work Supervisor*. Open University Press.

Hawkins, P. and Shohet, R. (1989). *Supervision in the Helping Professions*. Open University Press.

Heath, G. (1989). *Staff Development, Supervision and Appraisal*. Longman.

Marken, M. and Payne, M. (1987). *Enabling and Ensuring* (2nd Edn.) National Youth Bureau.

Part 3

Legal Responsibilities

The contract of employment

This should not be solely taken to be a piece of paper. There is no requirement in law to have a written document spelling out **all** the contractual conditions. Regardless of whether there is a written agreement, a contract can exist between two parties: an employer providing remuneration, an employee selling their work. There is a legal requirement, however, under the Employment Relations Act 1999 (ERA) to supply a written Statement of Particulars which has to include certain matters relating to terms and conditions. This should be provided within two months of the commencement of employment. However, as you will see from the Model Statement of Particulars in Part 2, the best advice is to ensure that the written Statement is as comprehensive as possible.

This section sets out some of the main considerations relating to the contract of employment. Each phrase and concept could practically be a chapter in itself and their construction or meaning exercises the courts continually. Regardless of the complexity, and not touching on such things as fixed term contracts, frustration of contracts, or the question of remedies against broken contracts, this aims to be a succinct discussion of the main issues that should be taken into account when creating, changing, or considering contracts of employment. This section should also be considered alongside Part 2 and the Model Statement of Particulars set out there.

A contract of employment is a complex amalgam of components which constitute the employment relationship. It will include:

- The letter of appointment.
- Anything promised at interview, if the job offer is made and accepted prior to the letter of appointment.
- The Written Statement of Particular terms and conditions of employment.
- Any collective agreements that apply to the post.
- Specific workplace rules.
- Custom and practice at work.
- Statutory regulations (equal pay, health and safety, maternity, etc.). Note, that it is possible for any employer to require a worker to sign a contract which waives various statutory rights. Naturally, this should not be accepted in youth, community and play work if the commitment to social justice at the heart of the work is to mean anything.

A contract is a promise by an employer to pay wages in return for specified work. To form the contract there will need to be an offer of employment under certain conditions and an acceptance of those conditions, followed by an exchange of money for the work performed. The Written Statement of particulars should be as clear and comprehensive as possible and the precise requirements of work should be unambiguously established through the Job Description and regular supervision.

There are four main elements in contractual terms. These are:

1. The **express** terms of the contract: those terms which have been directly spelt out orally, or in writing.
2. The **implied** terms of the contract: it is often a question of legal interpretation in any case as to what these are, but generally they are terms of employment which:
   - are not explicitly stated because they are so obvious as to not warrant setting down.
   - are obvious common practice within the employing organisation.
   - have been accepted by both parties as demonstrated by their actions and behaviour over a period of time.
3. The **incorporated** terms of a contract: those terms which enter the contractual relationship as a result of collective agreements (JNC national negotiations for example), or the changes resulting from local collective bargaining on such items as TOIL, residential payments etc.
4. The **statutory** terms of a contract: those terms which automatically apply to any contract as legislation nationally determines: equal pay, health and safety, maternity pay, sick pay etc. (A full list of statutory rights is spelt out in Chapter 1.)

The law does not say what the detail of a contract should be except that it requires there to be details of statutory minimum periods of notice and the right of an employee to and the terms of, statutory sick pay and statutory maternity pay.

Where an employer seeks to get an employee to agree to waive statutory employment rights, certain conditions must be met. Such agreements must:

- Be in writing.
- Be in relation to a specified complaint.
- Permit the employee to obtain independent legal advice from a fully qualified lawyer concerning the effect of signing such a waiver in relation to their rights in industrial tribunal.
- Permit insurance cover against the risk of loss incurred by such a waiver.
- Name the adviser to the waiver.
- Specify that the regulating conditions governing such waivers have been met.

The contract of employment is entered into when a job applicant accepts a job. The letter of appointment forms the fundamental basis of the contract and should be a well thought out document. As the Court of Appeal said in 1980: 'It is the original words of engagement which form the contract' (*Deeley v. British Rail Engineering Ltd (1980)* IRLR 147).

So, it is extremely important to consider how specific and detailed this letter of appointment is. If it states that you will be a youth worker at Centre X you know what you are receiving. If it says that you are to be a youth worker at Centre X but your duties will be as required by the Director of Education from time to time and four years after you have been working at Centre X the Director asks you to be a community worker at Centre Y, you are unlikely to be able to prevent this move. Where there is such a requirement of flexibility, the terms under which it would be exercised and the process for changing your duties should be outlined. The letter of appointment should be sufficiently detailed to let the prospective employee see the conditions under which they will be employed.

Occasionally the detail of a letter of appointment may not be consistent with the job advertisement that appeared. It is a matter of good practice that it should be, but case law has disregarded the job advertisement as a part of the contract. Lord Justice Lawton ruled: 'The advertisement is not part of the contract, it is merely a document leading up to the making of the contract' (*Pedersen v. the London Borough of Camden (1981) IRLR 173*).

It is also important to ensure that any remarks made at interview about the future conditions of employment are actually consistent with what will be delivered. If a job is offered and accepted at interview on certain conditions, then an employee may be able to rely more on this promise than on any subsequent letter of appointment which offers alternative terms. It is therefore advisable that offers are made in writing following the interview and that clear letters of employment are sent after interview.

Once the job is accepted the employee starts working. It may be that not everything that they do is spelt out in their Contract or Written Statement of Particulars. They then run the danger of implying terms into their contract by custom and practice: something has become an obligation or a contractual term by doing it. Voluntary, unpaid overtime may be such an example from youth, community and play work, unless the Union or member of staff has made it quite clear that such work is voluntary.

There is a legal test to establish whether an element of work has become a custom; that is whether the performance of something has been reasonable and fair, definite and precise, notorious or well known, and universally recognised in the area of work concerned. An important point here is that the burden of proof in this area rests with the person who is claiming the task has become contractual by custom, but also that an implied term cannot override a specific and previously agreed contractual term. In all cases of this sort, if either side claims something is a contractual right by virtue of custom and practice, they will have to justify it as something that occurs to give 'business efficacy' to the performance of the contract of employment. In the absence so often of Authorised Establishments to determine the level of service required, and in the absence of proper supervision procedures, youth, community and play workers frequently slip into a range of tasks and work areas that actually support service delivery. Without entering the legally difficult area of arguing over implied terms of contract, work patterns and responsibilities should be regularly reviewed and monitored.

Changing the contract

The perpetual re-organisations of youth, community and play work provision, the constant introduction of inappropriate elements of human resource management techniques, usually borrowed inappropriately from other areas of work, and the ever evolving demands of the service, mean that working patterns and work responsibilities change quite frequently. The essential point is that such changes cannot be made by the employer unilaterally. If such a change is made unilaterally there may, depending on circumstances, be recourse to the County Courts for breach of contract, or if the member of staff resigns as a result of the imposed change, they may have recourse to Industrial Tribunal to claim constructive dismissal. In this latter circumstance, the employee must be able to demonstrate that the change required by the employer was a fundamental breach getting to the very root of the contract.

Variations in pay, benefits arrangements, working hours etc. are obviously fundamental, and regularly affect part-time workers who are increasingly offered (wrongfully) ultimatums to accept new, reduced contracts.

Changes to terms and conditions must have the agreement of the employee. Such changes can come about by:

- Negotiating the change with the employee orally or in writing.
- Negotiating the change through the collective bargaining arrangements (e.g. LJNC).
- The employee working the new arrangements over a period without objection.
- Including a term in the Written Statement of Particulars that allows for a variation in the contract. The most familiar of such clauses concern the location where the employee will work, or the catch all phrase 'or any other such duties as the employer may from time to time consider appropriate.'
- Incorporating nationally agreed change (e.g. JNC pay award).

Where there is no agreement by the employee to have their contract changed the employer has the option to make them redundant from their post and re-engage them. In youth, community and play work this has proved to be one of the most corrosive and polluting methods, invariably losing the commitment and loyalty of staff. It is never a simple thing to do and opens a legal minefield. It is usually a sign of significant problems when management consider this option. Imposing a change without agreement is confrontational and automatically leads to further conflict. In this situation the employee whose contract is unilaterally altered has four main routes to consider:

- Grin and bear it.
- Resign and claim unfair dismissal.
- Refuse to work the changed contract if it involves for example, new hours and duties.
- Stay at work with the changes under protest and duress and take an action to the High Court or County Court or Employment Tribunal.

Flexible and mobile workforce

Broad ranging flexibility and mobility clauses are also a sign that the employing organisation is covering all options and not perhaps anticipating a clear and guaranteed future for the postholder. You may find in a contract a phrase like: 'As a term of your employment you may be required to undertake such other duties and/or hours of work as may be considered reasonable and as commensurate with your grade and general level of responsibility within the organisation at your identified place of work or any other establishment under the aegis of the Director of Education.' Despite such open ended clauses, if challenged, the employer would have to prove that they exercised this contractual facility to vary in a 'reasonable' way following explanation, discussion and consultation. Again, it is very much a question of the employment practice matching the purpose and ethos of the work concerned and meeting the requirements of the law to be fair and reasonable. The quality of consultation will always be taken into account: again a matter directing us very much to the need for properly established LJNCs.

Employees are also able to change their contracts. Once a contract is accepted, it is not an unalterable tablet of stone. You may think at interview that the post is wrongly graded, you may say this and the employer may note your comments and still offer you the job on the inappropriate rate, and you may accept this. This does not prevent an employee submitting a claim for regrading on the first day of employment. This is because the *JNC Report* offers a system for regrading posts, and an incorporated term, if not an express one within a youth, community and play work contract, is the right to apply for regrading. It is always advisable for a new post holder to compare their contract with those of immediate colleagues and for the union to pursue any discrepancies. Consistency of contractual terms across a workforce is very important.

Obligations and implied terms

Within any employment contract there are a set of established obligations bolstered by legislation and case law.

A) **The employer** is expected to:
- Pay wages as covered in the contract and to spell out how pay during sickness will be met.
- Provide work where a failure to do so would break the contract where a person's earnings or reputation depend on that work being provided.
- Take reasonable care of an employee: this is usually confined to matters of health and safety.
- Co-operate with their employees. An interesting concept this! It usually refers to a general requirement to take positive steps to ensure that the functions of the contract are implemented properly. This could in some circumstances include taking action to ensure that an employee is working free from harassment. In one case, it was ruled, 'It is an implied term of a contract of employment that the employer shall render reasonable support to an employee to ensure that the employee can carry out the duties of his [sic] job without harassment and disruption by fellow workers.' *(Wigan Borough Council v. Davies (1979) IRLR 127).*
- Uphold the confidence and trust of employees.
- Explain employee's rights.

B) **The employee** is expected to:
- Show good faith toward the employer in the exercise of his duty of fidelity. This means that they should not:
  - Compete with their employer by supporting a competitor.
  - Disclose confidential information.
  - Accept rewards from others without the employers permission.
  - Take reasonable care in fulfilling their duties.
- Co-operate with the employer. Reasonable orders should be obeyed, an employee should not unreasonably impede their employer's business. However, employees are not expected

to obey orders which are unlawful, or which fall outside the scope of the contract. This notion will also include adherence to reasonable work rules and the disciplinary procedure.
- Work with care.

Further reading and reference

See also the Select Bibliography and details of addresses in the Appendix.

I have chosen to recommend one accessible source which contains one brief section on contracts. This is a very reasonably priced publication which covers the whole gamut of employment issues:

Slade, E., Griffin, N., AEEU, and Lawford and Co. Solicitors (1999). *Employment Handbook* (9th Edn.). Tolley Publishing Company Ltd. This is available from the Amalgamated Engineering and Electrical Union.

You will find many aspects relating to contracts in other sources referred to in this publication. There are plenty of separate resources, just on contracts. Look out especially for anything from Income Data Services on contracts.

Part 4

'Us and Them'

The dynamics of disagreement

Employment practice and policy are about dealing with disagreement and managing change. This section comments on various forms of disagreement that exist in youth, community and play work and suggests some ways of using negotiation and procedure to gain more pleasure from it than pain. Although youth, community and play work is itself built on disagreements and various formulations of change and conflict management, its employment frame is becoming increasingly limiting and contradictory.

Tension, obstacle, conflict, lack of guideline, the inevitability of the unexpected are all vital components of the every day working experience of informal educationalists interested in developing individuals and groups and achieving collective victory over difficulty and injustice. When employing youth, community and play workers employers should seek to relieve the pressure of these factors in the employing base from which they work. Equally, employment practices should be established which fully and unequivocally reflect and fit the nature of the work. The contract of employment, working guidelines and supervision that nurture informal education practice should be a warm welcoming nest, not a nest of surprises and vipers as it unfortunately so often is. This is best done by building into the system organised and professional ways of handling disagreement.

Employers, management and workers

The extent to which employers and workers have shared interests is the subject of many great philosophies but not the subject of this book! What concerns us here is the level of understanding amongst employers about youth, community and play work practice and the way in which employers and their staff manage their shared and contradictory interests. Managers are intermediaries in this and need to play more of a transparent and less of a determining role, since the interests of managers and workers may be much closer than the service thinks. A reflection of this is the continuing inability of NAYCEO and CYWU to merge; the service as a whole would be strengthened if managers and workers got together more to put realistic demands to the actual employers and empowered the employers to take full responsibility for the direction of the work.

In local authorities, elected members have historically kept away from the policy, direction and management of the youth, community and play service, which has been delegated, sometimes inadvertently, or unconsciously to Senior Education Officers. Many elected members have been part of Youth Service Management Committees and Community Associations, indeed, many of them have been brought into political life by this route. But in general terms, the youth, community and play service has been led very much by the Principal Officers in charge. Education Committee agendas have been packed with schools business, few authorities have had sub-committees specifically to deal with youth, community and play work despite DfEE encouragement to do this.

However, this is beginning to change; considerable political interest and involvement in youth, community and play work is being awakened. Councillors are beginning to place membership of the management committee of the ward Community Association, or Community Education Council on a par with school governorship. Indeed, cynics would say, there are often more votes in it. A well resourced Community Centre with two thousand adult members is an attractive prospect within a ward! This is how it should be if the intentions of, for example, the Local Government Association's commitment to community development are to be fulfilled.

But the key to greater employers' involvement within the local authorities is the active participation by elected members in the Local Joint Negotiating Committee (LJNC) which is established to consult and negotiate on all aspects of the service. Where there is an active voluntary sector employing youth, community and play workers, they should also be represented on any consortia arrangement established to negotiate here.

In the voluntary sector, the employers, i.e. a local management committee, are often closely involved in day by day activities, but lack the experienced professional personnel department that can be deployed within local authorities. Also, there is usually a built in contradiction with voluntary sector management committees and their staff, one role of the youth, community and play worker being to enable and strengthen the management capacities of the management committee itself. The worker is sometimes being employed by, or seconded to, an employer who is insufficiently aware of their roles and responsibilities as an employer, or the worker is being given instructions by an employer while the worker is trying to instruct the employer. There can of course be straightforward resentment too; after all the worker will very often have better terms and conditions of employment than those they are working for and with. The youth, community or play worker in a small project may themselves be the equivalent of the education committee in a local authority, in that they determine budgets, apply for grants, manage those delivering the service, have responsibility for buildings and future planning etc. Some are compelled even to write their own contracts of employment and job descriptions! They almost, but never totally, become the employer and the employed at one and the same time.

In smaller projects, which cannot be part of wider consortia for negotiating purposes there are a number of possible solutions. The project, particularly if it is grant aided by the local authority could be subject to a range of conditions of grant aid negotiated by management and unions through the JNC. The project could agree regular more informal meetings with the local union representative. The project could obtain the contractual assistance of a third party. Where the project is part of a larger national or regional organisation, it could press for its personnel and other matters to be handled separately at another level. The disadvantages of complete autonomy in personnel management are far more dangerous to the well being of the project than more centralised structures.

Another major step forward made by the New Labour government was to introduce the first legislation to give trade unions rights of recognition. The overwhelming majority of employers in the community work and youth work voluntary sectors continue to try and ignore this legislation and to leave their industrial relations in a primitive state. Whether an employer recognises a trade union or not, every individual at work now has the right to be accompanied in a meeting with management by a union representative of their choice.

Towards a LJNC

One of the best ways of bringing the employers together with managers and workers, is to establish a forum for consultation, negotiation and problem solving. Where this has been done the service and staff morale have invariably been lifted. Such a forum reflects the ethos of the work itself which is about involvement and empowerment. It is better for management to take staff with them and better for the employer to take both along. Whatever the size of the workforce, if it feels excluded from the decision making processes, it will store up trouble for the system. There is special relevance to establishing separate negotiating structures for JNC staff. Even relatively small employment groups such as those on *Soulbury Report* contracts, have written into their national agreement, a clause facilitating the establishment of LJNCs. As youth, community and play work is generally low down the political agenda, it would be quite wrong to try and merge its interests with broader bargaining committees for larger groups of workers.

Most local authorities have now seen the sense of having separate bargaining arrangements for staff on JNC terms and conditions. In the voluntary sector, consortia of employers and unions are often formed across a geographical area and they form a staff side and an employers' side to work as a committee under a common negotiating constitution. Once this has been formed, all of those voluntary projects which are signatories to the agreement must abide by the decisions of the committee. A negotiating constitution, and a commitment to regular meetings acts on the collective level like supervision does on the individual level. Where supervision reaches its limit then management may resort to discipline and workers to grievance. Where an LJNC reaches its limit employers have recourse to imposition with all its risks, and workers have recourse to collective grievance or the procedure outlined in the Failure To Agree (FTA) mechanism. Like the individual procedures discussed in earlier chapters, the collective procedures that flow from negotiations under an LJNC are designed to reach agreement and resolve problems. The model procedure which follows reflects many successful and actual working arrangements and is designed to be equally applicable in local authority, voluntary sector consortia, or national voluntary organisation settings.

The principles which underpin effective operation of such a constitution are:

- Regular meetings.
- Minuted meetings.
- Effective ways of communicating decisions back to the appropriate constituency. Usually agreements reached on an LJNC would be circulated for inclusion in the staff handbook.
- Complete openness and access to relevant information.
- Clear and swift system with timescales of dealing with Failures To Agree.
- If a Failure To Agree is recorded, the status quo on the issue will obtain: nothing should change until the disagreement has been resolved.
- Regular involvement of the most senior representative possible of the actual employers rather than just management and where managers are involved, the most senior possible.
- Adequate working time for staff and management to prepare for, attend and follow up meetings.

Model Constitution for a Local Joint Negotiating Committee (LJNC)

1. Title

The Committee shall be known as the Local Negotiating Committee for staff paid under the terms of the Joint Negotiating Committee for youth, community and play workers (full and part-time workers).

2. Purpose

2.1   It is important for efficiency and good industrial and human relations that employees should feel that:

2.1.1 They are kept informed by employers on matters which concern them.

2.1.2 Their views are sought by employers on existing practices and on proposed changes which would affect them.

2.1.3 They can raise any issue relating to their terms and conditions of employment.

2.1.4 They can raise any issue related to equality of opportunities.

2.1.5 They can make representations in their interests through their own organisations, regarding the general objectives of the service.

2.2   Specifically the Committee shall operate:

2.2.1 To bring together employers and staff in consultation, with the object, as a matter of mutual concern, of maintaining an efficient service.

2.2.2   To afford a regular basis for consultation and negotiation on matters relevant to this objective and also on matters relating to industrial relations, productivity and working and other arrangements.

2.2.3   To discuss in relation to local conditions, the implementation of matters which have been prescribed or recommended at national, provincial or other agreed local level.

2.2.4   To give staff a wider interest and greater responsibility in these matters.

2.2.5   To maintain an effective means of reporting back to staff.

3. Functions

3.1   The Committee may consider any matter concerning:

3.1.1   Youth, community and play workers.

3.1.2   Other related informal education occupations as may be agreed.

3.1.3   Local authority part-time youth workers conditions of service, which supplement the national agreement negotiated through the Joint Negotiating Committee, or relates to aspects on which there is no existing national agreement.

3.2   In pursuance of these general principles the terms of reference of the Committee will include:

3.2.1   Management objectives.

3.2.2   Organisation, or re-organisation.

3.2.3   Equal opportunities.

3.2.4   Efficiency:
  - Issue and revision of working rules in the interest of efficient working.
  - Improvements in methods and organisation of work.

3.2.5   Working Conditions:
  - Work place layout.
  - Outreach and detached settings.
  - Generally.

3.2.6   Personnel Arrangements:
  - Administration of conditions of service.
  - Provision, specification and use of equipment.
  - Maintenance of essential services in emergencies.
  - Design of buildings from the point of view of working conditions.

3.2.7   Welfare facilities (except where this is a function of a Departmental Safety Committee) for physical and general welfare and safety.

3.2.8   General:
  - The investigation of any other circumstances conducive to the efficiency and satisfactory running of the Education Department and such other matters as are of common concern.
  - Content and conduct of local training programmes.
  - Procedure for selection for promotion.
  - Procedure for personal development and staff development and training.
  - No question of individual grievance, discipline, promotion or efficiency shall be within the scope of the Committee.

4. Constitution

4.1   Membership

4.1.1   The Committee shall comprise of the relevant Senior Education Officer (SEO), a representative of personnel and three CYWU representatives.

4.1.2   A substitute member of equivalent position may attend the Committee in the case of the listed member being unavailable.

4.2   Advisors

4.2.1   Either side may arrange for the attendance, in an advisory capacity, of other officers or full-time trade union officials where it would be helpful to the issue under discussion.

4.2.2   Such attendances shall be notified in advance of the meeting.

4.2.3   A representative of the personnel department should be present at all meetings in an advisory capacity.

5. Meetings

5.1   At least four meetings per year shall be held during working hours at reasonable intervals and there shall be provision for special meetings.

5.2   Reasonable facilities shall be provided for meetings of the employees side of the Committee, normally during working hours.

5.3   All meetings shall be convened by the SEO who will also respond to requests from either employers or staff for emergency or special meetings.

5.4   Special meetings shall be called as quickly as possible and in any event not later than within one week of a request by either side.

5.5   The employers accept that the meetings will be conducted without loss of pay to the participating Committee Members and all practicable steps will be taken to provide cover for the work of staff representatives.

5.6   Both sides should submit items for the agenda to the SEO within a reasonable time and not later than seven days before a meeting. The SEO is responsible for circulating the proposed agenda items. Business other than that on the agenda may not be introduced excepting with the agreement of both employers and staff.

5.7   Recommendations shall be reached by a consensus. All decisions of the Committee will be recorded by employers and in the event of the decisions requiring confirmation elsewhere e.g. Continuing Education Committee, Personnel Committee, employers will report on the Committee's decisions. In the event of a 'Failure to Agree' the employers will, if requested by the staff side, report to the appropriate committee giving the views of both the employers and the staff. In this eventuality the staff side will be allowed to make representations to the Committee which is making the final decision. In such circumstances the status quo will be maintained until the issue, or dispute has been resolved.

5.8   Any agreement made by this appropriate Committee shall be notified to the employers, staff and the Union and incorporated in all documents which will be available for reference within 18 days.

5.9   Minutes of the meetings shall be recorded by the clerical support provided by the employers side and circulated within 14 days of a meeting.

Signed

Signed

Date

Making it work

Words, and constitutions, and procedures are one thing, practice is another. It is often quite a cultural shift in youth, community and play work to introduce a mechanism for collective negotiation of the sort we expect young people and community groups themselves to achieve on issues that affect them. Perhaps the two most important principles underpinning the operation of the model constitution, relate to access to information and dealing with disagreements.

Access to information

Education has as a key hallmark, the transmission of anonymously created knowledge from one group or generation to another. Within youth, community and play work practice it is essential to inform, advise, and generally make children, young people and community groups aware of rights, responsibilities, laws, and opportunities. Paradoxically the face to face educators in such a service are themselves denied access to knowledge, frequently deprived by accident, or design of the essential information that they need for job security, high morale, planning work and developing creativity. Union membership and negotiating rights usually give the access that is essential to the development of professional practice and good industrial relations. Employers and managers do not have a right to exclude workers from essential information.

Section 181 of the *Trade Union and Labour Relations (Consolidated) Act 1992* requires employers to provide representatives of recognised, independent trade unions with information which is either:

1. Information without which the trade union representative would be materially impeded in carrying on collective bargaining with the employer, or
2. Information which it would be in accordance with good industrial relations practice to disclose for the purposes of collective bargaining.

Additionally, ACAS has a Code of Practice (No. 2, *Disclosure of Information to Trade Unions for Collective Bargaining Purposes*) which outlines the sort of information which it expects employers to disclose.

These include:

- Financial matters: all aspects of budgeting, planning, the financial environment, predictions and expenditure, liabilities, etc.
- Productivity and performance data.
- Workforce information, numbers employed, age and sex, labour turnover, etc.
- Conditions of service, details and policies, health and safety, etc.
- Pay and benefits arrangements, all aspects.

ACAS concede that their list (substantially more detailed than mine above) is not exhaustive and 'other items may be relevant in particular negotiations'. There are naturally some restrictions on access to matters relating to national security, personal confidentiality and the vulnerability of employers, but generally within the youth, community and play context, it is best to assume that the emphasis of the law and the Code of Practice is that all relevant information should be revealed. This area of industrial relations is much under-used in youth, community and play work, and there is nothing like good information to inform the management of a workforce. Any recognised officials of CYWU denied such information should obviously refer the matter to the national Union HQ which can have redress to the Central Arbitration Council. Again, taking on board ACAS' recommendations, it is useful for employers and unions to agree perhaps at a fixed point each year, usually around the budget setting period, the kind of information that should be shared, and the form it should take, as local authority budget printouts, can be an interesting mixture of science fiction, fantasy and entirely incomprehensible figures.

Access to good factual information is particularly essential when services are likely to be transferred, and additional entitlements to information are contained in the *Transfer of Undertakings (Protection of Employment) Regulations (1981)*, see Part 6 below.

Dealing with collective disagreements

Let us imagine that at the LJNC on Monday 10th, the employers representatives say that they intend to paint all workers' offices dark purple by Monday 17th. The union representatives, not having been forewarned about this at the previous LJNC meeting, or at any other time, and knowing that their members all prefer green, argue that the employer should not go ahead. The employer says they must because the leader of the voluntary organisation for whom they work is crazy about purple. The Union records a Failure To Agree. This freezes the situation as it is. Painters cannot move in until this FTA has been resolved. The status quo, and the non-purple office, is retained. Union and employer would then refer their case to the next arbitrator within the procedure.

Say, as is often the case in our small service, that this arbitrator is the purple-crazed leader, who is unlikely to uphold the Union's objection. If both sides persist, negotiations have broken down. There are then three options:

1. Pursuing the disagreement through industrial action: i.e. union members will ballot for strike action or some other dreadful form of non co-operation, if the painters move in with their vile purple cans.
2. Involving an expert third party to attempt conciliation, arbitration or compromise. Usually ACAS would be called in. The third party has to be mutually acceptable and any agreement reached with them would have to be binding on both employer and Union.
3. Trying another available procedure if it exists, like the Collective Disputes Procedure. This has the advantage, particularly in the larger national voluntary organisation, or in the local authority sector, of ensuring that the disagreement is likely to be reviewed and considered by another set of individuals.

This third option is one that should be built into any fair industrial relations framework. Third parties like ACAS will very often not get involved until all local procedures have been exhausted. In the absence of such a procedure, the prospect of endless talks about talks looms on the horizon.

Like an individual grievance procedure, a disputes procedure helps take the heat and emotion away from key individuals and personalities. It is designed to resolve a problem or disagreement swiftly and fairly, and therefore, again like an individual grievance procedure, should have clear stages for progress with definite timescales. Because of the under-use within youth, community and play work of such an important procedure, here is a model.

Model Collective Disputes Procedure

Introduction

It is envisaged that this procedure shall only apply where the normal process of collective bargaining and processing disagreements through the Local Joint Negotiating Committee has not enabled the resolution of a disagreement, or where a group of workers are collectively aggrieved.

During any dispute, whatever practice, or agreement which prevailed prior to the difference shall continue and there should be no industrial action or change in working pending a settlement or until this procedure has been exhausted. Once the procedure is invoked the status quo shall return.

The procedure will not apply to those issues of pay and conditions of employment where national or local collective agreements apply unless the dispute concerns alleged failure to observe those agreements. The right of trade union representation applies at each and every stage of this procedure. Conciliation procedures shall be available at each stage as mutually agreed.

Stage 1

1. Where a group of employees has a dispute or difference that has not been resolved through the LJNC, the employees should raise the matter with their senior officer. Alternatively, employees can approach the accredited trade union representative and discuss the matter with them, and the trade union representative may then take up the matter with the senior officer in the first instance.
2. After the initial approach, the senior officer should reply as soon as possible and in any case before the end of the next working day. If the accredited trade union representative is involved they should also be informed as soon as possible and in any case before the end of the next working day.
3. If the trade union representative has not represented the members and the members are dissatisfied with the reply, the employees should see the accredited trade union representative who may then try to resolve the matter at senior officer level.
4. If there is a failure to resolve the problem or if the matter is outside the scope of the senior officer, then the matter will be passed to Stage 2 of the procedure.

Stage 2

Where the matter cannot be resolved under Stage 1 of the procedure, the matter should be referred in writing to the appropriate principal officer who shall, with the appropriate trade union representatives, convene a meeting of all the interested parties within 14 days. (Every effort will be made to convene a meeting within a shorter timescale where time is a factor in the situation).

Stage 3

1. If the matter is not resolved the departmental principal officer, or other senior officer, shall in conjunction with the appropriate trade union, within ten working days, convene a meeting with the appropriate committee's Elected Members, or management committee members and attempt to resolve the problem at this level.
2. If the matter is still not resolved at this level, then it will be passed to the next stage of the procedure.

Stage 4

If the matter is not resolved at Stage 3 within five working days, it may be referred by either side to whichever is appropriate:

a) The Local Authority Personnel Committee or similar.
b) The national Joint Negotiating Committee.
c) The Local Advisory, Conciliation and Arbitration Service.

A meeting shall be convened as soon as possible and the parties will be invited to attend to present their case.

The decision of the appropriate body shall be given at the end of the meeting and shall be confirmed in writing. The decision will not prejudice the rights of either side to progress the matter under appropriate external machinery.

The more that policy development, organisation, budgeting and collective issues can be challenged through the LJNC, the less likely it is that the Collective Disputes Procedure will have to be marched through the committee room. Other mechanisms that, if properly handled, minimise the damage that can be done by unresolved disagreement should be integral to any good working environment.

When disputes are on it is often the case that union members will withdraw their goodwill. In a service which relies on goodwill, this is an incredibly difficult form of collective discipline to apply. However, sometimes the levels of exploitation or disregard for workers' concerns is so great that enough is enough. Withdrawing goodwill means refusing to deploy all those little areas of work that are not set out in your contract of employment and job description. It is a form of protest if you like that seeks to unite staff against a temporarily hostile management.

Withdrawal of goodwill can include the following depending on local contracts and circumstances.

Model Withdrawal of Goodwill List

Youth and community services rely very heavily on paid staff undertaking tasks and duties and adopting responsibilities over and above those agreed in their job description or contract of employment. This has both positive and negative sides. On the positive side enthusiasm for work is a good thing and pride in the skills you deploy and the effort you give is a great motivating factor. However, the negatives far outweigh these aspects. Every unpaid task performed masks the under resourcing of the service. Extra duties can create a dependency culture amongst those you work with. Extra duties can become extra stress. Additional work can have blurred professional edges, are you really acting as an informal educator when you go to the cash and carry?

When a dispute is on the very first form of action that workers may undertake if their collective views are not being considered properly is to withdraw good will to support their negotiators in their claim for some improvement or to stop some injustice or something unfair or something which reduces terms and conditions.

This form of support for union negotiators involves the immediate stopping of tasks at work which you are not contractually expected to perform. Things that do not appear in your job description or contract should not be done. They are somebody else's job. There are a surprisingly wide range of such tasks in your work if you start to look. Employers will naturally seek to classify them as contractual and determine that your refusal to undertake them is a breach of contract or an illegal union action. It is a question of holding nerve and getting union advice in such circumstances. What follows is far from an exhaustive list and is meant to stimulate your own thought as to what can be legitimately done. Remember the principle apply to this form of solidarity action is the same as any other, it is to press a point against the employers not harm the public and young people we work with, though let's face it there may always be an element of this, but this will always be less damaging than the effecting of letting service cuts and other negative employer developments go unchecked. A withdrawal of good will is also a time when you can check that the employer's systems and contractual obligations are being met. This is important particularly in larger organisations where you can make demands of personal departments.

Time

Work no more than your contracted hours.
Remember the Working Time Directive. Take your breaks on time.
Stop doing three session days.
Take all the TOIL owing to you.

Non supervision work

Do not undertake any new initiative or any work that has not been properly considered in supervision.

Duties and responsibilities

Immediately stop any task or duty not covered by your contract or job description.

Training

Are you owed some training time?
Put in a request for training.
Refuse to undertake any duty you have not been trained for.
Refuse any employer training related to service development.

Health and safety

When did the activities you are involved in last have a risk assessment?
Stop all activities that have not had a risk assessment.
Request a stress risk assessment on your position.
Request a Health and Safety check from the employer's and union's representative.

Administration

Stop answering the phone.
Refuse to answer any mobile or home calls.
Stop filling in forms you do not have to fill in.
Financial admistration?
Banking moneys?
Stock control?

Other duties

What work are you involved in which you shouldn't be?
Cash and Carry trips?
Driving minibuses?
Answering the telephone?
Completing time sheets?

Use of car

Is your car insured for business use? If not stop using it for work. Go to all management related meetings by bike or bus.
Are you an essential car user? If so check the terms with personnel.

Insurances

What is your responsibility for insurance in your job and what is the employers' cover for you? Time to check this complicated area out before you continue with your routine work.

Disagreeing with the workers

Disciplinary procedure and action

A Model Procedure is set out at the end of this section. This section contains some observations on the good underlying principles that should apply to any disciplinary procedure and the operation of disciplinary action and provides a checklist against which readers should be able to assess which part of the procedure applies to them. If you think that your procedure falls short, then ask the union to amend it by negotiation with the employer through the LJNC.

Capability procedure or disciplinary?

Before considering a checklist for a good disciplinary procedure and subsequent action, it is important to look at the increasing use of capability procedures within the service. In the Model Disciplinary Procedure below, discipline is distinguished from another procedure relating to capability. This distinction is important. The capability procedure should also not apply to problems arising from ill-health, or fulfilment of probationary periods.

   Capability relates to a generic area called 'performance'. Naturally one manager's view of performance may differ from another's. Performance needs to be as objectively defined as possible, through regular supervision, and good job descriptions and work planning. Where supervisory meetings have identified problems of performance over a period and required improvements have not been forthcoming, then applying the capability procedure can be considered. If there has been no regular supervision and no objective identification of problems through supervision, there should be no invoking of capability procedures. In these circumstances the kinds of principles outlined below, that apply to the disciplinary procedure, should be incorporated into any procedure. The monitoring of the desired improvements is then important and there should be a mutually agreed review period. If there is no improvement, there should be at least two stages of cautioning prior to a dismissal hearing under the capability procedure. Capability procedures are usually insidious in their operation and both management and unions are advised to discuss them very carefully indeed before implementing them and before actioning them. Capability procedures should only be used in the most exceptional of circumstances. They should be entered into in good faith with the recognition that performance improvement is possible and not invoked on the basis that the necessary improvement will not be achievable.

Action under the disciplinary procedure

A good disciplinary procedure will contain:

- An explicit statement that the procedure is based on the principles of natural justice.
- An explicit statement that the procedure is based on the *ACAS Code of Practice*.
- A clear commitment to thorough investigation prior to any disciplinary hearing.
- A right to trade union representation at every stage.
- Written and adequate notice (ten to fourteen days) of all meetings.
- Advance circulation of all materials pertaining to the case.
- Reasonable duration of warnings on file. (See Model Procedure.)
- The right to appeal against any disciplinary action to a party, or parties with knowledge of the case.
- A right to bring witnesses and character witnesses in your defence.
- A right to have temporary redeployment considered as an option instead of suspension.
- A time limit to suspensions. (Without this you can be kept hanging around in agony for ever.)
- A right to copies of notes taken at disciplinary and investigatory interviews.
- A right to approve, or disapprove of such notes.
- A right to access throughout the proceedings to all documentation considered by the employer.
- A right to have ample time to have your defence considered and to prepare your case.
- Alternatives to disciplinary action especially at the stage of dismissal.
- A recognition that discipline is different from capability, ill health or other procedures.

The absence of any one of these elements in a procedure makes both managers of the procedure and those to whom it applies, often one and the same, vulnerable to abuse.

In criminal and civil law, you can be guilty of a crime, win your case on a technicality, return to work and lead a peaceful career. In youth, community and play work you can be totally innocent, have a trumped up case made against you and not just lose your job, but your entire career in education. Teachers, and youth, community and play workers who are dismissed by employers for certain offences, can end up on *List 99* which effectively puts an end to any employment opportunities within education. If employers hear unlikely wild allegations against professional staff and on the balance of probabilities chose to believe the allegations rather than the sworn statements of professional workers, as they frequently do, then one result of their actions again is being listed and losing an entire career. Worse things can happen if employment discipline is mishandled, than if the worker had faced the criminal courts.

Fair disciplinary action will:

- Be based on the principles outlined above.
- Be entirely confidential.
- Adhere exactly to the procedure agreed. (If not take collective dispute as a union.)
- Clearly spell out what course of action and support will be undertaken to prevent future recurrence of the problem.
- Fit the offence.
- Treat different offences differently and not add them together.
- Be conducted in good faith. As soon as homophobia, racism, anti trade unionism, vindictiveness, and such like is suspected, with reasonable grounds, the person suspecting or alleging the breach of discipline or investigating the allegation, should make sure their suspicion is recorded.
- Be based at all stages and in all ways on the principles of natural justice.

Model Disciplinary Procedure

1. This disciplinary procedure shall apply to all staff within the employing organisation. The disciplinary procedure exists to ensure that disciplinary problems at work are solved as quickly and as fairly as possible. The disciplinary procedure may be invoked by the employer where your work, conduct, or action warrant such a measure and in order to improve performance and working relationships. It is envisaged that most problems of performance and responsibility will be dealt with initially through professional supervision or mutually agreed supervision in order to avoid disciplinary action.

2. This procedure operates within the ACAS Code of Practice concerning discipline at work and within the employer's overall commitments to see natural justice operate in relation to all workers. The employer sees natural justice as comprising the following:
    *   The nature of the allegations must be known to the employee in advance in sufficient time to consider them.
    *   The manager hearing the case should not be the same person investigating or presenting it. Appeals panels must be composed of those unaware of the detail of the case.
    *   The employee must be given a full opportunity to state their case and be represented.
    *   Those investigating, bringing, or hearing a case must demonstrably act in good faith.

3. It is envisaged that the employer's commitment to an open style of management and staff support through regular monthly supervision will mean that recourse to this procedure will be only in the most exceptional of circumstances. Breaches of the employer's rules and stated guidelines and confidentiality will automatically lead to disciplinary action. You are encouraged to ask through supervision for clarification of any rule, guideline or procedure.
    *   This procedure exists to deal with misconduct, wilfully deficient performance, refusal to follow instructions, negligence or similar situations.
    *   The assessment of employment probation is outlined in a separate procedure.
    *   Separate guidance exists for dealing with perceived failure of performance resulting from ill health or from alcohol dependence.
    *   A separate procedure known as the capability procedure exists for dealing with perceived failures in carrying out the duties and responsibilities of a post through lack of aptitude, skill, or ability rather than any lack of willingness.

4. This Disciplinary Procedure can only be invoked in relation to you by your line manager. Any complaint by a third party, except in the circumstances of Paragraph 7 below, will be discussed with you initially through the scheduled supervision meeting or a specially convened supervision meeting.

5. This Procedure has four stages as set out below. At each stage of the Procedure you have the right to be represented by your trade union representative. At each stage formal records shall be kept and the result of each stage shall be confirmed in writing within the timescales detailed. You are entitled to keep your own records and also to record your disagreement as to the accuracy of the formal records or of the result.

6. No disciplinary action will be taken against an employee who is a union representative until the circumstances of the case have been notified to a national official, or a full-time official of the trade union of which you are a member.

7. The employee shall be informed in writing of the complaint against them and will be advised, in writing, of their rights under the Disciplinary Procedure. The employee shall also be provided with documents to be referred to at the disciplinary hearing, lists of witnesses to be called and a list of all members of the disciplinary panel, at least five working days in advance of the hearing, and in sufficient time to consider these.

8. The employee and trade union representative shall be allowed a reasonable time to prepare the employee's case and the date and time of (any) disciplinary hearing(s) shall be agreed between the employee, and the trade union representative and the representative(s) of the employer.

9. At each stage of the Disciplinary Procedure there shall be a disciplinary hearing to allow the employer to put their case and the employee to put their case for their defence. The conduct of disciplinary hearings shall be as follows:

a) The employer shall form a disciplinary panel consisting of not less than three representatives. The members of this panel should have no prior knowledge or involvement in the case. The membership of this panel should be made known to the employee as soon as possible, and the employee and their representative should be given the opportunity to challenge the membership of the panel if they believe that members of the panel have prior involvement in the case. One member of the panel shall be elected Chair.

b) The representative of the employer bringing the charges shall present the complaint against the employee, will state the investigation that has been carried out and where appropriate will refer to documentation that has already been made available in advance to the employee. No new written evidence may be introduced at the hearing by either the employer or employee. During the presentation the employers' representative may present witnesses. The witnesses shall be called in turn and shall be questioned by the employers' representative followed by the employee's representative and finally if required by the panel. At the conclusion of the presentation, the employee's representative may question the employer's representative.

c) The employee's representative presents the employee's case, referring where necessary to appropriate documentation and may call witnesses at any stage as part of the presentation of the case. Witnesses shall be called in turn and questioned by the employee's representative followed by the employer's representative and finally if required by the panel. At the conclusion of the presentation the employee's representative may be questioned by the employer's representative.

d) Both sides are finally asked to sum up their respective cases, without introducing new evidence.

e) The panel will consider the case in private. The decision of the panel will be notified to the employee at the end of the hearing and shall be confirmed in writing.

f) The panel shall advise the employee of their right to appeal which they shall have at every stage of the disciplinary procedure.

g) All warnings given will be clearly specified and be accompanied by a clear statement of the improvement required with a clear timescale and a strategy for training and support to enable the employee to improve practice and performance.

h) No disciplinary action shall be commenced if there is a grievance from the employee pending.

Stage one: first oral warning

This is the only part (except in the case of gross misconduct or summary dismissal) of the Disciplinary Procedure that may be issued directly by the line manager. The line manager shall explain the reasons for taking disciplinary action and discuss plans and timetables for overcoming the problem. The line manager and employee shall discuss what action should be taken to prevent further disciplinary action, and a plan for assistance, training, support, and review, and appropriate timescales shall be agreed. A verbal warning shall be confirmed in writing. The first verbal warning will remain on the employee's file for three months. It will then be expunged and all records destroyed. (At all stages as an employee you have a right to inspect your personal file with seven days written notice. All matters relating to your employment, work record and supervision will be kept within this one file.)

Stage two: second oral warning

If after the review, the employer considers that progress on the matter of the first verbal warning is unsatisfactory then a second disciplinary hearing shall be called. Following the hearing, a second verbal warning may be issued. Again a plan of action and support, review and clear timescales for improvement shall be agreed. The verbal warning shall be confirmed in writing. The second verbal warning will remain on the employee's file for six months.

Stage three: written warning

If after the second review, the employer still considers that progress on the matter of the second verbal warning is unsatisfactory, then a third hearing shall be called. Following the hearing a written warning may be issued. The written warning shall clearly state the precise nature of the problem, what improvements or action are required, by when, set out a plan for assistance and state that subsequent lack of progress will result in the termination of employment. The written warning will remain on the employee's file for one year.

Stage four: final written warning

Should progress not be made by the time of the final review, the employee shall be made fully aware of the reason why the written warning is being implemented, and a final disciplinary hearing shall be held. References, at the discretion of the employer, may be given to the employee, and assistance may be afforded in obtaining suitable alternative employment.

Gross misconduct

a) The employer reserves the right to dismiss without notice for reasons of gross misconduct:
  - criminal acts at work
  - theft
  - fraud
  - malicious damage
  - deceit
  - assault
  - serious breaches of:
    - the employer's equal opportunities policies
    - health and safety policies
  - unauthorised disclosure of confidential information
  - gross disregard of rules about, or endangering the life or safety and well being of any person
  - engaging in unauthorised employment during working hours when contracted to the employer
  - conscious disregard of a reasonable employer's instruction, policy or procedure not currently subject to dispute with the recognised trade unions
  - negligence in the custody of cash or property
  - sexual, racial or general harassment or discriminatory behaviour

b) In cases of alleged gross misconduct that could seriously threaten the employer's assets, public commitments or trust, the employee shall be suspended on full pay and the employer shall carry out a thorough investigation which shall seek to determine all of the relevant facts of the situation and relevant evidence. It is recognised that the employer has a duty to ensure that the suspension is of limited duration, is the only realistic alternative, and that it is professionally explained to staff and clients. It is recognised that suspension in itself is not a disciplinary sanction.

c) Following the investigation a hearing shall be called, using the procedures outlined in section 9 of this procedure. In addition, the employee shall be advised that if the complaint is upheld it could lead to their dismissal. Where the nature of the problem is not likely to mean that the employee is a danger to the public or clients, every opportunity for temporary secondment to other duties shall be explored in place of suspension. A suspension shall be for a maximum of one month unless agreed otherwise by the employee and their representative.

10. The employee shall have the right of appeal at all stages of the disciplinary procedure, including gross misconduct. Notice of the appeal shall be made in writing within ten working days of the

employee receiving written confirmation of the employer's disciplinary decision. Appeals shall be heard by an appeal panel constituted by the employer. This appeal panel shall have no prior knowledge, nor involvement in the case. Where this is impractical the employer shall make alternative arrangements, perhaps using mutually agreed third parties such as ACAS, or the professional staff of other related employers.

11. Depending on the precise circumstances, disciplinary action could result in:
    a) A written warning indicating the improvement required and, where appropriate, the time-scale for its achievement.
    b) Allowing employees to resign, without duress and with clear advice as to the effect of this course of action.
    c) Dismissal with notice.
    d) Dismissal without notice.

12. Alternative action to dismissal may be considered. The employer has no contractual right to impose these alternatives unilaterally, and therefore the agreement of the individual employee concerned must be gained. The following may be considered:
    a) Relegation to a junior post.
    b) Transfer to another post.
    c) Suspension on reduced pay for a fixed period.

13. The employer shall take reasonable steps to ensure that professional legal advice is obtained throughout the operation of any disciplinary action.

Rules, regulations and being clear: the importance of the staff handbook

Better the Staff Handbook that buckles the shelf
Than one as light as an elf.

Some local authority employers have established huge staff handbooks in which are placed all of the rules and regulations, and guidelines that apply to youth, community and play staff as agreed from time to time through the LJNC and by committee.

Such handbooks can give the impression of too much bureaucracy and ineffective administrative control, and in themselves do not guarantee effective communication of agreements, or successful administration of their contents in practice. They can give the impression that instead of educating children, adults and young people, workers will be continually filling in forms.

However, I share the view of the *ACAS Code of Practice on Discipline* which advocates the issue of clear guidelines and communication of employers' expectations. In the vulnerable work terrains that youth, community and play workers enter there is so much that can go wrong: hazardous pursuits, the drugs culture, crime related confidences, inadequate financial controls, conflict with authority on behalf of young people, sex education, conflicting perceptions, etc. Professional judgement is open to continual re-interpretation as political cultures and moral public panics come and go.

A staff handbook can only be of use if it is based on a system of regular negotiation through an LJNC and regular and open consultation with those working in the field, which assists in clarifying the employers' professional expectations and objectives. With the further fragmentation of an already small service into autonomous areas or districts within one employing authority, and the different patterns and objectives in different voluntary sector organisations and, more recently new employers in unitary authorities, it has become even more important to hold onto concepts of common expectation and standards. It is simply not good enough for area team X to have a completely different culture on how to report drug abuse from that of neighbouring area team Y in the same Authority.

Next the principles which should accompany the issue of a good staff handbook are considered and a checklist of those items that should be included within it is provided, along with some model guidelines, or rules, because the absence of such has, in my experience, been the cause of unnecessary casework. These concern sex education, acceptable behaviour, the misuse of prohibited substances and alcohol abuse among young people.

Model Staff Handbook Contents List

JNC Report.

Local agreement for part-time workers.

Staffing ratios policy.

Vulnerable situations policies.

Child abuse guidelines.

Staff contracts.

Job descriptions.

Staff development policy:
- Equal opportunities.
- Induction pack.
- Employment probation guidelines.
- Supervision statement of intent and guidelines.
- Performance appraisal guidelines.
- In service training.

Pension scheme that applies.

Details of employers' insurance.

Equal opportunities policy:
- Recruitment and selection.
- Policies at work.

Recruitment and selection procedures.

Redeployment procedure.

Redundancy policy and procedure.

Health and safety.

Procedures, policies or structures:
- Reporting accidents and emergency situations.
- Insuring vehicles and foreign visits.
- First aid boxes and training.
- Coping with asthma, diabetes, epilepsy and other diseases.
- Drugs and medication guidelines.
- Safety audit checklist.
- The Electricity at Work Regulations.
- Driving minibuses and other vehicles.
- Safe use of ladders.
- Tower scaffolds.
- Information and Communications Technology Policy.
- Dangerous substances at work and COSSH regulations.
- European Directives on use of VDUs etc.
- The Food Act.
- Dealing with violence at work.
- Trespass.
- Outdoor activity procedures and guidelines.
- Hazardous activity guidelines.
- Protective equipment regulations.

Sexual harassment guidelines and complaint procedure:
- Job share policies.
- Detached work policies.

Guidelines on taking responsibilities during work (e.g. secretary of Association, leaseholder).

Parental leave procedures.

Carers' leave procedure.

Policies on violence at work.

Employers welfare support structures.

Sick pay procedures and policies.

Financial management guidelines:

- Approved audit procedures
- Handling petty cash.
- Financial assistance available.
- Lettings regulations.
- Paying part-time and casual employees.
- Ordering and invoicing.
- Approved accountancy procedures.
- Financial security.
- Budgeting.
- Unit financial plan submission.
- Retention of records.

Disciplinary procedure.

Grievance procedure.

Collective disputes procedure.

Regrading procedure.

Facilities agreement.

Local Joint Negotiating Committee Agreement.

Time off in lieu arrangements.

Residential pay arrangements.

Travel and subsistence allowance schemes and guidelines.

Complaints procedure (how does authority respond if a member of the public complains about you?)

JNC regrading form and procedure.

Compassionate leave scheme.

Policy on writing references.

Authorised Establishment figures for JNC posts.

Lists of all full and part-time JNC posts.

Name and addresses of national and local support services.

Security of employment agreement.

Accident at work report forms.

Official conduct guidelines. Important examples are:

- Behavioural standards.
- Whole time service.
- Interests of officers.
- Information concerning officers.
- Contact with the press.
- Sex education guidelines.
- Dealing with abuse of prohibited substances.
- Dealing with alcohol abuse.
- Visits off site.
- Model parental consent form.
- Indemnity form for visits and travel.
- Guidelines for visits and overnight stays.
- Approved qualifications for specialist activity instruction—weightlifting, canoeing, etc.

A thrilling list I am sure you will agree; exhausting, but not exhaustive. Aren't all staff teams entitled to be clear on what all of the above entail?

Sex education

Youth, community and play workers deal with issues relating to sexuality and health education in ways that are different from teachers. Our approach is more akin to health education specialists in many senses and reflects the now suppressed spirit of a Health Education Authority more than the suggestively rampant puritanism which has been promoted by the DfEE and which applies to teachers. Given that youth, community and play workers are mainly employed within education departments, this clash of culture has already caused some problems, particularly where schools have seen the sense of inviting youth workers in to develop personal and social education programmes but assumed that the DfEE guidelines apply, thus rendering the youth worker's approach impossible. There have already been instances of youth workers who promoted sex education and sexuality awareness in *their* professional way, being disciplined, simply because this method conflicts with the political, and sometimes parental expectations, more common in schools and colleges.

It is absolutely essential therefore, that all employing organisations should have a clear and comprehensive package of guidelines regarding youth, community and play workers, and sex education.

Acceptable behaviour

Youth, community and play work projects are open to public and professional scrutiny by a range of agencies and individuals. Often standards of behaviour amongst users, expected as the norm in other institutions, are the exception within ours. Such moral transfers rarely assist and the parameters of working relationships with 'clients' are less easily defined. After all, in some of the best practice, the worker's deployment of professional skills might appear like a form of close friendship. In many respects the behaviour tolerated or worked with by youth, community and play workers covers a wider, more unpredictable spectrum than in more formal areas of education. While advocating that projects are openly against oppression and in favour of equal opportunities practice, declaring publicly to users and staff what is and what is not considered acceptable professional conduct, nevertheless all employing organisations and staff teams should consider specific advice in relation to certain problematic and potentially, or actually, illegal or unacceptable behaviours of which youth, community and play workers are aware, or which they witness on an almost daily basis.

Also, there is the question of risk minimisation. The natural sympathies of youth, community and play workers can lead them to protect young people or adults, by putting themselves in vulnerable situations. For example, what guidelines do most employing organisations give on taking young people home if they cannot get them into the local homeless shelter, or if the young person has been ejected from the home in a blaze of violence and there is no local hostel?

Moral and professional ethical dilemmas abound in this area, and perhaps the safest advice is to say, again, that through clear line management and induction, the parameters of work should be abundantly clear. In my experience however, this is simply not enough, and the disciplinary measures that management are often forced to take against staff in the climate of moral panic that often exists, result from a strict lack of guideline. No worker is going to condone drug taking or pushing, prostitution, petty crimes like theft, misuse of alcohol and the like. But in order to support young people in coming to terms with the dangers of these, youth, community and play workers frequently have to live with the problem, become more aware of its impact on the young person's life, and understand its full dimensions, in order to educate around and through the problem.

Additionally, it is recognised professionally that youth, community and play workers relate very differently to their client groups than do teachers, the Police or social services workers. To put it at its starkest: the problem adult client of the local social services team, may be a leading member of the Management Committee of the community centre where the youth and community worker is seconded. Or, the criminal statistic and neighbourhood nuisance may be the young person with whom the youth worker has established a unique and trusting relationship.

The young person alienated from school, social welfare techniques, work and the local peer groups and community networks, may well be the subject of the youth worker's closest educational attention. The young person may only agree to meet the worker in the pub or amusement arcade. Alternatively, the articulate college student and local youth forum chairperson may look to the youth worker to support the promotion of anti-homophobic work. The local youth centre may be the only venue where the ten and twelve year olds in a community of high rise flats can really let off steam. It may be incredibly noisy and chaotic when the local councillor visits, and the young people may be swearing and shouting.

Neither professional training nor endless procedural guidelines will prepare workers for the range of dilemmas that they will face. Yet again, the emphasis is on the importance of supervision. It is in regular supervision sessions that the worker is able to share their perception of the vulnerable or perplexing situations they have faced. If their responses have been deemed to be unacceptable, or it is thought that they are unnecessarily at risk they should be informed of this. Equally, workers have a responsibility to inform line management between supervision meetings of any doubtful or risk laden situation they are likely to enter. The complex ethical debate about confidentiality and complicity cannot be avoided in employment guidelines and in management supervision. Indeed by dealing with it in these places, workers are assisted in coping with intractable problems more effectively.

In the following two sets of guidelines we are dealing with the parameters set by the employer for dealing with common, but illegal matters. In some senses the principles underlying these would apply to other situations where persistent behaviours do not quite fit the exact shape of the law books. What employers and particularly external agencies such as the police need to appreciate more in relation to this area of work, is that the successes of social education in youth and community work depend on the establishment of trust and confidentiality between the worker and individuals concerned. I have never seen this recognition spelt out in an employment policy.

The other side of this appreciation is the recognition that youth, community and play workers are frequently those most intimately involved with supporting for example, the victims of racial and violent crime, the bereaved families of victims of drug overdoses, and the families distraught by the effects of unemployment on their children. The following model procedures have drawn on a number of actual agreements in terms of concepts and particularly heavily on procedures in Staffordshire. In issues of this complexity, and bearing in mind that drugs workers are specifically employed to reduce drug taking, or health education youth workers are employed directly to improve health awareness at all levels, any model procedure will be deficient and unable to catch all of the permutations of circumstance. What is more worrying though, is the number of employers with no guidance to staff whatsoever.

Model Procedure on the Misuse of Prohibited Substances

Preamble

The Authority recognises that a long established element of youth culture is the experimentation with drugs and alcohol and that it is the professional task of youth, community and play workers to encourage involvement in creative educational activities and to discourage the misuses of stimulants, prohibited substances and alcohol. In order to be effective in such work, the worker will often have to become aware of the extent of abuse and the culture surrounding drug and alcohol usage. All knowledge of this should be recorded in writing and related in supervision meetings and assessed. It is important that the youth and community service is not associated with actions that could be interpreted as condoning drugs or alcohol misuse and that sufficient facilities are provided for constructive social education programmes among young people.

Premises

Immediate action must be taken, involving the police as expedient, to curtail the following activities which place both the worker and the service staff at risk of prosecution:

- Smoking cannabis on youth and community premises.
- Supplying alcohol or illegal drugs on youth and community premises.

Simple possession of illegal drugs by young people on the premises does not in itself put the person responsible for the premises into the position of having broken the law. However, youth workers should ban all illegal drugs, solvents and alcohol from premises, which includes any land within the boundaries of the premises.

It is recognised that in many situations and locations, enforcement would be difficult and that it should be left to the youth worker's discretion to deal with situations, bearing in mind the law. The worker will ensure that when exercising their discretion they record their decision and discuss this through supervision or more urgently with their line manager.

Responsibilities for premises and liability

Under the Misuse of Drugs Act and other legislation, anyone responsible for the management of premises, including centre-based youth workers, is liable if particular illegal acts are committed on those premises. For example, anyone responsible for management of premises upon which cannabis is smoked, or alcohol is sold (the premises being unlicensed) is liable for a fine and/or imprisonment.

However, the mere fact that an act is illegal does not in itself make the centre worker liable. They are only liable if the act is one covered by the legislation on management of premises.

It should be clearly established prior to any residential, foreign exchange or trip exactly, what rules will apply to these matters, and the situation should be fully discussed with all participants. Such rules and agreements should be made explicit to parents prior to undertaking the visit.

Confidentiality

Youth workers may maintain confidentiality and are not obliged to take any action in the following circumstances:
- Being told that a young person has used alcohol, solvents, or any illegal drug.
- Observing the possession or use of illegal drugs off youth and community premises, (e.g. in detached work).

Observation must be recorded in writing and communicated confidentially through supervision.

Youth workers may often decide it is in the best interest of the young person, themselves or the service to take action, which may or may not involve the police, or parents.

Obstruction

Youth workers must not obstruct the process of investigation.

Obstruction involves a positively obstructive act, such as the physical concealment of illegal drugs or of a person who possesses them, or helping such a person to escape the police, e.g. by creating a diversion or providing means of transport.

Drug possession

In the case of the young person who possesses small amounts of drugs for his or her own use, the youth worker (or any other member of the public) may receive the illegal drug from the young person with the intention of giving it to the police or destroying it at the earliest opportunity.

The transfer of the drug from the young person to the worker should be witnessed by at least one other adult so that the worker has a defence against any suggestion that the drug might be their own. Likewise, if the drug is destroyed (e.g. by flushing down the toilet), then this too should be witnessed.

Contacting parents

Under normal circumstances, when dealing with the younger age range, that is, under 18's, as opposed to young adults, parents should be contacted and a written record of this contact kept, in cases of confirmed and repeated use of alcohol, solvents or any illegal drug, because of the serious risk to health. Whenever possible, the worker should first negotiate such contact with the young persons concerned, so that it may be done on their terms, as far as possible.

In cases where the worker judges that family relationships are a significant contributory factor to drug use, or where they suspect contact with parents may not be beneficial for the welfare of the young person concerned, the situation should be discussed in the first instance with the line manager before any decision not to contact parents is taken.

Alcohol abuse

Those scrutinising, visiting, and sometimes professionally inspecting youth and community services may have different standards of what is acceptable behaviour amongst users and young people, from those of youth, community and play work professionals. I have dealt with one case where a visiting inspector reported a youth worker for permitting unruly behaviour in her centre. The worker was disciplined. It transpired through evidence, that the unruly behaviour involved 12-year-old boys shouting loudly, not swearing or acting violently, at the time of the World Cup, in the presence of a distinguished guest but in the absence of the usual two part-time members of staff who worked with them and were off sick on that occasion!

Model Practice in Relation to Alcohol

This guidance is intended for youth, community and play workers. It aims to set out the legal, health and social aspects. It cannot prescribe rules for every situation. Discussion with line management and thorough supervision should seek to clarify situations.

1. Legal framework
Children under five

It is against the law to give any child under the age of 5 years alcohol of any kind, except on doctor's advice, or in a medical emergency when a responsible person judges it necessary.

Children under fourteen

By statute, children under fourteen must not be in a bar during 'permitted hours', that is the hours during which alcohol may be sold or supplied for consumption on licensed premises. The exceptions to this are:

1. If they are the children of the licensee.
2. If they are resident at the licensed premises.
3. If they are passing through the bar to, or from other parts of the premises and there is no other convenient means of doing so.
4. Family rooms and pub gardens. Some pubs have a family room or pub garden. Children under fourteen can be admitted into such a room or area if it is distinctly separate from a bar, and there is no alcoholic drinks service, either through a hatch or by table service.

Young people aged fourteen to eighteen

At the licensee's discretion they may be allowed into a bar, but must not under any circumstances drink alcohol in that bar or be sold alcohol.

Off-licences (including supermarkets)

As off-licences do not contain a bar, there is no restriction on the age at which children may enter them. However the sale of intoxicating liquor to under-eighteens is prohibited and it is an offence for a young person to buy or attempt to buy alcohol on such premises. An off-licence is any category of retail outlet which has a licence to sell alcohol, including supermarkets, grocers and other shops.

Persons under the age of eighteen may not make any sale of alcohol unless the sale has been specially approved by the holder of the licence or by a person over the age of eighteen authorised to act on their behalf.

Employment of young people

Young people under eighteen, including the licensee's family, must not be employed in a bar when it is open for the sale and consumption of drink. No person under the age of eighteen may be employed in any capacity between 10 am and 6 pm where alcohol is regularly sold after 11 am. Any work, even without payment, is regarded as employment.

The basic age for restaurants, hotels etc.

In a restaurant, dining room or eating area clearly set apart for meals, young people aged sixteen–seventeen may purchase beer or cider to drink with a meal. They must not purchase wine or spirits, but are allowed to consume them, if bought by an accompanying adult, with a table or counter meal in a room set apart and made exclusively for such meals.

Young people under sixteen are allowed to be in a restaurant dining room or eating area set apart and used exclusively for table (or counter) meals when alcohol is only served, or consumed as an ancillary to a meal. They may not purchase any alcohol whatsoever. At the licensee's discretion, they may be allowed to consume alcohol with a table meal, but only if it is purchased by an accompanying adult. In practice, licensees will generally expect the adult concerned to be a parent or other responsible guardian.

Under licensing legislation, anyone responsible for the management of a premises including club-based youth, community and play workers, is liable if alcohol is sold, unless the necessary licence has been obtained.

Immediate action must be taken, involving the police as expedient, to curtail the sale, supply or consumption of alcohol on youth, community and play premises. Alcohol should be banned from the premises, which includes any land within the boundaries of the premises.

Special permission must be obtained from the Principal Youth and Community Officer in conjunction with the Authority's legal department to apply for an occasional license.

2. Youth and community premises

Some centres have rules agreed with members; in others the staff decide on the admission or not of a young person who is under the influence of drink. However rules are arrived at, they should be made known to existing members and new members, and appear in writing either on a notice board, membership card or other medium.

In all cases, the health and safety of the staff, the young person concerned and other members are paramount and the following guidelines may be of help to workers in discharging their duty of care.

1. The staff will probably know the young person who demands entry while under the influence of alcohol. They may be able to assess the degree of drunkenness, taking account of their knowledge of the person's usual behaviour, and must decide what action to take. The following must be considered:
    - The risks involved in refusing entry, e.g. is the person so drunk that they are likely to be a danger to themselves or to others?
    - When or whether to contact parents, take the person home, ask a friend to accompany the person or allow them to go home alone.
    - The youth and community worker should find a suitable opportunity, as soon as possible after the incident, to discuss it with the young person.

2. If a young person is very drunk, the following procedure should be followed:
    ● Assess situation to determine appropriate action.
    ● Treat drunkenness as poisoning. Remember that alcohol taken with any other drugs is a dangerous combination of poisons.
    ● Ask friends what kind of alcohol and how much has been consumed and whether it was combined with any other drug.
    ● Call an ambulance. Place the person in the recovery position. Do not leave them alone and keep the person warm. One youth worker (if possible) should travel in the ambulance unless a parent or relative is available.
    ● The youth worker should consider using their own transport only in cases of extreme emergency and only if the worker is fully aware of the most direct route to hospital, the insurance cover they have for such use of personal transport and if they have left details of their arrangements either with the young person's parents or a colleague.
    ● Find out if a parent or nearest relative is at home and contact them immediately; it is important for all centres to have complete lists of all users addresses.
    ● As soon as practicable, record the incident and the action taken in the Incident Book.

3. International exchanges

Licensing laws and cultures relating to alcohol vary from country to country, and frequently exchange trips will be organised to countries with more relaxed licensing laws. It is important that prior to the trip any agreements or rules in relation to the consumption of alcohol while on the trip are clearly understood and discussed with all participants and that resulting agreements are made known to parents and guardians in advance.

4. Continuing social education work

In all cases where young people are involved with alcohol misuse, the worker should seek to negotiate with the young person about any contact with parents, whilst hoping it may be made on their terms. However, in some cases, it may be necessary to inform parents without the agreement of the young person.

In the case of under-eighteens, parents should be contacted if a young person is a confirmed and repeated abuser of alcohol or if there appears to be any indication of risk to health.

If the worker judges that family relationships may be a contributory factor to alcohol abuse or if they suspect that contact with the family might not be beneficial to the welfare of the young person, the situation should be discussed with the appropriate designated officer before any decision to contact parents is made.

In the case of over-eighteens, if the young person regularly and repeatedly drinks too much, the worker should encourage them to seek help from one of the agencies specialising in support of people with alcohol problems.

In every case, the worker should offer continuing support.

5. Community centres with bars

As a general rule, the Authority will not encourage and support the development of social clubs and bars within community centres.

Bars in community centres should be additional complements to fund raising activities and not the centre of activities, or the focus of financial dependency.

It will be important for staff in community centres with bars, to establish precisely their legal and professional responsibilities for the bar operations. *Community Matters*, the Charity Commission and the Registrar of Friendly Societies are able to give guidance on all matters relating to bar management in community centres, and additional support should be obtained from the Authority's legal department.

The employer does not expect youth, community and play staff to take legal responsibilities relating to bar operations, licensing, financial and stock control and staffing. Where this is required by the Community Association a full schedule of expectations, induction and in service training will be provided.

Similarly all applications for occasional licenses will first be referred to the Principal Youth and Community Officer who will consider the request initially in consultation with the Authority's legal department.

6. Community awareness

The Authority will actively support work to make suppliers of alcohol in every neighbourhood, where there is a youth and community centre aware of the Authority's youth, community and play work policies, and attitudes to alcohol misuse.

Information communication technology policy

The universal adoption of information technology with our places of work has led to a new kind of casework and problem. Youth, community and play centres tend to be very accessible, as are the offices where computers are stored. Many other centres are the local neighbourhood resource for information technology and large computer suites are increasingly common in centres. The trouble is that computers have very good memories, that are difficult to erase and staff are increasingly faced with actions against them as a result of inappropriately sent or downloaded messages and access to websites. Often they are wrongly accused as a result of unauthorised public access or the absence of a procedure to deal with how they relate to technology and how they use it with clients old and young.

This model policy seeks to create a framework for consideration of managing this area and needs also of course to be read in conjunction with the Code of Ethics and other common sense employment procedures.

Model Information Communication Technology Policy

The number of cases involving youth and community workers and the use particularly of e-mails and the internet has multiplied. Skilled youth workers with absolutely no computer literacy whatsoever have been dismissed on suspicion that they permitted young people to access inappropriate websites and the like on employer's owned computers. You might think that in these days of sophisticated firewalls and password systems, that every youth centre computer would be safe and secure and impenetrable. Unfortunately not. Young people are often more proficient in the use of ICT than their youth workers. So, as with all employment related policies the principles are that the rules must be transparent and clear and that staff must be fully trained into awareness and competence in the area for which policy is being developed. This draft policy therefore errs on the side of detail and caution and is set down as an initial draft for all local employers and staff groups to discuss.

The draft imagines mainly working within a local authority setting possibly with a network system. It may need amending therefore for smaller organisations. It assumes the existence of an IT support specialist and Help Desk. It also takes on some issues wider than just access within youth and community centres. Some of the work of www.youth.org.uk has been helpful in considering this draft.

1.   Responsibilities

1.1   This policy applies to:
Clearly specify all groups covered by this policy. Will you treat full, part-time and volunteer staff any differently?

1.2   It is the responsibility of each employee and other person mentioned in Section 2.1(2) to familiarise themselves with and adhere to this policy.

1.3   Adherence to this policy is a condition for using council equipment and networks.

1.4   This policy is designed to conform with standards used throughout the public and private sectors and is the council's first step towards compliance with British Standard (BS) 7799 – Code of Practice for Information Security Management.

1.5   This policy has had full consultation with all relevant trade unions.

2.   Internal e-mail

2.1   The following should be strictly adhered to when using the council's internal e-mail system:
- Do not send e-mails that may breach council policy or government regulations. This includes messages that may harass or offend someone. Harassment can take the form of argumentative or insulting messages or any other message that the sender knows, or might reasonably be expected to know, would cause distress to a recipient.
- Do not use e-mail for gossip.
- Do not send e-mails from someone else's account, except under proper 'delegated' arrangements (proxy) that retain individual accountability.
- Do not forward information known or believed to be confidential without the approval of the sender or information owner.
- Do not reply to all recipients where an answer to the originator will suffice.
- Do not use e-mail where an alternative form of communication (e.g. telephone, memo) may be more appropriate.
- Do ensure that Public Groups are used appropriately. Section 3.2 below deals with all user groups specifically.
- Do carry out regular housekeeping of mailbox items. All messages, even old ones, can take up valuable system resources and should be archived locally or deleted as soon as they become obsolete. Users are encouraged to set preferences for archiving personal (diary) items that they wish to retain.

3.   Youth and community centres

Every youth and community centre shall have a clear policy relating to access and use of computers in publicly accessible buildings. All computers in youth and community centres shall be protected by firewalling and password protection systems and shall be regularly inspected. Training support and advice shall be regularly available to all staff in relation to these aspects. Users of council computers shall register their use and its purpose and shall all be made aware of the code of good conduct model for the use of the internet.

Instruction in the ethical and proper use of the council's computer equipment shall be given to all users of equipment and shall be considered a valid part of the informal education work with young people, adults and community groups. Consideration should be given to issuing each user with a certificate verifying the fact that they have had awareness training relevant to their user needs prior to using the equipment. The council does not consider excessive use of computer equipment to play games to be a valid use of educational resources.

Each centre shall design its own access and use policy relevant to the needs of users. Particular attention should be given to creating an understanding of the definition of offensive material given in paragraph 5.6 below.

Consider adopting a set of rules for NET use which are publicly displayed, discussed with users and incorporated into the centre's rules of conduct.

Code of Conduct

- I will use the computer in the centre for educational purposes and not for games all the time and for gossip and chat.
- I will only access the computer when my youth worker knows about it and has agreed how long I can go online. I will leave a record of when I log on and log off.
- I will always try to be with someone else when using the computer.
- I will not give out personal information such as my gender, address, telephone number, nor anyone else's nor the owner of the computer.
- I will report any misuse of the computer and any unwanted mail.
- I will tell a youth worker if I come across any information that makes me feel uncomfortable or if I have not requested it.
- I will never agree to get together with someone I meet on line.
- I will not respond to any messages that are vulgar, insulting or make me feel uncomfortable in any way. I will inform a youth worker if I get a message like that or become aware of anyone else from the centre sending such messages.
- I will not copy information created by other people and claim it as my own work. This includes stories, pictures, information and art.
- I will not seek, search, publish, download or transmit information/pictures which may be offensive or illegal. If in doubt I will always ask my youth worker.
- I appreciate that my youth centre has sought to ensure that the internet use on this computer is as free from offensive material as possible and I will not seek to disable any of the filtering and blocking software.
- I will not pass on to anyone else any information about the computer equipment at this centre or the passwords and other protections it uses.

4. External (internet)—e-mail

4.1 Access to the internet (for external e-mail and world wide web) is provided to individual users to support council goals and those of the educational programmes of individual educational establishments including youth and community centres.

The following points apply specifically to employees who use this facility:

- Where e-mail is used to communicate with suppliers, customers etc. staff should note that e-mail must be treated in **the same way as formal business correspondence**.
- The e-mail account details of other individuals or Services should not be given to external sources without gaining their consent.
- Anyone receiving excessive junk mail should consult IT Technical Support (Help Desk) about the use of mail filters and other ways of blocking unwanted correspondence.
- Staff should not re-send e-mail chain letters and should use caution with any e-mail that asks the reader to forward it to others. This includes forwarding any verified e-mail virus warnings as such e-mails are almost always chain-mail hoaxes. Staff should retain such correspondence and report the matter to IT Technical Support (Help Desk).
- Staff should not reply to *external* e-mails sent to them by mistake.
- Be aware that any distribution list publishes the names of all people to whom the message is sent. Do not send the names of other employees in this way without their knowledge and consent.

4.2 Employees should be particularly careful about what they commit to e-mail (either internally or externally). In particular, communications must be free from any statements that are defamatory, libellous or slanderous. In general material should not contain anything that could be seen as insulting to any individual or group; it should not be damaging to the personal or professional reputation of any individual or group.

The Telecommunications Act 1994 makes it an offence to transmit messages or other matter via a public telecommunications system (including the councils digital networks and telephone systems), that is indecent, obscene or menacing. This includes causing annoyance, nuisance or needless anxiety to another by a message that the sender knows to be false.

E-mails can be used as evidence in industrial tribunals and formal enquiries, including internal disciplinary and grievance hearings. Deleting an e-mail does not guarantee that it will be erased from network systems.

Users receiving mail falling into the description outlined above should inform their manager and the IT Technical Support (Help Desk) immediately.

5.   Use of the world wide web/other internet services

5.1   Access to the internet must be used responsibly and legally. Users must not take *any* action which could bring the Council into disrepute, cause offence, interfere with the Council's work or jeopardise the security of data, networks, equipment or software.

5.2   Until such a time as a disclaimer can be added automatically to all e-mails, staff posting items/comments to newsgroups should add the disclaimer:

The views contained in this post are those of the originator. They are not the views or opinions of the council, unless specifically stated.

5.3   Under no circumstances should staff make use of council facilities to access chat lines or similar services.

5.4   With the advent of e-commerce, staff should beware of committing the council to purchase or acquire goods or services without proper authorisation.

5.5   Staff should not attempt to download or install unauthorised software.

5.6   The internet contains far more useful information than it does offensive material. However, offensive material does exist and members of staff should be aware of the following definition of 'offensive' as far as the Council is concerned:

Offensive material is anything that is pornographic; involves threats or violence; promotes illegal acts, racial or religious hatred or discrimination of any kind. It also covers material that the person knows, or might reasonably be expected to know, would offend a colleague with particular sensitivities.

5.7   People receiving offensive or sexually explicit mail should inform their manager and the IT Technical Support (Help Desk) immediately. Such material may not be identifiable until an e-mail is opened and in these cases staff will not be held responsible providing they report it immediately.

5.8   Newsgroup messages often link to web pages and staff should be aware of the risk of accessing inappropriate sites. Anyone accidentally accessing offensive material should inform their manager and the IT Technical Support (Help Desk) immediately. Accidental access will not result in disciplinary action but failure to report it may do so.

5.9   Staff who have to monitor offensive material as part of their jobs, e.g. child protection, equal opportunities and trading standards, may access relevant material with the permission of their Head of Service. Permission must only be given to named individuals and a record placed on file.

6.   Monitoring use of IT systems/privacy

6.1   The Council logs all messaging activity and monitors internet use.

6.2   The Council provides e-mail internet to facilitate communication and the sharing of information among its employees and external business and community partners. This system is the property of the Council and is intended for Council sanctioned use only. Whilst the Council does not routinely access or monitor an individual's use of IT systems, there may be instances that require mail items/files to be retrieved by the Council, its authorised agents, or legal regulatory agencies.

7.   Security

7.1   The definition of 'user' in the context of this policy document is any person or persons granted authority to use a system or systems whether such authority is granted to them individually or by reason of their being a member or part of a group authorised to use a Council system. Authority is granted to a user on the basis that that user agrees to be bound by the conditions in this policy document.

A 'User Id' is a unique identifier which is given to a user which, together with a personal password of the user is used to identify and authenticate the user when accessing a council system.

Because passwords provide the principle means of validating a user's authority to access a computer service, all users should adopt, wherever possible, the following procedures:
- Create and use *individual* passwords to maintain accountability.
- Keep password confidential.
- Avoid keeping a paper record of passwords.
- Change passwords regularly, and whenever there is any indication of possible compromise select a password with a minimum length of five characters.
- Avoid basing passwords on any of the following: months of the year, days of the week, family names, car registration numbers, company names, birth dates etc. Such passwords are easy to guess and may lead to unauthorised access.
- Log out of screens when leaving your desk unattended (or at least save and exit from current application back to desktop).

7.2   The Computer Misuse Act makes it an offence to access any computer system for which access authorisation has not been given. Thus any attempt to interfere with or try to bypass the security controls on a computing system is an offence. Similarly trying to obtain information such as users' passwords or accessing or modifying files belonging to other people who have not given access authorisation is also an offence.

7.3   In exceptional circumstances, IT Technical Support will install stand alone systems with their own Internet connection. In these cases the Head of Service is responsible for ensuring that the connection and associated equipment adhere to the security and access standards defined by this policy.

7.4   Any member of staff using floppy discs (e.g. to transfer files between home/office) should ensure that such disks are scanned for viruses before use in council equipment. Anyone using these work practices should, therefore, ensure that their home PC is appropriately protected using up to date virus protection software.

8.   Confidentiality

8.1   A user processing personal data should ensure that they are aware of their obligations under the Data Protection Act. The council maintains a registration under the Data Protection Act. Should any user be in any doubt about their obligations under the Act, they should, in the first instance, consult their administrative general manager who may wish to refer the matter to the council's data protection officer. Guidance material is currently being developed for issue to all Service Units.

9.   Unauthorised downloading or installation of software

9.1   Using the internet to download or otherwise copy copyrighted software, information or other material without adhering to its licensing conditions is an offence under the Copyright, Design and Patents Act. The council has a statutory obligation to comply with licensing conditions. Thus all licensing requirements, payment conditions and deletion dates associated with software installed on council systems must be met.

9.2   To ensure licensing regulations are strictly complied with, it is the role of IT Technical Support *exclusively* to install software on council owned equipment. Only software installed in this way will be regarded as 'authorised'. Any deviation from this principle will require the written approval of the IT Technical Support Manager (such approval to be retained by the user).

9.3   Individual users should not, therefore, attempt to download any software from the internet (this includes any executable file -exe file) or otherwise install personal software (this includes screensavers/wallpapers, CDs from magazines/games etc.).

9.4   Any unauthorised software found either locally (on a user's PC/laptop) or on the council's network will be deleted without reference to the installer.

10. Personal use of equipment

10.1   All ICT facilities are provided for council business. However, incidental personal use is not prohibited, but should be kept to a minimum. It is subject to the discretion of managers provided:
- It does not interfere with council work.
- It does not relate to a personal business interest.
- It is not used for commercial purposes, including the sale or purchase of goods and services.
- It does not involve the use of chat lines, inappropriate sites or similar services.
- It complies with this policy.

10.2   Managers are responsible for monitoring time spent by their staff on personal use of ICT equipment. Excessive use will be regarded as misuse. Time parameters for such use and its timing will be agreed in writing.

10.3   Staff wishing to spend significant time outside working hours using the internet—for example, for study purposes—should obtain their manager's prior approval and inform the Help Desk of their late working requirements.

10.4   The use of council ICT equipment should under no circumstances be used for playing games. Some of the original games that form part of the Windows operating system may still exist on some PCs, but their use is prohibited.

11. Failure to comply with ICT Policy

This document provides staff with essential information regarding their use of the council's ICT systems and sets out conditions to be followed by all users of those systems. It is the responsibility of all to whom this policy document applies to adhere to these conditions. Failure to do so may result in:
- withdrawal of ICT services
- informal disciplinary processes
- formal disciplinary action

Additionally if, after internal investigation, a criminal offence is suspected (for example under the Computer Misuse Act or Telecommunications Act), the council may contact the police or other appropriate enforcement authority to investigate whether a criminal offence has been committed.

Glossary

firewall—Network security system used to restrict external and internal traffic.

ICT—Information and Communication Technology.

ISP—Internet Service Provider. Company that sells access to the internet.

newsgroups—Use net message areas or discussion groups, organised by subject hierarchies.

spammers—Individuals who inappropriately post the same message to multiple newsgroups or e-mail addresses.

zip—PC file compression format that creates files with the extension.-zip using PKZlp or WinZip software. Commonly used to reduce file size for transfer or storage on floppy disc.

Links between CYWU and NAYCEO

The CYWU Code of Conduct reprinted in Part 2 offers an opportunity to involve the Union in solving work related problems before they become grievance or disciplinary matters with management. The Union is composed of professional colleagues and can act as conciliator and problem solver.

CYWU Officers meet regularly with NAYCEO Officers. One positive aspect of their close national working relationship is that there is an agreement that the General Secretaries of both Unions can be referred to by local branches if there are any potentially conflicting situations at local level. If one of the Unions thinks members of the other are acting unreasonably or against trade union principles, the offices of the national officials can be used to try and resolve the matter before it gets worse.

Sexual and other harassment: policy and procedure

Regrettably forms of harassment and bullying can exist between worker and worker; management staff clearly do not have a monopoly on bad behaviour. The hierarchies of power resulting from the interface of full-time worker, part-time worker, and volunteer, and the cultural misunderstanding of who is the employer, have led to all sorts of problems. Clearly harassing, bullying and victimising is unacceptable anywhere but most of all in an area built on anti oppressive and anti discriminatory values. An employer's failure to support a worker who is subject to such harassment that it becomes an obstacle to them fulfilling their work requirements, could in certain circumstances, lead to the employer being charged with breaching the employee's contract and failing to support them.

Model Code of Practice on Harassment at Work

1. This procedure recognises that there can be various forms of intimidatory and harassing behaviours. This procedure recognises the anti oppressive, and anti discriminatory nature of youth, community and play work and in particular reasserts the wording of the 1990 Ministerial Conference on the youth service which agreed a Statement of Purpose for the Service in England and Wales as follows:

   The purpose of youth work is: to redress all forms of inequality and to ensure equality of opportunity for all young people to fulfil their potential as empowered individuals and members of groups and communities…

   This is achieved by offering opportunities which are designed to promote equality of opportunity

   …through the challenging of oppressions such as racism and sexism

   and through

   celebrating the diversity and strengths which arise from those differences.

2. In the light of this statement and the Equal Opportunities Policies of this employer, harassment is an unacceptable form of behaviour which will be treated seriously by the employer possibly as a matter that can result in disciplinary action against the harasser. It is recognised that the perception of the harassed person is the basis for concern in handling such cases and can involve a range of harassments, such as unwelcome and unreciprocated looks, jokes, contact, advances, physical approaches, comments, or other behaviours or unprofessional conduct. This procedure recognises that certain forms of harassment can be contrary to the Sex Discrimination and Race Relations Acts.

3. In recognising the stress and hurt that can result to the victim of harassment, this policy believes that the right to complain, without fear of recrimination and in anticipation that the complaint will be treated fairly and seriously are essential features of this policy and procedure.

4. This procedure recognises that harassment can occur between:
    - colleagues
    - young people and young people
    - young people and staff
    - children and staff
    - adults in the community and their peers
    - adults in the community and staff

5. All incidents of harassment will be recorded using the attached forms. *(These of course would be locally agreed.)*

6. Management committees of youth, community and play centres will be encouraged as a condition of grant aid to issue and display an Equal Opportunities Policy and to incorporate a procedure for dealing with harassment at work into their constitution and staff contracts, and to promulgate acceptable standards of behaviour to all of their users and members.

7. The employer does not expect its staff to work in locations where harassment exists and will consider immediate and temporary or permanent withdrawal of staff from situations which are considered to be harassing and potentially or actually harmful. Furthermore, the employer recognises the right of staff to withdraw immediately from situations considered unacceptably harassing. Where staff are considered to be working in vulnerable positions, mobile telephones or other supportive equipment will be issued. In conjunction with line management and staff meetings, staff will be expected to devise strategies for challenging and eradicating harassing behaviour between user groups and members. The employer does not expect its staff to be subject to harassment, abuse, or violence or other forms of abuse in working with children, young people, community activists and community groups. In addition, staff supervision meetings are recognised as the official line of communication between management and staff and the views of Committees or elected members would be conveyed through these rather than informally or on an ad hoc basis.

8. The employer will endeavour to provide support for all victims of harassment whether that harassment takes the form of racial, sexual or other harassment in the form of unwanted behaviours, jokes, graffiti, references, approaches, threats, name calling, printed materials etc.

9. Alleged harassment between colleagues will be dealt with swiftly and seriously according to the timescales and stages laid out in the Grievance Procedure. But additionally, in recognition of the feelings and stress that can be present in the victim of harassment, the complainant will be offered informal meetings as and when required with full rights to representation by their trade union representative or friend in order that the employer can consider ways of dealing with the procedure as sensitively as possible. No such reasonable request shall be denied and the employer shall make every effort to provide the appropriate professional, managerial and emotional support that is necessary to investigate the allegation of harassment, and remedy it where it is found to exist. Within this procedure, the employer recognises that the requirement to repeat the details of a case or allegation at a number of different levels can be an additionally and unwarranted pressure on the victim, often a deterrent to pursuing a case further. The employer recognises that:
    - the quality of the record of the initial complaint should be as detailed as possible
    - victims of harassment are not themselves expected to appear at all chosen stages of the procedure
    - by the nature of much individual harassment there is little written evidence or witness
    - consideration must be given to the actual distress and perception of the victim.

10. The recognised purpose of pursuing a case of harassment against a colleague, is to:
    - seek a remedy
    - prevent repetition
    - in a proven case, the harasser must alter behaviours

- where an act of harassment has damaged a professional working relationship, in many circumstances the harasser should be removed from that situation.

11. Staff found guilty of harassing behaviours through this procedure, will automatically be subject to separate disciplinary action which will be taken up by the officer investigating the harassment grievance at its conclusion. It is recognised that the victim of the harassment may not feel it appropriate to give evidence in the disciplinary procedure and that it will be most appropriate for the investigating officer on behalf of the employer to present the case against the proven harasser.

As some readers will have guessed, the CYWU believes in promoting clear, step by step procedures for most circumstances. However, these can be mechanistic, intimidating and inappropriate for cases of harassment, particularly those involving sexual harassment. The essence of a procedure, is the extent to which it conveys a recognition of the emotional complexity of complaining about harassment and the extent to which it offers to be flexible in order to diminish the hurt and anxiety victims invariably feel. It is vital that women workers feel able to pursue a complaint with as much confidentiality, adaptable management, personal and trade union friendship or employer support as possible. The nature of sexual harassment often means that the harassed person is considered 'guilty' especially if the perpetrator is proven innocent, while the perpetrator even if found 'guilty' can often be declared innocent at appeal by an all male panel, because they fail to categorise the incident properly. There is a case for the various forms of harassment to be distinguished one from another and dealt with by different procedures. This model procedure has simply aimed to set down some over-riding principles which should be incorporated in a sympathetic procedure.

There is a close inter-relationship between the Equal Opportunities Policies pinned to the wall, employers' 'Statements of Intent' which are more loosely worded, and the actual operation of the procedure once a complaint is made. This connection is expressed entirely in the quality of the fairness and supportiveness of the management's handling of the case.

Disagreeing with management

What right do management or supervisory staff have to raise a problem that has not been broached in supervision first? What right does a worker have to raise a grievance whose elements have not been raised first in supervision? Once again in the concept of effective supervision becomes a cornerstone of good practice and a means of avoiding unnecessary conflict.

Having said that, supervision cannot solve everything. For a start supervisors may not have the authority to alter certain circumstances, nor can that appallingly right wing and increasingly anachronistic concept that 'management has a right to manage' be relied upon. Usually when this is used, it is synonymous with 'management can do whatever they want.' Of course they cannot, and integral to 'good management' is the recognition of the need for negotiations with representative trade unions, the right of staff to be represented and the need to take staff with an idea rather than impose it upon them. Again, it is on this terrain that freelance consultants have been particularly dangerous by endorsing outmoded dictatorial management techniques.

Grievance procedure

Often a grievance may be about the quality of supervision, or the unhelpful style of the supervisor. Many matters are best dealt with by a grievance. In this Model Procedure below, a worker seeks to prevent something happening which they see as being terrible, or seeks redress for something terrible that has already happened.

It is a procedure for changing things for the better. It is a positive thing. It recognises that something must be resolved and not permitted to poison an otherwise free flowing river of productivity. The culture surrounding grievance is always unhelpful and grievances are often seen as things taken out by over-bolshevik members of staff or inveterate moaners. However, a good thunderstorm, no matter how loud it gets, clears the air, while a stagnant pond just gets more stagnant.

Something which is perceived as a persistent problem, can be an undue contributor to stress. A grievance is a professional process whereby persistent problems that cannot be sorted by any other means, have a chance of getting sorted. It does not represent an attack on managerial staff. Instead, it represents a way of helping to *manage* a problem. Taking out a grievance against someone or something, does not mean that you do not like them, or that you want them disciplined!

To be successful a grievance must be precise from the outset. It should:

1. Specify who or what the grievance is against. Be careful with this. If the perpetrator of the terrible deed is a line manager acting on behalf of the employer use a formula like: X acting as agent of Y Borough Council. If it is against a seemingly inanimate employer's decision, make this clear too. Ask yourself, is it the individual manager, their actions, or the orders they have been given that are the problem. If it is the orders the managers themselves have been given, there is usually good cause for a collective grievance.

2. Specify exactly what you are aggrieved about. 'I am aggrieved about the fact that X acting on behalf of Y Borough Council has persistently cancelled supervision meetings and thereby not upheld my employer's contractual commitment to staff development as specified in the Staff Development Policy contained in my Staff Handbook'. Alternatively, the problem may be more specific: I am aggrieved that X swore at me in supervision sessions on November 24th, 25th and 26th.'

3. Give an outline of the kind of remedy that you seek. 'I would want the employer to guarantee regular supervision meetings placed in the diary six months in advance.' Or, for the swearing incident: 'I require an apology and a new line manager.'

4. Ensure that the Grievance Procedure is followed to the letter. If it is not, this in itself is cause for a collective grievance or dispute promoted by the Union.

The seven most important elements of a good grievance procedure are:

1. The right to representation by a friend or trade union representative at all stages.
2. Clear stages of progressing the grievance with reasonable timescales between each stage (between seven and fourteen days).
3. A general intention to apply the principles of natural justice to the whole procedure.
4. Reasonable notice of meetings and distribution of paperwork for meetings in advance.
5. Written details available to all parties.
6. The final stage should be in front of the highest authority possible. In the case of local authorities, this should be councillors. In smaller voluntary sector projects, it should be whatever is most appropriate—a committee of management including representatives of main funders, perhaps.
7. An explicit recognition that invoking a grievance will not lead to any personal detriment or victimisation.

Check that your local grievance procedure includes these elements.

Model Grievance Procedure

1. Individual grievances

1.1   This Grievance Procedure shall apply to all staff. The aim of this procedure is to settle any grievances as quickly, fairly and as amicably as possible and to resolve working problems where normal approaches, through line management and supervision, have not worked to the satisfaction of the employee. It is recognised that all employees have a positive right to complain constructively in the interests of their professional role.

1.2   It is envisaged that the Authority's commitment to an open style of management and staff support through regular monthly supervision will mean that problems arising from work will be resolved professionally through that process. It is therefore envisaged that any matter of concern to the employee can be raised directly with the employee's line manager in supervision. Should matters not be resolved to the employee's satisfaction in this way, then the employee has the option of using this procedure to lodge a formal grievance.

1.3   Should the employee have a potential grievance against another employee of the employer or against a member of the employer's management, the employee should in the first instance, in all cases, indicate this to their line manager and seek to resolve the matter directly with the member concerned.

1.4   Should the employee's concern not be resolved through supervision or informal discussion with the person directly involved, they should put their concern in writing as a grievance as soon as practicable and forward this to their line manager. They should clearly indicate in their letter that they are invoking this individual grievance procedure and state the nature of their grievance and where appropriate how they think this may be best remedied. Should their concern be with their line manager and be unresolved, they will be able to refer the matter to the next manager or officer in line.

1.5   The employee's line manager may discuss this matter further with the employee, but in any event they will reply to the employee's grievance within seven working days.

1.6   Should the employee remain dissatisfied with the written response of their line manager they will indicate this in writing to them within seven working days, clearly stipulating the deficiency of the response as they see it.

1.7   The line manager will then forward this response to the appropriate superior officer, within seven working days. This officer will then convene a three-person grievance panel within 15 working days at a date mutually agreed with the employee and their union representative.

1.8   At the grievance panel meeting the employee or their union representative will be given a full opportunity to present their case and the line manager to respond. The decision of the grievance panel shall be conveyed to the employee in writing within five working days.

1.9   Should the employee remain dissatisfied with the response of the grievance panel they have the right to appeal to the appeals committee. The employee should write to their line manager within seven working days of receiving their response from the grievance panel and request that the employer considers the appeal. The employee's letter should state clearly, the deficiency within the response as they see it. The employer will then consider the appeal at its next scheduled appropriate meeting, or at its earliest convenience thereafter, should it think that the formation of an appeals panel would most fairly consider the appeal. The decision of the appeals panel shall be final and be conveyed to the employee within five working days in writing.

1.10 At all stages of the grievance procedure employees may, and are advised to, obtain support and representation from their trade union.

1.11 All paperwork pertaining to any grievance in any instance shall be stored confidentially by the employer for a period of at least two years. Taking a grievance where regular line management and supervision has not resolved a problem shall be viewed by the employer as a reasonable course of action for which the employee shall not in any way be penalised or disadvantaged.

Disagreeing with the union

Disagreements with the Union need to be taken up through LJNC meetings. There needs to be more appreciation, both amongst workers in the field and officers, that active union membership, participation in its training courses, meetings and conferences is a positive thing within the service. Trade unions are after all the largest voluntary and community sector organisations in Britain and their underlying principles are not dissimilar from those in youth, community and play work. Time spent by staff on union duties should not be begrudged. Indeed, some local facilities agreements advocate paid time off to attend branch meetings and CYWU national conferences.

It should also be realised that accredited trade union representatives have slightly more protection. If the employer intends to discipline them for example, the full-time official of the Union should be contacted first. Inevitably, if the employer proceeds wrongly against an active union member their actions can often be construed as forming a pattern of constructive behaviour which can lead to victimisation.

Disagreeing with the employer

Who is the employer? In local authorities, it is the elected members not Principal Youth and Community officers or area officers, or full-time workers. The right to hire and fire, rests with the employer not the manager. For part-time workers, this means that it is particularly important to ensure that permanent contracts are issued by the employer, so that managers do not have the insidious right whether or not to renew a fixed term contract. While there should be no limit to the extent of delegation, there should be no limit to the close understanding of the employer as to the day to day control and functioning of the work.

In smaller voluntary sector projects at neighbourhood level, the employer can be a management committee which knows little about the worker's professional qualification or employment practice generally. It is important that every opportunity is made to train the management committee in its responsibilities and that it clearly designates some from amongst its number to take on the specific function of staff management, and, where appropriate, industrial relations.

Often management and employment problems originate in strategic decisions and policy objectives made by the employer either by default, or design. There are many ways to influence the politics of an employer of course, outside of the LJNC and the relationship between employer and employee. Youth, community and play workers are after all voters, or their friends and family may be members of the community association for which they work. There are legitimate ways of influencing the policies which determine the nature of the employment. The key to doing this successfully is ensuring that employers exercise their political responsibility for employing through appropriate involvement at the most strategic level. This does mean participation in the LJNC, and the creation of youth, community and play committees for a defined political constituency.

Furthermore, it means taking every opportunity for employers and employees to meet as equals with an equal interest in the development of the service. Labour party controlling groups can meet CYWU and NAYCEO branches as equals within the Labour movement. To an extent, the same can be done with Liberal Democrat groups, who meet as equally free citizens. Tory groups will often do the same. A trade union can meet with a voluntary sector management committee to discuss policy and strategy.

Within the confines of an LJNC meeting, which more often than not will not include a direct representative of the employer in the form of an elected member, management and unions may find it useful to make joint representation to an employer. What is wrong with an LJNC paper being submitted to full Education Committee saying that both management and unions agree on something? Why couldn't an LJNC make a strategic policy suggestion to elected members? Again, this is very much part of the youth, community and play work sector making its political presence felt with the real employers, the real holders of power over the service. It is part if you like, of the empowerment of the service of itself. Unions have been so busy trying to empower others, they have forgotten to do it for themselves, and tremendous cuts and losses have been the result.

Disagreeing with public allegations and complaints

Youth, community and play workers are vulnerable to misunderstandings and allegations from the public and local community leaders. This arises from the informal nature of the work, and the mixed perceptions of their role which is not as clear as that of a teacher, or social worker, or local councillor. It arises from the nature of befriending, and building close, confident, working relationships. It arises from having to deal with social justice, lifestyles, attitudes, anti oppressive work, health education, informal relationship building and the contexts in which those kind of curriculum specialisms are developed. Certain styles of work can be mistaken for intimacy, or condoning bad practices. The availability of remedies to those with whom youth, community and play workers frequently practice is also very often minimal, and the experience of using established structures to complain is not always familiar in already disenfranchised communities. It is easier to phone up the local councillor, who then phones the Director of Education, than to tackle the problem professionally and through lengthy procedures. And of course, people are prone to the old truism— there's no smoke without fire—and are wont to create some fire even though there may be no smoke.

In other words, a youth, community and play worker is more likely than not to have a wild allegation made about them at some stage during their career, usually to a senior councillor, or officer. Often this can have criminal, political or sexual overtones.

Again this sort of situation has the potential to be dealt with very differently. A Director of Education, receiving an allegation of sexual abuse about a Level 3 JNC worker in their employ, is likely to have to deal with this differently from the chair of the local management committee receiving a similar complaint from their next door neighbour about the worker employed in the community centre. In the British justice system you are still, just about, innocent until proven guilty. Not so, in youth, community and play work. Totally innocent workers have been sacked on the basis of gossip, and innuendo, and unproved allegation.

How can this increasing phenomenon be dealt with more professionally? For the organisation to be prepared might be the first step. Most local authorities now have elaborate procedures for dealing with general complaints from the public. Few though have anything established for youth, community and play work. It would be interesting to see how they would handle a complaint that the general level of provision across an area was inadequate.

Each organisation employing youth, community and play workers should establish some form of protocol. The prime objective of this would be to establish the good faith and reasonableness of the allegation in the first place. Each organisation should identify an officer to whom complaints should be made. Is it really reasonable to suspend a youth, community or play worker immediately when any form of allegation is received? Is it reasonable as an employer to expect that if the complaint about the employee has also been made to the police, that the employee will be unable to comment on the complaint to the employer until the police investigations are over? Many of the principles that underpin a fair way of dealing with complaints about staff from those outside of the immediate line management structure are contained within the Model Procedure for dealing with allegations of abuse or serious professional misconduct. In less serious, more routine cases the following may act as a guide.

Model Complaints Procedure

Preamble

It is recognised that staff work closely with young people, adults and children, and with networks of agencies seeking to provide informal education, and social and welfare services, and that to be successful staff must establish a confidential, trusting relationship with 'clients'. It is further recognised that staff may work individually and less obviously as part of staff teams than colleagues in other agencies.

In addition to established procedures dealing with allegations of a serious nature, the Authority will adopt the following policy in relation to complaints of a less serious nature.

Procedure

1. As far as is practicable the Authority shall appoint someone within each unit (the Complaints Officer) to whom any complaint shall be referred.
2. Should a complaint not be received initially by the Complaints Officer, the receiving officer shall refer it to the Complaints Officer and inform the complainant of the action taken.

3. These procedures shall be made known to all elected members who will also be expected to follow them.

4. All complaints will be immediately recorded and the complainant will be called to an interview at which it will be expected that the complaint will be put in writing, dated and signed. Such record shall distinguish between complaints about individuals and complaints about delivery of service by the employing organisation or its administration.

5. Anonymous complaints will be referred to the employee immediately along with their line manager and shall not be acted upon in any form, nor shall they be recorded in any way on the employee's file.

6. The Complaints Officer will immediately consult the staff supervision notes to establish whether the subject of the complaint has ever in any way appeared in staff supervision.

7. The Complaints Officer will seek to establish immediately the credibility of the complainant and the existence of witnesses or corroborative evidence.

8. The lapse of time between an incident complained about and the complaint, the nature of the complaint, the views of the employee complained about and their line manager shall be taken fully into account prior to any investigation under the established investigatory and disciplinary procedures.

9. It is important at all stages to inform the complainant and the employee complained about of the action being taken on the matter and to provide the employee complained about with counselling where requested and the right to trade union representation at all meetings related to the complaint.

10. Only those complaints which following investigation are found to have some substance shall appear on the personnel record of the employee complained of. No entry shall be made in any personnel record of the fact that an unsubstantiated complaint was made.

Dealing with allegations of physical or sexual abuse or serious professional misconduct

This has been a long standing problem, paradoxically heightened rather than alleviated by the Children Act 1989. The model includes the wider notion of serious misconduct. This is because casework experience has demonstrated that the position of youth, community and play workers makes them vulnerable to a host of allegations on a range of unacceptable behaviours.

Not only do youth, community and play workers become the first to detect signs of abuse in young people and children, they very often become aware of the perpetrators of such abuse. It is not unknown in CYWUs case work files for perpetrators of abuse to be members of management committees which manage professional youth, community and play workers. Nor is it by any means unusual to find allegations made by members of the public against elected members with whom youth, community and play workers work. In fact, judging by the frequency of incidents, an untrue allegation of abuse is seen as a particularly paralysing tactic in malfunctioning community politics.

The model guidelines have been informed by discussions on this matter that have taken place and by the guidelines drawn up by the six teacher organisations and the local authority associations. They also reflect some exceptionally tragic casework undertaken by CYWU on behalf of members, and I record here with sadness the loss to the service of two exceptionally professional colleagues forced out by unsubstantiated allegations so appallingly mishandled by their management. The ability of allegations of this nature, even when they are totally false, to destroy the self esteem and entire work, confidence and character of a professional, is always heart rending to witness.

Model Procedure for Dealing with Allegations of Abuse or Serious Professional Misconduct

Preamble

1. It is recognised that youth, community and play workers (hereinafter 'staff') work in the informal education context in which trusting personal relationships and interpersonal confidence and trust are significant features of the educational approach. A greater degree of personal familiarity between staff and clients is required within informal education practice than in related areas of more formal education relationships. Personal friendship between staff and some clients is an accepted element of the work which can lead to misunderstandings amongst those witnessing the relationship.

2. It is further recognised that staff will be employed by a variety of employing organisations, ranging from large local authority departments to small voluntary sector projects, and it is the intention that the principles underlying this procedure and the structure, can be applied across a variety of employment settings.

3. Staff work closely with children, young people and adults and frequently are the first group of professional workers to detect signs of abuse, or behavioural alterations caused by receiving or indeed perpetrating abuse. Furthermore, because of the nature of the involvement of staff with the client groups with which they work, they themselves are extremely vulnerable to allegations of abuse. Allegations can be false or true, malicious or misplaced, deliberate or accidental. The consequence of allegations whether true or unfounded can devastate professional careers and the individual concerned and should consequently be considered as exceptionally significant and requiring close, methodical examination and handling.

4. The initial response to an allegation of abuse is particularly important. A decision to suspend the subject of an allegation immediately, can permanently damage professional confidence and render completely untenable that person's ability to operate within a given community context in the future. It is therefore recommended that the guidelines below be followed. These guidelines are constructed to complement *Working Together: A Guide to Arrangements for Inter Agency Co-operation for the Protection of Children from Abuse* (Home Office, Department of Health, Department of Education and Science, Welsh Office, 1991).

5. Staff can work at the interface of complex relationships of authority and power. For example when local authority employees are seconded to voluntary sector management committees, they will find their work scrutinised by clients, the wider community, the management committee, local elected members, the local authority employer, related local authority departments, other voluntary agencies, as well as their peers. It is likely that allegations could be made anywhere within this recognisable, but not necessarily coherent system. It is therefore important that early consideration is given to how the allegation is made within this nexus, and that one definite initial investigating officer with knowledge of the dynamics of such systems is identified.

6. This procedure recognises that frequently staff will be expected to work with voluntary management committees and that while staff are legally 'managed' by such committees, very often a recognisable part of the member of staff's role is to train and develop these committees into employing bodies that are responsible and aware. In this sense it is vital that every organisation has attached to it a designated officer to assess such allegations. Equally, every member of staff should be clear to whom they are expected to report any suspicions, or allegations of abuse that they receive.

7. This procedure acknowledges that in addition to allegations of and problems concerning sexual or physical abuse, staff may be especially susceptible to allegations concerning other equally serious forms of misconduct, or may become aware during the course of their work of real problems within communities. A non exhaustive list of examples may include: arms offences, drugs related offences, violent crime, and burglary. It is therefore hoped that the principles devolved strictly for cases of alleged sexual and physical abuse will be applied to other serious forms of potential misconduct.

Guidelines

Information and training

All staff should receive adequate in service training in matters relating to observation of, reporting of and procedures for sexual and physical abuse, and should be familiar with these and the *Working Together* Guidelines and any locally applied Child Protection Guidelines and Procedures.

Each institution where staff are employed should be provided with a copy of these documents and the Authority should record the training and induction provided by the agency in their use.

The operating procedures, working practices and structure of the local Area Child Protection Committees should be made available by the Authority to every organisation employing staff.

Allegations

One person should be designated within each organisation to be the first point of referral for allegations. Should an allegation be about that person, it should be clear that referral will be to an agreed third party placed within the child protection or personnel system. Where an allegation is against a member of staff, an immediate assessment should be made of the substance of the allegation. Among the crucial factors that should be taken into account are:
- The probity and likely intent of the person making the allegation.
- The probity and likely intent of the person to whom the allegation was made.
- The probity and likely intent of the person against whom the allegation was made.
- Relevant timescales associated with the allegation.
- The nature of the allegation.
- The nature of any corroborative evidence.
- The likely immediate impact of the allegation on the person about whom the allegation is made and the person whom it is alleged has been abused and the risks to either.

The assessment of these and other factors should wherever possible be made by the superior officer involved and the appropriate officer from personnel, or social services departments. It is the purpose of this assessment to establish whether further investigation is necessary, not to construct a view on the case. Subsequent investigation will seek to establish whether the allegation can be substantiated. Confidentiality is also essential at this stage.

Discovering the facts

Where possible the responsible officer should seek to obtain the detail of the allegations in writing and should personally interview the parties involved and make a written record of such interviews. Any written statements should be signed and dated. It is clearly vital that the facts of the situation and the exact allegations made are properly recorded as these will form the substance of any later investigation. Further measures may be necessary at this stage to discover the facts surrounding an allegation. This is undertaken purely with a view to establishing facts and not to suggest guilt or evidence. Such measures would seek for example to determine whether there were witnesses, whether the parties could have been together, what exact details relate to the allegation in terms of place of occurrence, times and dates.

Different investigations

Should the initial assessment officer consider that there are reasonable grounds for further investigation, an immediate referral should be made to either:
- The social services department, in the case of Child Protection Procedures.
- The National Society for the Prevention of Cruelty to Children.
- The police, where a reportable criminal offence is possible.
- The employer.

Effect on contract

If such a referral is made, consideration should be given to the impact of this upon the employment contract, maybe requiring disciplinary action. Advice from personnel officers should be sought and in the case of the voluntary sector there should be a local agreement to access such advice free of charge from the local authority.

Upon initial investigation it may be deemed that no one is at risk, or has been harmed, and that no reportable criminal offence has been committed and that further, less serious investigations are required.

Communication with those involved

The person making the allegation, the person about whom the allegation is made and any other relevant parties should be informed of the course of action adopted immediately, and the need for confidentiality and discretion in the matter.

Police enquiries

Allegations may be made in tandem to the police. The police should be given every assistance in their enquiries, though interviews should not normally be conducted at the workplace. It would be expected that times for police interviews would be arranged with minimal disruption to the normal working patterns of any staff or assessment officer.

Separate investigations

As a matter of good practice, employing organisations should consider police investigations or social services enquiries to be completely separate from their own investigations. Indeed it would be advisable in many instances to permit the police or other third party investigator to pursue their enquiries prior to taking employer action, unless it was reasonably assessed that the continuing employment without suspension of the member of staff, or further investigation by the employer put the public at risk, or significantly disrupted the employment relationship. The quality and fairness of an employer's investigation are paramount.

Suspension from work

The decision to suspend from duties should be taken very seriously indeed and in such a way as to ensure that suspension is not perceived by any parties as itself a form of disciplinary action or an admission of guilt by default. Strict confidentiality should be maintained throughout a suspension. All alternatives to suspension should be considered. Very often it would be sufficient to redeploy a member of staff temporarily from a project or neighbourhood, in order to undertake a specialist piece of work. In considering whether a suspension is appropriate the responsible officer will need to consult with specialist personnel colleagues and act by reference to the disciplinary procedure that applies. Suspension can be considered where:

- Children, colleagues or the public are at risk.
- The allegation, if proven, or in itself is so serious, that dismissal for gross misconduct is possible.
- Not suspending may seriously impede a fair investigation.

In every case, the reasons for suspension should be clearly outlined in writing to the suspended member of staff and they should be advised to consult their Union. The general right to representation should be extended to every stage or meeting related to this procedure. In any instance where the member of staff concerned is an accredited union representative, no action should be taken or meetings arranged without firstly contacting the most immediate full-time official of the union concerned.

In every case the member of staff should be interviewed prior to suspension to ascertain their views on the situation. It should be recognised that in certain circumstances, staff will be advised by their trade union or solicitor at this stage not to comment. Such a response should in no circumstances be considered negatively. The arrangement, timing and location of the meeting should be by mutual agreement and take place as soon as practicable. It should be made clear that the interview does not constitute any part of the disciplinary procedure itself and that the member of staff should feel able to answer accurately and in an informed way and has the right to be fully represented where appropriate.

Communicating courses of action to wider public and those involved

In recognition of the way in which even an unfounded allegation, or a completely malicious allegation can permanently damage the reputation of a member of staff, advice will need to be sought as to how best to communicate to colleagues and clients what action is being taken both in relation to the individual and the person making the allegation. Any disclosures should seek to protect all concerned. It is recognised that parents, in particular, and other clients generally may require considerable reassurance, and appropriate steps should be taken with the designated agencies to provide any support and counselling that may be necessary.

No action to suspend

Where no action to suspend is contemplated and no further investigation is required, or where a part investigation is required, a meeting should be held with the member of staff to offer support and guidance and to agree a satisfactory way of proceeding within an ineffective working environment.

Suspension: information, conditions and stress

Suspension of staff can create enormous stress and uncertainty. It is therefore important to expedite an investigation as soon as practicable and to provide a contact officer to whom the suspended officer may refer in order to seek an update on the progress of investigations. It should not be necessary to prevent the member of staff concerned from visiting places of work, or having social contact with colleagues, except where such would prejudice a fair investigation. Separate notes on investigations are given below.

Lifting a suspension

When a suspension is lifted a meeting should be held to discuss in detail the nature of the return to work, and what support can be given to the member of staff, and what needs to be communicated to clients and others who may have been aware of the allegations. The employer should clarify exactly what will appear on the personnel record in relation to this event.

There is a special responsibility of the employer and staff representatives to ensure that normal professional working relationships are restored as soon as possible. In the youth, community and play work context, this may entail ensuring that community activists, or those known to the person who made the unsubstantiated allegations, have it made clear to them that any member of staff defamed, slandered or libelled or professionally undermined has legal courses of redress.

An equally important element of community development responsibilities is to ensure that those making innocent but unfounded allegations, especially if they are minors, receive counselling and support following such a sequence of events.

Recording events

All aspects of a case should be fully recorded. The member of staff should be informed of what will appear in their personnel file and access to this file will be arranged according to the local procedure. Where a member of staff resigns before the completion of a disciplinary process, or where they are dismissed, they should be informed of the employers statutory duty to inform the Department for Education, Teacher Misconduct Section.

It is not customary within the youth, community and play service to keep records of individual young people or community activists. In the case of proven malicious allegations, it may be advisable to seek advice on an appropriate method of recording events.

Investigative procedures and protocols

An investigation is embarked upon in order to establish facts. If facts give rise to concern that warrants disciplinary hearing or other action, it will be through these processes that allegations are proved or disproved. An investigation precedes disciplinary action and is separate from it. All evidence compiled during an investigation should be available to all parties in any subsequent disciplinary action.

Those making allegations should be required to sign and date their statements following a process of interview. Interviews should be witnessed and fully recorded and conducted in a manner conducive to establishing facts.

An investigating officer should seek appropriate advice from personnel or other relevant department and local authorities should offer support to the voluntary sector in such instances.

An investigating officer will seek to determine the credibility of the person making the allegation, verify corroborative evidence, establish witnesses, and focus on key areas for investigation.

If during an employers investigation, new evidence comes to light that requires a referral to the police or Child Protection procedures, the employer's investigation shall be held in abeyance until the investigations of the third party have been concluded.

At the earliest opportunity the member of staff against whom the allegation was made shall be informed of:

- The course of action to be taken.
- Their rights under the disciplinary procedure that applies.
- Their right to be accompanied by their trade union at all stages.
- The contact person to whom they may refer queries on the progress of the investigation.

All meetings with members of staff will be minuted and the minutes agreed by all concerned. It is recognised that the member of staff has the right to respond or not to respond at any stage during the procedure.

Disagreeing with authority

Successful youth, community and play work will occupy a difficult position within all power structures and in relation to most forms of authority for it will be seeking to empower groups and individuals, and encouraging them to challenge and oppose and often replace forms of authority perceived as being inimical to group, neighbourhood, or community interests. Often youth, community and play workers, as a collective workforce themselves will be challenging the decisions of their employers in relation to youth, community and play work policy, the government in relation to the way in which they are treating local authorities and the voluntary sector, or particular local policies adopted by councillors.

Rather than celebrating our ability to train staff to be active on issues of social justice and collective decision making, employers, in local authorities in particular, have tended by and large to consider youth, community and play workers as troublemakers. How dare such well-paid youth, community and play workers encourage low paid residents of an area to bite the hand that feeds them!

In challenging abuses of power, administrative mismanagement and social injustices, workers will frequently advise individuals and groups how to take the local authority to court, how to challenge the decision of the Department of Social Security, how to refer some local authority decision to the Ombudsman for maladministration.

In a country now dominated very much by unelected bodies like quangos and commercial interests, an important element of employment practice will be to appreciate the combative, challenging, and democratic basis of youth, community and play work practice. Whether it is the active citizenship laughingly advocated by the Tories, community politics praised by the Liberal Democrats, or the local democracy put forward by Labour, the role of youth, community and play workers is not to be underestimated, nor stifled in restrictive employment attitudes.

Changing things

Disciplinary procedures provide a mechanism for improving individual work performance. Grievance procedures provide a mechanism for ensuring that problems with management do not fester. Local joint Negotiating Committees provide a mechanism for negotiating all aspects of change. Re-deployment procedures and safeguarding agreements provide mechanisms for processing change in moments of crisis. Good supervision allows change to be filtered down to individual work performance by way of fixed, clear contracts and job descriptions. Staff development procedures keep staff fresh, and alive, and alert. Policy Committees bringing together the local authority and voluntary sectors at the level of strategic planning. Annual reports on the development of youth, community and play work and adult education are submitted in every local authority area. What more could we want? Time off for trade union duties, to begin with, so that there is ample time and resource available to representatives of a workforce to negotiate change.

If the sum of changes is to be managed effectively and if the commitments to monitoring equal opportunities and health and safety are to be enacted, there needs to be formal recognition of the role of trade union representatives, and time and facilities allocated for them to fulfil their role. If change is to be effected with the good will of the majority of staff and their understanding and support, it would seem entirely logical to ensure that they fully participate in change. Both the *Soulbury Report* and *JNC Report* advocate the establishment of negotiating mechanisms locally and this automatically implies a commitment to providing facilities for local trade union branches to operate. This section provides therefore a Model Facilities Agreement and some brief observations on it.

Partnership is best

This book has tried to demonstrate that disagreement is natural and is professional when managed through clear procedures that admit to its necessary presence. But conflict was the order of the day in most workplaces for over twenty years. With the election of the Labour government in 1997 a new culture of shared responsibility and partnership was fostered. The Department for Trade and Industry, the TUC, and the Confederation of British Industry were drawn into some creative thinking about how to foster a new culture. CYWU sought to be an active part of this culture and extend its work to develop good industrial relations with employers.

As a result a simple distinction between old style bad management and new style good management cultures was drawn up:

Old style	New style
Executive vision	Partnership
Workplace excluded	Workplace included early
Workers instructed and supervised	Workers trained and empowered
Solutions/Negotiations	Solutions found through shared problem solving
Suspicion	Communication, trust and respect
Minimise staff concerns	Security of employment
Minimise costs	Focus on partners
Paid for job	Reward, mutual success

You may want to assess where your employing organisation fits on these scales, old or new style?

Having identified early on that better management was desperately needed in this sector in the light of the new legislation and culture, CYWU like many other unions set about establishing a model partnership agreement to establish with all employers. Staff debate, the appointment of a new national officer, and NEC approval led to the adoption of the following Model Partnership Agreement which the Union thought best captured the new culture.

Model Partnership Agreement: the Principles of Partnership

Introduction

The purpose of this agreement is to create flexible, innovative industrial relationships, which support both ('the Employer') and the Employees of the Employer to achieve future strategic direction.

In order to implement the above both CYWU and the Employer recognise the following points as being essential:

- The need for good communications at all levels.
- The involvement of the Employees in change.
- The Employees to be taken along by the Employer as willing allies rather than reluctant followers.
- Working together to meet common goals and shared objectives.
- There will be an increased level of union membership resulting from the Partnerships Ideals.
- The promotion of best practice.
- Joint training initiatives.
- Better skilled and more knowledgeable trade union representatives.
- The need to engender a sense of pride in membership of a trade union and of being an Employee of the Employer.
- The need to have effective approaches to resolving disputes.

Principle One: the commitment to the success of the organisation

We all have a vested interest in ('the Organisation') and in delivering as high quality a service and in being as successful as is possible. In order to achieve this it is recognised by all that there needs to be a climate of trust.

Training is an important part of this process and joint training will be undertaken on an array of issues including:

- Health and Safety.
- Grievance and Disciplinary Procedures.
- The JNC Report.
- The structures of the Organisation.

This training programme will be agreed jointly.

The training will enable all to understand what is going on and to contribute their ideas. The structures that will be put in place will create a culture where information is widely shared, where problems are solved quickly and fairly on a joint basis and where team spirit is maintained.

A local joint negotiating committee (LJNC) shall be set up where equal numbers of delegates from CYWU and the Employer meet monthly. The chair shall alternate between the two sides.

Principle Two: recognising legitimate interests

Effective and constructive Partnership embraces the notion that at any time there might be quite legitimate differences in interests and priorities between the Partners. This Partnership Agreement, if effective, will embody a degree of trust and respect that should aid the resolution of such differences, but ultimately each Partner will respect the need of the others to listen to and properly represent their respective constituencies.

Principle Three: commitment to employment stability

There is little argument about the importance of this issue. People who feel secure are more likely to adapt to changes, challenges and future developments than those who feel threatened. What is needed is a combination of measures to maximise employment security within the Organisation i.e. limiting the use of compulsory redundancy, joint agreement on staffing levels and improving skills and qualifications.

There are two main issues here:

1. Historically the reduction of staffing levels has been seen as nothing more than cost reductions, because decisions have been made without consultation and negotiation. What have been missing are procedures for ensuring agreement. If partnership is to mean anything, then the issue of staffing levels is of prime importance. A LJNC should look at this issue, to make the Employees feel they are part of a process rather than just recipients.
2. Those Partnership Agreements that have achieved the greatest success have placed high emphasis on training. Employers have been able to demonstrate that they value staff and do not just see them as profit makers but as adding value to the organisation.

Principle Four: focus on the quality of working life

By adding to the educational training of the Employees we can jointly begin to enhance skills and help to improve the quality of working life.

It is very difficult to motivate people to feel part of a team if their experience is at best ignored or at worst belittled. It should be recognised that managers do not have a monopoly of good ideas.

The area in which partnerships can most effectively contribute to an improvement in the quality of working life is that of personal development. There are two main areas of action:

1. In job related training, by jointly agreeing the Employees will feel a greater affinity to this process.
2. There is the whole issue of personal development outside of the workplace which should be achieved by enhancing educational opportunities during working time. By doing this the employer is arming itself with a well-trained and dedicated workforce.

Principle Five: transparency

There is a need for everyone in the Organisation to understand that this is not a game of one-upmanship. It is not a chance to gain points over the other side, perception is all here. If either the Employer or CYWU feels that this is the case any attempt at partnership will fail and industrial relations will regress rather than progress.

If Partnership is to be meaningful then it must be based upon a real sharing of information and a willingness to discuss plans and thoughts about the future when they are at a very early stage. Equally the process of consultation and negotiation must be genuine, with a commitment to listen to cases for alternative plans.

Principle Six: adding value

The hallmark of an effective Partnership is that it taps into sources of motivation, commitment and resources that were not accessed by previous arrangements.

As is explained above, by involving everyone to the full, by enhancing training and opportunity to participate without fear of detriment then the Employees can add value to the service. There is a lot of inherent talent and skills that at present is untapped. To uncap this the Partners should be looking at what currently encourages or deters the employees from contributing ideas or suggestions.

These six principles are a good starting point; there has been discussion about involving everyone and training will be needed to ensure this partnership will succeed. Some other areas that could be looked at will include communications, mutual benefit, understanding trade union and management concerns.

Recognition of the Union

Having established these principles of partnership by agreement and signed a document to that effect, it is also recommended under the new trade union legislation that a formal written recognition agreement is written and agreed.

Model CYWU Recognition Agreement

Agreement between: (Name of employer)

and

Community and Youth Workers Union

Preamble

This Agreement is made between (Insert the name of the employer) (the Employer) and the Community and Youth Workers Union (CYWU) with the intention of maintaining and furthering the best possible relationship between the Employer and its staff.

1. General principles

The Employer and CYWU have a common objective in ensuring the long-term provision of high quality and effective Youth, Community and Play Work.

Both parties commit to working together in a spirit of mutual confidence, partnership and co-operation to achieve fairness and equality in the treatment of staff. The Employer and CYWU agree that it is mutually beneficial for the CYWU to be involved in the Employers' decision making process.

Both parties agree to make every effort, by joint discussion, to resolve any difficulties which may arise, and to ensure that this Agreement is effective.

The parties to this Agreement are committed to the development of positive policies to promote equal opportunity in employment regardless of workers' sex, marital status, sexual orientation, colour, disability, religion, race, ethnic origin, age or holding of trade union membership or office. This principle will apply in respect of recruitment, training, and allocation of work and promotion. If any employee considers that they are suffering from unequal treatment then they may make a complaint, which will be dealt with through the agreed procedure for dealing with grievances.

2. Recognition and scope

2.1   CYWU recognises the duty of the Employer's Management:

2.1.1 To plan, organise and manage effectively.

2.1.2 To agree the duties and responsibilities of employees and reward them according to these duties and responsibilities, subject to JNC terms and conditions of employment negotiated by CYWU.

2.1.3 To communicate with employees in furtherance of the operation of the organisation.

2.1.4 To ensure the well being and welfare of employees through good employment policies and practices.

2.2   The Employer recognises the right of CYWU to protect and advance its members' interests through consultation, negotiation, representation and organising and in consequence:

2.2.1 Accords CYWU sole negotiating and bargaining rights on all matters relating to the terms and conditions of employment of staff employed by the Employer in the bargaining unit as defined in Section 4. No terms and conditions of employment shall be amended without prior negotiation and agreement between CYWU and the Employer;
    And accepts the right of CYWU:

2.2.2 To represent any individual member of CYWU employed by the Employer who invokes the Grievance Procedure.

2.2.3 To represent any individual member of CYWU employed by the Employer on any other matter.

2.2.4 To organise and train so that it can be a democratic Union and reflect the need of its members.

2.3   In negotiations under 2.2.1 above the CYWU members shall be represented by such representatives as CYWU may chose, including a full-time officer of CYWU.

2.4   Representations under 2.2.2 and 2.2.3 will be made by an accredited Representative or by a full-time officer of CYWU.

2.5   The organising and training of representatives under 2.2.4 will be arranged by CYWU.

3. Membership of CYWU

The Employer recognises that it is desirable for all employees, who are within the scope of this Agreement, to be members of CYWU. All such employees will be free to join and remain in membership of CYWU.

The Employer will advise new employees of this Agreement and will encourage them to join CYWU. The Employer will inform CYWU of the names and locations of each new entrant.

Where the Employer holds an induction programme for new employees, the CYWU will be entitled to provide a briefing at the induction to explain the role of CYWU in the workplace. Where this facility is not available, employees will be introduced to CYWU on an individual basis.

4. Bargaining unit

CYWU has the right to negotiate and represent on behalf of its members who are employed in Youth, Community and Play Work or allied fields.

Where an individual member is outside the bargaining unit as defined above, CYWU is entitled to represent the individual.

5. Facilities

See attached Model Facilities Agreement.

6. Negotiations

A proper Local Joint Negotiating Committee will be formed.
See attached Model Constitution for Local Joint Negotiating Committee.

7. Organisational change

The Employer agrees that before implementing any changes in established work practices or structures the Employer shall negotiate these changes and any consequent issues with representatives of CYWU through the negotiating procedure.

8. Training

The Employer and CYWU recognise that all employees should undertake appropriate training as necessary and that the Employer has the responsibility to improve and develop the skills of its employees to meet current and future requirements.

In recognition of this it is agreed that the Employer will invite representatives of CYWU to periodical meetings for the purpose of:

a) Agreeing a policy on training.

b) Agreeing plans for training for the next six months.

c) Reporting on training provided since the last meeting.

9. Failure to agree

It is in the interest of both parties to this Agreement that all negotiations will be carried out as expeditiously as possible and that every effort will be made to reach a mutually acceptable settlement.

If the Employer and CYWU are unable to come to agreement on an issue that is subject to negotiation, and subject to the agreement of both parties, the matter may be referred to the Advisory Conciliation and Arbitration Service (ACAS) in an effort to reach settlement. Both parties commit to making all reasonable efforts to reach a settlement prior to reference to ACAS.

Neither the Employer or CYWU will take any detrimental action until this procedure is exhausted.

10. Procedures

The following procedures, negotiated between CYWU and the Employer will be used at all times:

a) Disciplinary Procedure.

b) Collective Grievance Procedure.

c) Individual Grievance Procedure.

All procedures will be operated to ensure a speedy resolution of all matters arising.

11. Termination of agreement

This Agreement can be terminated by two thirds of all staff in the defined bargaining unit voting in a ballot in favour of termination.

The Employer is required to give CYWU three months notice of its intention to hold a ballot. A ballot to terminate this agreement will be conducted by ACAS. The Employer will bear the costs of conducting such a ballot.

If a ballot to terminate this agreement is unsuccessful, the Employer cannot initiate another ballot for a period of three years.

12. Review of agreement

Both parties agree to review this Agreement on a regular basis to ensure that it continues to meet the needs of the Employer and Union.

A ballot of CYWU members must agree any changes to this agreement.

This agreement is made day of

Agreeing facilities for the union

Having established the principles of partnership and the trade union recognition that follows from it, it is necessary to agree the facilities that the employer will agree to enable the trade union to carry out its part of the bargain.

There are four matters or principles integral to such an Agreement:

1. It covers the local authority employees and those organisations with whom the authority is in partnership to provide the service.
2. It recognises the need to cover for work when time off is being taken.
3. It recognises the need to provide trade union facilities for part-time staff also.
4. It is based fundamentally on the recognition that it is preferable to manage change through negotiation with a represented workforce than with isolated individuals.

Model Facilities Agreement

General

1. This agreement is between the .... County Council (the Authority) and the Community and Youth Workers Union (the Union).

2. Both parties fully support the system of collective bargaining and believe in the principle of encouraging harmonious industrial relations by discussion and agreement and, for this purpose, recognise that it is to the mutual benefit of the Authority and its employees to be represented by properly constituted trade unions. Consequently, the Authority recognises the right of the Union to represent staff employed under the terms of the Report of the JNC for Youth, community and play workers and part-time workers under additional local agreement.

3. Such representation is manifest by the election, from the Union, of branch officers and of the negotiators, caseworkers and health and safety representatives. The Authority agrees to make reasonable facilities available in accordance with this Agreement to enable such representatives to fulfil their role.

4. The Union recognises that it is the responsibility of management to plan, organise and manage the operations of the Authority in order to achieve and maintain maximum efficiency, subject to appropriate consultation through the Local Joint Negotiating Committee in matters affecting the interests of both the Authority and its employees.

5. Both parties recognise the need to work within the national, provincial and local agreements and procedures and undertake to take reasonable steps to ensure that these are observed by individual managers and employees and that there is a good understanding of these procedures throughout the workforce.

6. The names of elected union representatives and any changes shall be notified to the appropriate Chief Officer or Head of Department by the Union.

7. It is recognised that the industrial relations functions of a union representative are as important in their normal duties as other employees of the Authority. To perform such functions it is agreed that reasonable time off during normal working hours without loss of earnings will be given by the Authority for the following purposes:

    a) To negotiate and consult with local departmental management on industrial relations matters covered by current legislation and relevant to their accredited constituency.
    b) To inform their members in the constituency about relevant discussions or consultations with management.
    c) To liaise and seek advice from branch officers or full-time officials on matters of concern.
    d) To investigate matters arising under, and represent members of their constituencies at meetings called in accordance with the Authority's grievance and disciplinary procedures.

e) To meet new employees and to be involved, where practicable, in the induction of new employees as organised by local management.

f) To attend, as a nominated representative of the Union, appropriate meetings of properly constituted Joint Negotiating Committees within the Authority and national bodies of the Union when matters relevant to the development of youth, community and play work services will be discussed.

8. Requests for time off to perform the above duties should be made to the line manager. As much notice shall be given as is reasonably practicable, stating the nature of the business for which time off is required, the intended location and the expected duration of absence. Such requests will not be unreasonably requested by the representative or refused by the Authority.

9. In order to assist representatives in effectively fulfilling their industrial relations functions the Authority will provide:

a) Reasonable use of interview facilities, as and when necessary to discuss industrial relations matters with members of their constituency both individually and collectively.

b) Use of notice boards sited within the constituency for the display of official Union information.

c) Where there is no access to Union facilities and by prior agreement, the use of existing simple reprographics and photocopying equipment.

d) Use, where reasonable, of an official telephone with such reasonable access and privacy as may be practicable for industrial relations matters and branch functioning.

e) Use of the internal mailing system to circulate general Union literature up to four times a year, provided no significant additional administrative burden fails on the Authority.

f) The facility for all Union members to meet at their scheduled branch meeting during normal working hours.

g) The facility of additional sessional payment for a part-time member of staff elected to represent, or negotiate on behalf of the Union.

h) The facility of travel, support and normal subsistence allowances for elected delegates to attend the annual conference and training event of the Union.

10. Reasonable time off during normal working hours without loss of earnings and with cover for the work will be given:

a) To negotiate and consult with management on particular issues that are relevant to more than one area within the Authority and/or which have not been resolved at constituency level, i.e. Joint Negotiating Committee meetings.

b) To investigate matters arising under, and represent members of their area at meetings called in accordance with the Authority's grievance, regrading, disputes, complaints, capability and disciplinary procedures.

11. The Secretary of the Union shall be allowed one session per week with cover to administer the affairs of the Branch.

12. It is recognised that the demands on the branch chair to be involved in matters of an industrial relations nature between the Authority and its employees will vary from time to time. Consequently, no finite limit is stipulated as to the amount of actual time off allowed during normal working hours but it is generally expected that this will not exceed one session per week.

External commitments

13. The Authority recognises that from time to time, the branch chair or elected caseworker negotiator may be called upon to represent members who are employed by the Authority at external Employment Tribunals. The elected official will be granted time off during normal working hours without loss of earnings and cover for work to attend such tribunals or meetings.

14. It is recognised that facilities and training for elected health and safety representatives are covered by statute and the Authority's own local agreements.

Training of representatives

15. The Authority and the Union recognise that industrial relations within the Authority will be aided by the provision of adequate training of both supervisors and representatives in their respective industrial relations roles.

16. The method and extent of such training will be jointly agreed to meet individual circumstances but may be under the auspices of the Authority, the Union, the Provincial Council, the TUC, the GFTU, ACAS, CYWU or other such body agreed to be appropriate. Release for jointly agreed courses concerned with industrial relations functions and held in working hours will be granted without loss of earnings.

17. The Authority will pay the cost of reasonable tuition fees and tutors expenses for jointly agreed industrial relations courses. The Authority will also reimburse excess travelling expenditure, accommodation and subsistence at the locally accepted rates.

18. When requested the Union will provide the Authority with the appropriate syllabuses for training courses. The Union will normally give the Authority (through the appropriate Chief Officer or Head of Department) a minimum of three weeks' notice of nominations in order that adequate consideration for time off can be given. The Union will also supply to the department such details of past training received by individual representatives as may be appropriately requested.

19. The Authority values the partnership with the voluntary sector and recognises that in the interest of good industrial relations throughout the service partnership, recognition should be given to representatives drawn from the voluntary sector and assistance be given by recognised representatives to the voluntary sector.

The right to be accompanied

The right to be accompanied by union representatives at disciplinary or grievance hearings is now guaranteed to workers for the first time. This new right is part of the Employment Relations Act 1999 and was passed in September 2000.

This means that every trade union member now has the right to be accompanied by a trade union representative of their choice at disciplinary and grievance hearings. You have this right from the first day in your job—and it does not matter if the trade union concerned is recognised by your employer or not.

However, the right is to be 'accompanied', rather than represented although in most circumstances the employer will allow full representation. In any case even the most obstructive employers are unlikely to know the difference between accompaniment and representation.

Depending on the case, you will be accompanied/represented by either a full-time officer or a caseworker from another workplace. A colleague can also accompany you from your workplace and CYWU is running courses to equip members to do this.

You have the right to be accompanied at any disciplinary hearing, which could result in you getting a formal warning. You also have the right to be accompanied in certain grievance hearings—those involving a 'breach of duty' by your employer.

In detail, the act states:

- An employer 'must permit' a worker to be accompanied.
- A union representative as a 'companion' chosen by the woker can address the hearing and confer with the worker during the hearing.

- A companion can be a full-time trade union official, a lay official certified by the union or a co-worker on paid time off.
- If a companion is not available for a hearing a worker can propose an alternative time withing five working days.
- If an employer fails to comply with the act by not allowing a companion to be present the worker can complain to an employment tribunal and gain compensation.
- An employer cannot victimise or detrimentally treat workers for being accompanied (or the companions accompanying them).
- An employer cannot unfairly dismiss workers for this, however long they work on the job and however old they are.

A useful publication setting out these and other rights is contained in: *Your Rights at Work: A TUC Guide* (published by Kogan and Pace at £8.99) offers information on workers' rights from when they are applying for a job to facing redundancy.

It covers the national minimum wage, working time rights, family rights, health and safety, stress, discrimination, dismissal, redundancy, and how to enforce all these rights.

Copies can be orderd from TUC publications by calling 0207 467 1294 or direct from the publisher on 01903 828800.

The TUC also has a Know Your Rights Line which is available from 8am–10pm on 0870 600 4882.

Further reading and reference

See Appendices for relevant addresses and Select Bibliography.

In this section, the sources listed are those which are most readily accessible and within the budget of even the smallest youth, community and play work unit.

The nature and culture of informal education practice:

Butcher, F. et al. (1994). *Community and Public Policy*. Pluto Press.
Smith, M. (1994). *Local Education*. Open University Press.
Young, K. (1999). *The Art of Youth Work*. Russell House Publishing.
Hugman, R. (1991). *Power in Caring Professions*. Macmillan.

The closest thing to an employer's description of the work is:
Community Development, published by the now defunct Association of Metropolitan Authorities. Much of this thinking has now been transformed within the Local Government Association's thinking on Local Democracy.

The only thing approaching an authoritative political statement is a Socialist Educational Association publication (1994), *Youth Service, Adult Education and Community Education*. No major publication has yet followed from a political party.

However, the comprehensive policy framework for children and young people in Wales goes a very long way to embedding the value and principles of informal education in formal government policy. See National Assembly for Wales publications: *Putting Wales First* (October 2000), *Plan for Wales* (Autumn 2001), *Children and Young People: A Framework for Partnership*, *The Learning Country*, *A Paving Document for a Comprehensive Education and Lifelong Learning Programme to 2010 in Wales*, *Extending Entitlement: Supporting Young People in Wales*, *Learning is for Everyone*, *Extending Entitlement*, *Supporting Young People in Wales Consultation on the draft Direction and Guidance*.

Industrial relations

In the general context of industrial relations today and the developing trends, four publications may be of use:
TUC. *Workplace Representation*, available from the TUC at Congress House.
TUC (1999). *Partnership at Work*, available from the TUC at Congress House.

Disclosure of information

ACAS. *Disclosure of Information to Trade Unions for Collective Bargaining Purposes.* Code of Practice No. 2.

Discipline

I have found nothing better on discipline than the ACAS *Briefing Paper Practice on Discipline* and their booklet *Discipline at Work.*

Handbooks

Two particularly shelf-buckling Staff Handbooks are from Nottinghamshire and Staffordshire and can both be referred to in the Information Centre of the National Youth Agency, where others can also be found. In addition, AMAZE, the Association for Christian Children and Youth Workers, has produced a manual aimed at Christian employers, while *Groundwork* has produced a handbook for trusts about taking on the Youth Work model.

Sex education

Stockport and Wigan Youth Services have produced particularly useful and comprehensive guides on this subject.

Working practices

There is a huge bibliography of materials relating to working with children, young people and adults at risk and guidance in relation to behavioural problems, violence at work, drug and alcohol related problems. The best starting point for advice in this area is again the Information Centre at the National Youth Agency.

Sexual harassment

The best sources I have found have been trade union publications. These can frequently be obtained from the unions even though you may not be one of their members. Sometimes local law centres, Citizens Advice Bureaux or Trade Union Resource Centres will have copies of these. The Transport and General Workers Union, UNISON, and the National Union of Teachers have helpful publications in this area, and I would pick out Northumberland County Council as an employing organisation with a reasonable agreement.

Grievance

If you can find anything on grievances at work, other than what is written here and what CYWU has produced, I would be very pleased to hear from you.

Arbitration and conciliation

The position of ACAS is outlined in the publication *What is ACAS?*

Child protection guidelines

All workers should be familiar with the local procedures and in addition be provided with copies of *Working Together: A Guide to Arrangements for Inter-agency Co-operation for the Protection of Children from Abuse.* Home Office, Department of Health, Department of Education and Science, Welsh Office, (1991). In addition, the important publications and recommendations of the National Council for Voluntary Youth Services in this area are essential reading. They were mainly published by them in 1999 and 2000.

Part 5

Employment Law

The basics

> *Employment law is an instrument of economic policy…It changes according to political, economic and industrial pressures.*
>
> *Most employment rights can be enforced in an industrial tribunal, but negotiation and direct action are more reliable methods.*
>
> McMullen, 1983

Disappointing though it may be to many, there is no such thing as a beautifully pure set of laws designed to protect staff from exploitation, harassment and bad management, while they lead fulfilling lives at work. There is minimal protection in law, huge gaps on key aspects such as discrimination against workers on the grounds of disability or sexuality, and seeking redress under law is usually a drawn out, highly intimidating and stressful process. It is usually also an individualistic route. As youth, community and play workers who have been ill will know, it can be a costly and risky and daunting route. It is still possible to lose a case spectacularly, with all sorts of costs awarded against the worker.

To succeed in proving discriminatory treatment, for example, a worker will have to compare their individual position with that experienced by others. The law in some situations simply cannot act quickly enough to be of any use to the individual. Furthermore, even if it can be proved that an employer has acted illegally, in most circumstances, the worker will not receive a good material remedy. Compensation awards are almost always low and even if you unfair dismissal were proved and an Industrial Tribunal ordered reinstatement, the employer is not obliged to re-employ the worker.

It is legal to export billions of pounds sterling from Britain each week to invest in financial speculation on money markets. It is legal to run down essential public services and to de-regulate health and safety legislation. It is legal to put five million people out of work. It is legal to turn an island of coal with fertile land in a productive sea into a place without a merchant shipping fleet, without coal mines, with *set-aside* agricultural land, with no manufacturing base to speak of and fish stocks and oil reserves plundered. But it is illegal to express your disgust with a management decision and walk off the job with your workmates. It is legal in some situations to sack someone on the unsubstantiated suspicion of misconduct, but illegal to take industrial action to support that person if they work for a different employer. Employers can relatively easily take out an injunction against a union which has infringed a minor aspect of the industrial action legislation, but it is horrendously difficult to prevent an employer from unfairly dismissing someone or making an illegal redundancy.

Every aspect of trade union organisation is strictly controlled by law. Practically every aspect of the City of London's financial affairs is de-regulated. An employer can use a pension fund as they want, they can even profit from any surplus made on it, yet it is not apparently illegal to create circumstances where pensioners freeze to death each winter.

Though it may seem from this, that employment law and trade union law are a bit biased, nevertheless relentless rounds of trade union and employment legislation over the last fifteen years have fundamentally tilted the nature of legislation and its use.

This is not of course to say that all is lost and that legal redress should be discounted as irrelevant. It should not, but it is salutary for a youth, community and play workforce to be aware of the limitations of legislation when considering its position. A brief but excellent guide to the impact of legislation on everyday work is *The Law at Work* published by the Labour Research Department. This is something that should be an essential reference tool for every youth, community and play worker.

Many aspects of legislation have been dealt with in other chapters of this book: part-time workers' rights, European Directives, redundancy, transfer of undertakings, discrimination, and so on. This book does not deal in depth with legislation as it affects trade union organisation or taking industrial action, nor in detail with wages or sick pay regulations, nor to the maternity leave and pay arrangements, or pension schemes. It should also be clear from the part on part-time workers that legal entitlements now depend on what kind of worker you are: whether you are full-time or part-time, whether you have worked for 729 days for the employer or 731 days. Whether you are black or white can obviously make a difference in certain circumstances. What this section will do is to give some outline of the legal framework, to discuss the use of Industrial Tribunals and consider the question of dismissal from work and redress against this.

Framework

There are three sources of law:

1. **Statutes**

   Laws passed by Parliament are called statutes and can themselves provide for the making of Statutory Instruments to empower Ministers to rule or legislate on specific points of detail. It is also worth mentioning that Codes of Practice set by, for example ACAS, are not in themselves legally binding documents but have considerable weight in relation to courts.

2. **Case law**

   The precedents set by Judges and juries in coming to a verdict on a case.

3. **European law**

   English Courts are increasingly applying European laws where no equivalents exist, and where they are directed to by the European Court of Justice. There is a general trend following a 1992 case, for individuals to have a right to sue their own state for its failure to implement European law. There are also wider international laws and international bodies, such as the United Nations or International Labour Organisation which set some standards often taken into account in legal proceedings.

As youth, community and play workers will be well aware through their support of children and young people, for criminal proceedings there are Magistrates Courts and Crown Courts with judge and jury, where punishment may be fines or prison etc. There are County Courts and High Courts for civil actions, where compensation may be awarded, or injunctions granted etc. There are various tribunals to deal with non industrial matters, for example, appeals against immigration restrictions from the Home Office.

Then there are the more industrial informal hearings. Familiar to most youth, community and play work practitioners will be the Social Security and Medical Appeals Tribunals which can be heard before Social Security Commissioners and Tribunals and so on. If a union fails to receive information from the employer pertinent to their collective bargaining they can refer to ACAS, and if they receive no satisfaction there, they can appeal further to the Central Arbitration Committee. Health and safety problems, as opposed to individual claims for negligence can be heard by Industrial Tribunals or Magistrates Courts. All cases, wherever they start, have a final right of appeal to the House of Lords. Increasingly individuals have access to the European Court of Justice (ECJ) and the working of our national systems is more and more determined by European directives and laws.

What concerns us here are the Employment Tribunals (ET) and the body to which any disputed ET verdict is referred, the Employment Appeal Tribunal (EAT).

Employment tribunals

ITs were established theoretically to give quick and relatively cheap informal legal hearings to ordinary workers. However, it is advisable to proceed only to tribunal with full legal backing and legal support. Matters over which ETs have jurisdiction correspond to the list of rights outlined in Chapter 1:

- Equal Pay.
- Guaranteed pay.
- Insolvency of the employer.
- Itemised pay statement.
- Maternity rights.
- Medical suspension rights.
- Occupational pension schemes.
- Race relations.
- Redundancy rights:
  - Consultation with unions.
  - Payment under protective award.
  - Redundancy payment rights.
  - Sex discrimination.
- Time off for:
  - Health and safety representatives.
  - Public duties.
  - Seeking alternative work and training if declared redundant.
- Trade Union rights:
  - Time off for trade union duties.
  - Right not to be victimised for trade union membership or activities.
  - Not to be unfairly dismissed because of trade union activities.
  - Not to be unfairly dismissed for non membership of a trade union.
  - Not to be chosen for redundancy because of trade union activities.
  - Interim relief.
  - Not to be unreasonably excluded from a trade union.
- Transfer of undertakings.
- Right not to be unfairly dismissed.
- Written reason for dismissal.
- Deductions from wages.
- Contracts of employment.
- Minimum wage.
- Disability, race and gender discrimination.

Under each of these headings there are books of case law and precedents and interesting interpretations.

An employee's ability to go to an ET is limited by their ability to meet the length of service thresholds outlined in Chapter 1. There are different qualifying periods for different complaints. In addition, most complaints should be submitted to the ET within three months of the 'Effective Date' of termination or dismissal or the problem. In the case of claims for equal pay and redundancy pay, it is six months. If interim relief is sought pending a complaint of unfair dismissal for trade union reasons there are seven days to apply.

Form IT1 should be obtained from a Job centre, completed and returned to the ET. This needs to be accurate and precise and completed in all respects. A trade union official should advise on this.

The employer will have to make a written response on a form which will also be returned to the claimant (the person making the claim).

Either side has the opportunity now or at any later stage to request further details of the arguments and points made by the other side. The Chair of the Tribunal has powers to enforce disclosure of such information, and to summons both sides to a hearing to examine certain matters in the case and clarify issues.

Once this is submitted the battle begins. Initially, an ACAS officer may contact both parties to establish whether there is any room for resolving the issue out of court. Sometimes the Chair of the Tribunal will require a pre-tribunal hearing in order to clarify certain key points and establish in his mind if there is a case to proceed to full hearing.

Sometimes the opponent's representative will offer a settlement prior to going to court.

Both sides will exchange all of their documentation and the materials on which they intend to rely, prior to the ET. Neither side should be surprised by evidence on the day.

The ET office or ACAS can be called upon at any time for advice on ET procedure etc.

An ET can be cancelled at the eleventh hour if there is a settlement. Often such agreements can be reached under the aegis of ACAS and appropriate forms are available for signing and agreeing to the terms of the settlement.

Although a claimant is required to submit an application within a definite timescale the ETs do not have to hear the case within any particular time frame and the gap between your application and the court case will depend on the volume of work in the tribunal office.

Requests from either side for postponements can be entertained by the Chair of the Tribunal.

Requests for the tribunal to be heard 'in camera' without the press or outsiders present, can also be entertained by the Chair. Tribunal cases almost invariably hit the headlines and there is very frequently a court journalist present.

When the day for the ET finally arrives, the claimant will face three people, the chair, a lawyer, a representative of the business (employers) world and a trade unionist. Depending on the nature of the complaint either the trade union side or the employer presents their case first. The procedure continues much as a full court with witnesses as required, evidence presented to the tribunal members who sit to hear the case and full rights to cross examine statements and witnesses. The likely duration of the case should be considered in advance and will often be requested by the Chair. It is worth considering this aspect carefully, as it is surprising how short a tribunal day can be. A claimant should be prepared to take the witness box for the arduous exchange of evidence and possible distortion of truth from the other side.

A detailed written verdict is given at the end of the tribunal hearing and where a claimant is successful, various forms of compensation and awards can be made. The financial limits of these are set and in most cases when there is a win for the complainant, the other side may seek to reduce the amount of the compensation by arguing various contributory factors. A claimant interested in the money factor as well as the principle will need to be fully aware of the actual financial detriment, if any, they have suffered, and what they would accept as reasonable. Once an award is made it must be enforced and the claimant may have further recourse to the courts if the employer does not obey the IT decision.

If a claimant is dissatisfied with the ET verdict, they can appeal to an Employment Appeal Tribunal within a period of 42 days.

This is an outline of the basic remit and structure of the ETs. Of course, every aspect can be a potential minefield depending on the nature of the case, and slipping on a technical fault can fatally ruin an otherwise excellent case.

Please note that the payments made by Employment Tribunals are increased every February, you should consult CYWU or the DTI website for the latest figures. The full list is as follows:

Limit on guarantee payments	£16.70 per day
Limit on a week's pay	£240
Minimum basic award for unfair dismissal	£7,200
Maximum compensatory award for unfair dismissal	£51,700 (Note there is no limit where an employee is unfairly dismissed in relation to health and safety and whistleblowing)
Victimisation	£5,500
Minimum basic award for unfair dismissal	£3,300
Maximum award in breach of contract	£25,000

Dismissal

This potentially book-length subject illustrates some of the basics of employment law and some of the principles that will be entailed in seeking legal redress. This topic was chosen as it has been the most frequent serious complaint, dealt with by CYWU, by youth, community and play worker against employers, specifically the constructive dismissal category, and it is a problem most likely to occur in small scale voluntary projects. Also, the *Trade Union Reform and Employment Rights Act of 1993* introduced some new grounds for automatically claiming unfair dismissal which are worth bringing to attention. In the close quarters of youth, community and play services, it is an unfortunate reality that many managers and employers want to shed staff. Nevertheless, redundancies are now a feature of life but there are fair and unfair ways as is seen in more detail in Part 6.

There are five relatively straightforward forms of dismissal which if they occur will be considered as automatically unfair where the dismissal is:

- On the grounds of pregnancy.
- By reason of an individual's membership or non membership of a trade union or participation in trade union activities.
- For complaining to the employer or taking action on health and safety grounds.
- For seeking to assert a statutory employment right (e.g. right to an itemised pay statement, right to time off for public duties etc.).
- As a result of a transfer of a business or a contract, unless the employer can show an economic, technical, or organisational reason for the dismissal entailing a change in the workforce.

In a situation where a worker made a successful claim for unfair dismissal to an Employment Tribunal and the employer refused to reinstate them, then the Tribunal could order (on rates for January 2001) a basic award of up to £7,200, in addition to an award to compensate the worker for loss of past and future earnings of up to £51,700. Special awards of up to three years pay can be paid where the dismissal is also shown to be on trade union, or health and safety grounds. If an employer is ordered to reinstate a former employee following their successful ET claim and an ET order, there is an additional award of over £6,000 or loss of earnings (without limit) to the date of the reinstatement order, whichever is the greater. Rarely however, do such amounts compensate for the disruption of life, career, family and the painful stress factors involved.

However, no dismissal is particularly straightforward and a complaint against it certainly isn't. Indeed, 'dismissal' itself and what it entails is the subject of considerable debate. Legislation defines dismissal as covering three possible situations:

1. The termination of the employment contract by the employer with or without notice.
2. The expiry of a fixed term contract without its being renewed on the same terms.
3. The employee resigns with or without notice in circumstances such that they are entitled to resign without notice by reason of the employer's conduct; the employee claims constructive dismissal.

Dismissal on the grounds of redundancy may also lead to a claim of unfair dismissal where there has been inadequate consultation or unfair selection etc.

A fair dismissal is one where the employer can show that the reason for the dismissal was:

- For reason of redundancy.
- Related to the conduct of the worker.
- Related to the worker's capability, or qualifications for performing work of the kind they were employed to do. (Assessed by reference to skill, aptitude, health or any other physical or mental quality.)
- That the employee 'could not continue to work in the position which they held without contravention (either on their part or the part of their employer) of a duty or restriction imposed by or under an enactment.'

As is often the case with neat lists of definitions there is an additional catch-all phrase. This makes a dismissal fair if it was for 'some other substantial reason of a kind such as to justify the dismissal of an employee holding the position which that employee held.'

The two most common complaints in youth, community and play work are:

1. Employers acting in such a way as to render the contract of employment impossible (usually

in the voluntary sector), thus forcing the resignation of the worker who then goes on to claim constructive dismissal and

2. Workers claiming that their dismissal for misconduct, or poor performance was handled unfairly and unreasonably. The compensation awards are updated each year, the figures quoted are as of January 2002.

Constructive dismissal

An employer's conduct must be such that it entitles the employee to resign without notice. The breach by the employer of the employee's contract must be so fundamental that its essential terms are repudiated. The most significant ruling on this remains that of Lord Denning, then Master of the Rolls, in the case of *Western Excavating (ECC) Ltd v Sharp 1978* (1CR 221). He said:

> *If the employer is guilty of conduct which is a significant breach going to the root of the contract of employment, or which shows that the employer no longer intends to be bound by one or more of the essential terms of the contract, then the employees are entitled to treat themselves as discharged from any further performance. If they do, then they terminate the contract by reason of the employer's conduct. They are constructively dismissed.*

The intentions of the employer are in many respects irrelevant. They may want to keep the contract going, but do something which has the effect of breaking it.

In trying to prove to an ET that an employee has been constructively dismissed, an advocate will be arguing matters of reasonableness in much the same way as in a case of unfair dismissal.

As related in the section on the Contract of Employment, a contract is composed of a number of aspects. In cases of constructive dismissal, a representative will first have to show that one of the aspects of the contract of employment has been broken and then that the breach of the contract is serious enough to be fundamental. If an employer imposes a change of contract with new terms and conditions, the contract is likely to have been broken. Where workers accept the change, then the contract will merely have been varied.

Employers may sometimes give a clear and unequivocal indication that they intend to breach a contract and then, when the employer's plans can be seen to be absolutely unalterable, an employee could resign and claim an anticipatory breach of their contract. This is very rare and difficult and not advisable in most cases. More normally, an actual breach of the contract will have occurred.

Fundamental breaches of contract clearly relate to basic issues like pay. Courts have rightly penalised employers seeking to impose pay cuts, or failing to pay wages on time. The term pay can also include all other related benefits arising from the contract. Any increase in the number of working hours a worker is expected to perform will usually be considered a fundamental breach. Unilateral changes in the tasks customarily performed by a member of staff can also be construed as obvious breaches of contract. Where such changes are imposed, staff wishing to contest them, should be sure not to accept them in any way. Clearly defined temporary changes to tasks can be arranged in reasonable circumstances. The overall status of a worker's job, if diminished, can also constitute a fundamental breach of contract. If the employer fails to abide by its own disciplinary procedure, this, will usually be judged strictly by an IT as a breach. Failures in some circumstances to protect an employee from harm or harassment at work will be considered negligence rendering the contract broken. Similarly the general duty to ensure that a worker is able to work in a safe environment, if demonstrably broken, could enable a worker to resign and claim constructive dismissal. There is a general obligation implied in the contractual employment relationship of mutual trust and confidence, and the behaviour of supervisors is especially important in this respect.

Where a place of normal work is altered unilaterally in the absence of a mobility clause within the contract, a repudiatory breach will have occurred. Even where there is a mobility clause, e.g. 'Your place of work will be X Community Centre, unless otherwise specified by the Director of Education', the employer must be seen to take reasonable steps to move your workplace. Reasonable steps will include the following, in degrees dependent on the case:

- Reasonable notice of the move.
- Discretion to provide relocation will not be exercised in such a way as to make the performance of the employee's duties impossible.

- Employers must not act in such a way as to undermine the mutual confidence of the employment relationship.

If it can be established that there has been a breach of the contract by the employer which is fundamental, then two additional requirements must be met:

1. The worker's resignation must be directly caused by the employer's breach of contract.
2. The worker must not in any way have accepted the breach.

On this latter point, if an employee is forced to accept a change of contract, depending on the circumstances, they can resign or accept the change under protest, without waiving their right to claim a repudiation at a later date. However, the time delay between accepting, or affirming, anything under protest, and resigning, is always significant, and there is a general rule that the nearer to the breach of contract the resignation is, the better for the employee, if the delay is not of the employer's making.

Turning to some aspects of unfair dismissal, it should firstly be noted that unfair does not necessarily mean harsh. A member of staff can be dismissed for some relatively trivial misconduct, misperceived or perhaps exaggerated by the employer, but if the employer can be judged to have acted 'reasonably' and especially abided by their own disciplinary or other procedures in the process of the dismissal, the likelihood is that the dismissal will be considered fair. In a case of precedent, a 'reason for dismissal' was described as 'a set of facts known to the employer, or of beliefs held by him, which cause him to dismiss the employee' (*Aberbethy v Mott, Hay and Anderson, 1974 ICR 323, CA*). Where dismissal is on the grounds of capability or conduct, as it so often is within youth, community and play work, the employer only has to show that they genuinely believed on reasonable grounds that the worker was guilty of misconduct or incompetence. It should always be remembered that the employer does not have to prove the offence or inadequacy. An honest belief, even if it is wrongly held, will be enough to justify the dismissal. There are of course innumerable cases and interpretations seeking to define reasonableness.

One aspect of reasonableness particularly pertinent to youth, community and play work is the size and administrative resources of the employer's undertaking. Some of the worst problems have occurred within small, often voluntary sector projects, which may not even have disciplinary procedures, or trained and experienced managers. Following a morally unreasonable dismissal, the small project if challenged through tribunal will claim that their inexperience, their small size, their lack of expertise and so on meant that they could not behave in the way a larger, better resourced employer would. This could affect particularly, such factors as being able to provide suitable alternative employment, or being able to provide different people to form an Appeal Committee. Equally, it should be noted that size and administrative resources will not excuse a total absence of proper procedural steps. Most organisations within the youth, community and play sector can avail themselves of expert advice; no project actually is an island.

One of the most important aspects of employment practice, and stressed in this book, is that there is a collective responsibility throughout the whole sector to provide formal support for the employment relationship and practice. Local authorities grant aiding the voluntary sector should set minimum standards and requirements. Small projects should be supported by trained personnel from other organisations.

Further reading and reference

See also the Appendices for relevant addresses and Select Bibliography.

Any book on the detail of legislation written prior to 1993 should now be considered obsolete.

Farrer and Co. (1994). *Disciplining and Dismissing Employees: A Guide for Charities*, available free of charge. Useful in a small organisation and may, as it is nicely produced by a firm of solicitors, help to persuade the management committee of a small project to think twice.

Kibbling and Lewis (1994) (Legal Action Group). *Employment Law: An Advisor's Handbook*, 2nd Edn.

Hendy, J. Q.C. (1993). *A Law Unto Themselves. Conservative Employment Laws, A National and International Assessment*, 3rd Edn. The Institute of Employment Rights.

Part 6

Redundancy, Re-organisation, Re-deployment and Transfer

Redundancy

This Part covers this ever-changing and complex area in a straightforward manner, and with special relevance to the defence of youth, community and play services.

A redundancy happens only to someone with at least the minimum service requirements of eight hours per week for two years. It occurs when someone is dismissed from work for reasons attributable wholly or mainly to the fact that the employer ceased, or intends to cease to carry on the business, or the fact that the requirement to carry out the work of a particular kind has diminished. Changing a person's place of work can amount to redundancy so long as there is not a mobility clause in the person's contract. It is something that happens to a worker through no fault of their own.

Redundancy should be unnecessary in youth, community and play work. Youth, community and play workers are always required. There have never been enough staff to meet real needs and the work is more needed than ever before. There should be a permanently funded youth, community and play service resting on improved legislation that requires local authorities to establish sufficient provision. Britain spends less on its public services than most other countries in Europe and should spend a lot more. The country could actually afford to spend double or triple the amount it currently does (around £200m) on the youth service. All staff qualified to JNC level, having made the effort and sacrifice to go to college, should be entitled to lifelong employment in their chosen profession. Regrettably after so many years of lowered horizons workers have stopped thinking in aspiring terms. They should try to again.

Paradoxically, redundancies do happen and have happened with increasing frequency. Over the last few years, many skilled and experienced workers have been prematurely forced out of the service. This section seeks to advocate a protection of employment procedure, provide a model, remind the reader of key elements of redundancy legislation and procedure, and comment on the important aspects of re-deployment and provide a model procedure. It does not cover the decisive element of political and trade union organisation to avoid redundancy, overtly at least, and does not detail every device that can be used to remedy a bungled redundancy consultation or unfair dismissal.

The three underlying questions are:

- How can redundancy be avoided?
- If a worker can be re-deployed, how can it be done fairly?
- If it becomes inevitable how can redundancy be handled?

The context in which redundancies can occur within youth, community and play work, the reasons for them and the way they are handled vary according to the nature of the employing organisation. What happens in a local authority, a national voluntary organisation and a small local voluntary project varies enormously. The law, however, stays the same, as does good practice. A small voluntary organisation with one full-time JNC worker has less room for finding alternative employment within the organisation than a local authority. This argues, though, for some creative thinking not for further abuse. Conditions of grant aid and service level agreements should be adequate for providing permanent posts, access to local authority re-deployment schemes, and in any event funding for redundancy payments, for long term planning and for making use of the personnel support that the funding agencies can perhaps give. Also, if mechanisms for really developing the partnership between the voluntary sector and local authorities were in place and if both were working on the basis of improved statute to build a planned and sufficient service, the arguments for protected and expanded funding would be more evident.

A Local Protection of Employment Agreement at this stage becomes a useful part of the defence and promotion of the service. Again, the model is written with the need for local amendments in mind, and while hoping that ways can be found of extending its remit to all those voluntary sector projects in the field.

Note: This Agreement needs to be between each workforce and its employer, big or small, but also where possible, between the maximum number of employing organisations that are grant aided by similar sources and their workforces. It needs to be particularly geared to the political and social position of community work and youth work as distinct services within local government and the voluntary sector.

Model Protection of Employment Agreement

1. Preamble

This Agreement is based upon the recognition that youth work, community work, and play work, and the range of other informal and community education specialisms and occupations should be permanent and developing features of local authority and voluntary sector provision subject to the terms and conditions of the *JNC Report* as enhanced from time to time by local agreement. It is fully recognised that the professional development of staff determines the quality of service provision to children, young people and communities and that security of tenure is central to maintaining this professionalism and morale. This Agreement recognises that:

a) Although there is a requirement on local authorities to provide an adequate service to children, young people and communities the lack of more specific statutory duties to provide this area of work has meant that this sector has been historically underfunded and currently operates on insufficient staff and inadequate resources.

b) The shared interests of the local authority, representative bodies within the voluntary and independent sectors and staff and their trade unions enables joint representation and action in the protection of posts and resources and staff.

c) Community education services have proved themselves to be highly cost effective services involving an exceptionally high number of users of their activities.

d) These services would be best protected by separate definition within the Education Act to create a duty to establish sufficient levels of provision and appropriate funding through an identified element within the Standard Pending Assessment and Rate Support Grant and that all those involved with the service have a shared interest in working towards this locally, regionally and nationally as an integral commitment within an employment protection policy.

e) There is a real need to establish an effective and permanent partnership between the elected representatives in local authorities, the staff unions, and representatives of the community work, play work and youth work agencies (hereinafter Community Education) in the voluntary and independent sectors and that mutual support on funding, personnel practice, equal opportunities, training and policy development is a desirable objective. In order to achieve this a Community Education Partnership Arrangement (CEPA) shall be established with reference to the local authority Education Committee.

f) Forward planning, both financial and organisational is seen as the key to preventing redundancies.

2. Funding

In determining the level of required resourcing for Community Education the local authority will create mechanisms for permanent partnership with all representative bodies within the sector, user groups and staff unions in order to determine and publicly make known the desired Authorised Establishment for each post, the necessary level of resourcing to meet a sufficient level of provision and the forms of representation best suited to achieve this.

Annual funding reviews will take place through this joint forum and within the Local Joint Negotiating Committee for Youth and Community Workers. Funding plans will subsequently be submitted annually as part of the requirement under the Further and Higher Education Act and in recognition of the criteria contained within the HMI Framework for Inspection of Youth Services.

In addition to the above, more strategic financial planning will take place with plans presented for approval and consultation for periods longer than the annual reviews.

Grant aided voluntary and independent sector projects will be subject to conditions prevailing under the *JNC Report* for youth, community and play workers, employment legislation and agreements reached from time to time within the Local Joint Negotiating Committee. The grant aided voluntary sector shall have access to the advice and support of the local authority personnel department on matters of fact and legislation and local procedure. The local authority shall fund centrally costs arising from the safeguarding of salaries or, where unavoidable, redundancies throughout those employing organisations party to the CEPA. Suitable alternative employment requirements where identified shall be from within the employing organisations within the CEPA as a whole. The CEPA shall also maintain a central register of all those locally qualified part-time workers and national JNC qualified staff from this local authority area seeking employment within it.

3. Potential redundancies

The purpose of this Agreement is to attempt to avoid the necessity of redundancy and to agree that there will be no compulsory redundancies within the CEPA area. Where this becomes unavoidable in the most exceptional and unforeseen cases, the CEPA will seek to ensure that all participants undertake the fullest and earliest possible consultation with the Community and Youth Workers' Union and other trade unions representing ancillary staff in full accordance with Section 188 of the *Trade Union and Labour Relations (Consolidation) Act 1992* as amended by the *Trade Union Reform and Employment Rights Act 1993*. This Agreement fully recognises that the purpose of consultation defined in these acts is to avoid dismissals, reduce the number of dismissals proposed and to mitigate the consequences of any dismissals. Consultation will take place with a view to reaching agreement and in full accordance with all legislative requirements. *(Note: Sections taken from Key Elements of Redundancy Legislation could be incorporated here for local use and reminder.)*

Immediately upon declaring a likelihood of redundancy any party to the CEPA shall issue a notice under Section 188 of the *Trade Union and Labour Relations (Consolidation) Act 1992* as amended and shall inform in writing the Principal Community Education Officer and the CYWU representative of all those details required by the Act. At the first stage of notice all possible alternatives to redundancy shall be considered and the views of staff as to alternative proposals shall be sought. Should mutual agreement be reached that no alternatives are found then selection criteria for redundancy should be established which are made known to all staff, which are objective and fair and which are non discriminatory whether directly or indirectly on the grounds of gender, marital status, race, national or ethnic origin, religion, disability, age, sexual orientation or trade union activity. At this stage a further audit review shall be commissioned. On the preliminary selection for redundancy the employer will inform the affected members of staff first and shall ensure that no notification is made to the press or third parties prior to this notification unless otherwise agreed through the appropriate trade union. The right of appeal against redundancy and selection criteria shall be available at every stage including the preliminary selection and the CEPA shall ensure the prompt and fair hearing of all appeals for employing organisations within the arrangement. Full rights to those so selected shall come into effect as of the date of the notice of selection. At this stage also there shall be another search for suitable alternative employment.

Should redundancy occur at this stage, the CEPA shall ask that it be recorded formally at the appropriate local authority committee that priority should be given in future plans to restoring the post/s deleted and that the CEPA was opposed to the deletion. The work resulting from the deleted post shall not be distributed and shall not be replaced other than by a full equivalent of that which previously existed.

Separate Codes of Practice concerning re-deployment measures and procedures, protection of terms and conditions, early retirement, and voluntary severance arrangements are available on request.

It is recognised that youth, community and play workers are employed throughout their careers in both the grant aided voluntary and independent sectors, and local authorities, and that in such employment the *Redundancy Payments (Local Government) (Modification) Order 1983 SI 1983/1160* and the recognition of continuity of employment must be taken into account.

Key elements of redundancy legislation

Redundancy legislation has not prevented the biggest balance of trade deficit in history and five million citizens unemployed. The youth, community and play service in the light of its own ethos and value base, should seek to set precedents in avoiding redundancy: it is hoped that the Model Protection of Employment Agreement above will assist in this. Practice can be better than the law.

The law requires employers to consult appropriate trade unions about proposed redundancies in order that they can seek to avoid and reduce them. In a new development within the statute (Section 34 *TUERA 1993*) employers are required to consult 'with a view to reaching agreement'. This is an interesting and as yet insufficiently tested clause. What does 'with a view to' mean? It is highly likely that the courts will want to see good faith demonstrated, adequate information provided for the purposes of consultation and, on the basis of previous case law, will want to see the employers demonstrate that they have reasonably and realistically considered any alternatives to redundancy put to them by the unions. Evidence of written rejection of the union's alternative proposals will be required. Workers who are not properly consulted can claim a protective award and any compensation paid in this respect by an industrial tribunal cannot be offset against wages, or pay in lieu of notice. Consultation definitely means advanced consultation with workers' representatives.

A key element in the redundancy situation is the quality of consultation. This in turn depends on two things, the background to industrial relations and the involvement of the employers (particularly in the case of local authorities) in the long term planning of the service. Frequent LJNC meetings which are provided with proper information concerning budgeting and planning, and which are regularly attended by senior elected members, should broaden the responsibility for the long term profile and planning of the service. Where such LJNCs can work in harmony with education sub committees and representatives of the voluntary sector employers, so much the better. All too often the reality is that the Rate Support Grant figures are set globally, received by the Policy and Finance Committee and the cuts are then evenly distributed across departments with little, or no regard for the disproportionate effect a five percent cut can have in a small department, or sub department such as youth, community and play work. The reality is that most of our services are already below an acceptable minimum level of resourcing and the viability of some is seriously in question.

Redundancy consultation has to be based on clear information and the legislation requires the employer to give unions all of the following:

- Reasons for the proposals.
- The numbers and description of employees proposed to be dismissed.
- The total number of such employees in that description.
- The procedure for dismissing, taking into account local procedures, and the period over which the dismissals will take effect.
- Method of calculating redundancy terms.
- Ways of avoiding dismissal and mitigating the effects.

- Other information as may be required by the union for the purposes of industrial relations.
- Where more than ten but less than ninety-nine employees may be made redundant over a period of 30 days or less, at least 30 days notification for consultation must take place.
- Where a hundred or more employees are to be made redundant as much notice as possible is required.
- A decision to make redundant must not be taken prior to consultation on proposals to make redundant.

The employers also have to notify the Department for Trade and Industry of proposals to make redundancies within the timescales specified above. This is significant as the purpose of such notification is in order that the Department may provide help in re-deploying or retraining redundant employees.

Once redundancies have been announced, an individual declared redundant has rights to:

- Paid time off work to look for another job, or to arrange for re-training. (Two days a week is considered by some Industrial Tribunals as not being unreasonable.)
- Redundancy pay.
- Notice of termination.
- The right to a trial period in a post, if alternative work is available with that employer.

If there is an agreement that the employer will not make any compulsory redundancies, the employer will then advertise for voluntary early retirements, voluntary redundancies and a range of other measures. At the very least in such circumstances it is advisable for both management and union to get on record from the employers a commitment to prioritise the restoration of those posts as and when funds become available, and that they will jointly and actively seek a restoration. Even this rarely tried defence mechanism should be a fall back position in our drastically eroded services.

If the employers are unable to get enough volunteers for redundancy and retirement, they will have to select for redundancy among the group identified at risk. They cannot just select who they want. Selection criteria have to be objective and non discriminatory on the grounds of sex and race, they must be fair, and moreover, they must be applied reasonably. There have been many successful cases brought against employers magically selecting the active trade unionists for example. Also, within the youth, community and play service with the majority of part-time staff being women workers, it will almost always be automatically unfair to select part-time workers first, as it could be proven that this selection discriminates against women.

Once a set of 'fair' selection criteria have been agreed, where such agreement is possible, as very often an organised workforce will refuse to be part of this discussion, there must be an appeals mechanism built in to give any employee the right to appeal if they consider themselves unfairly selected. Like grievance and disciplinary procedures, this appeals structure must be according to the laws of natural justice, and must include stages with fair timescales. Any set of selection criteria needs to be reduced to the most objective factors that can be considered. But even if the affected group of employees does begin to consider these criteria with the employers its members will very soon discover that they are signing the termination papers of some of their number, individuals known by name.

Built into any fair system of dealing with redundancy, of course, is the need for the employer to demonstrate that they have offered reasonable alternative employment. Legally the employers must make any alternative offers before the contract that is being made redundant comes to an end. It is fair to offer:

- Counselling or career advice
- At least three alternative posts with at least one month trial periods in each. *(Note: an unreasonable refusal of an alternative job offer can jeopardise redundancy pay entitlements).*
- A written description of how the newly offered post differs from the old.

The suitability of alternative employment offered is assessed with reference to:

- Levels of pay.
- Levels of status.
- Place of work: any disruption, consideration of domestic (child care) circumstances etc.
- Working hours and deployment.
- Levels of skill required: are they commensurate etc?

Given the flexibility, adaptability and relevance of the skills of youth, community and play workers there is hardly a department in a local authority that could not benefit from a worker qualified to JNC level being involved.

Redundancy should be like industrial action, to be used as a last resort, and much more time and effort should be given through LJNCs in particular to avoiding it, especially in our meagre service with so many demands upon it. Again, this area stresses the need to establish Authorised Establishment lists for all youth, community and play posts and for determining, in conjunction with the voluntary sector, what is a sufficient level of service provision.

Re-deployment

Finding suitable alternative employment within the confines of a redundancy situation is a form of re-deployment of course. It is an enforced move because the existing post has become redundant. Youth, community and play workers may face re-deployment for other reasons: their work situation may become dangerous, or professionally unworkable, their post may change by mutual agreement, it may be mutually desirable to move elsewhere within the employing organisation. There should be equal opportunity within a Model Re-deployment Procedure for workers to request re-deployment as well as employers compelling it. Naturally the key element of any agreed procedure is the extent to which it protects terms and conditions. All aspects of remuneration; pay, travel allowance, incremental prospects, special allowances etc. need to be protected. A good agreement will protect every aspect of current employment benefit and guarantee no personal detriment. If, for example you have an area allowance and you are moved to an area without one through no fault of your own, then your current area allowance should really continue to apply. If you have a special responsibility allowance in your current post and are moved to one without that area of specialism, you should not lose that aspect of your grading.

Here, then, is a Model Re-deployment Procedure, which perhaps of all the model procedures outlined in this book, is the one most likely to require local adaptation. There will be considerable differences of concern when dealing with internal re-deployments within youth, community and play departments, or when dealing with re-deployments concerning full-time or part-time workers. Volunteers also should have an opportunity to be re-deployed if they still wish to work for a service but cannot develop their full potential within the current unit of operation.

Model Re-deployment Procedure

Guiding principles

1. Re-deployment as a consequence of redundancy will be subject to the principles of protection outlined in this Procedure, but in certain circumstances may be subject to procedures outlined in the Protection of Employment or Redundancy Procedures.

2. Re-deployment, whether initiated by management or staff, will be subject to no detriment in any term or condition of employment, and all existing contractual benefits shall continue to apply.

3. All aspects of re-deployment, the procedure, process and outcome shall be monitored by management throughout and be subject to consultation and negotiation with staff and their trade union representative.

4. It is recognised for the purposes of this agreement that re-deployment except in cases of redundancy, is an opportunity for management or staff, separately or jointly to develop the individual and the service, to respond to the needs of the service and for the individual employee to maximise the contribution of both. It is recognised that individual employees may from time to time face hazardous or unacceptably difficult situations in the workplace and that management may have requirements for staff within the service beyond their existing place of work. It is recognised that re-deployment may be time limited or otherwise and that the duration of the re-deployment should be clearly agreed.

5. Re-deployment whether requested by staff or management shall first be registered in a supervision meeting as a formal request with all of the appropriate reasons spelt out.

6. An agreed range of options and period of time to work within those options shall be negotiated at each stage and every reasonable effort shall be taken to reach mutual agreement.

7. An appeals mechanism shall be available for any aspect of the re-deployment process.

8. It is recognised that a mutually agreed re-deployment is in the best interests of the service.

9. This agreement is established without prejudice to existing procedures for grievance, redundancy, protection of employment and other contractual obligations.

The procedure

1. To establish suitable alternative employment options the employee will be interviewed by their senior officer, to establish the type of work to which they may wish to be re-deployed and to review their present job, remuneration, work location, skills, qualifications, capabilities, experience, and, where relevant, training or re-training needs. The field of re-deployment options will be as wide as possible and relevant to each particular case, following negotiation jointly with the employee and their trade union. Any employee who is dissatisfied with the re-deployment options may of course refer the difference to the grievance procedure and the appeal mechanism available at any stage throughout this procedure. The reasons for re-deployment will be established in a written record initially at a supervision meeting. The desired timescale for the re-deployment shall be mutually agreed at the outset of the procedure and reviewed and altered by mutual agreement.

2. All initial offers of suitable alternative employment will be made in writing by the principal officer.

3. An employee accepting alternative employment shall have an agreed trial period of up to eight weeks in their new post. This trial period shall be increased to offset any time spent on re-training for the post.

4. Any necessary re-training programme will be defined in writing and will accompany the written offer of alternative employment. Requests for re-training will be considered and be responded to within one month of request and all reasonable efforts shall be made to meet them.

5. The re-deployment will then be reviewed by the principal officer in consultation with the employee and the relevant senior officer and if satisfactory to all, the permanent, or if agreed, temporary, re-deployment will be confirmed in writing by the senior officer.

6. If it is jointly agreed that the re-deployment will not be appropriate then suitable alternative employment will be offered by the employer using appropriate procedures.

7. An employee who accepts alternative employment which would result in a reduction in their grade shall retain their existing grade on a no detriment basis together with all other aspects of remuneration and benefit associated with the current post, unless mutually agreed to the contrary.

8. Any employee who is required to move their place of work shall be paid re-location expenses in accordance with the provisions adopted by the employer.

9. This procedure can only work effectively given reasonable offers and acceptance of suitable alternative employment according to all the circumstances of each particular case.

10. At every stage of the re-deployment procedure an employee shall have the right to be accompanied by their trade union representative and an employee will be informed of this right at every stage of the procedure. Unless the employee specifically indicates otherwise trade union representation will be the practice. Copies of all correspondence will also be sent to the relevant trade union representative.

11. An individual employee may apply to their principal officer for consideration for re-deployment where changes cause real concern for personal reasons. Action is at the discretion of the principal officer and this provision will not apply to groups of employees. In the event of disagreement on re-deployment the matter will be considered through the internal grievance procedure.

Transfer of undertakings and protection of employment

A complex set of problems is faced increasingly by public sector workers, as a result of privatisation and the 'purchase' of local authority services by private companies. Although privatisation in the form known by, say, cleaning, catering and engineering and other local authority departments is less common in youth, community and play work (mainly because our work does not so obviously generate a 'profit'), parts of it have been contracted out, and some areas of youth work are now run by companies. More and more youth workers have been transformed from youth social educators into Business Unit Managers (an appropriate acronym!). Business Unit Managers put together the bids for funding from the local authority for their centres. If someone puts in a better bid, the underbidder has nowhere to go. Alternatively in some areas, voluntary sector consortia have put in bids to 'buy' those local education authority workers on JNC contracts, to run particular projects. Remarks about youth, community and play workers being worth more than famous, or infamous, footballers never seem to go down too well. Workers in difficulty have turned to the relatively progressive aspects of European legislation or Directives, often as a substitute for re-imposing the employment legislation and trade union rights that have been lost in the United Kingdom.

In any event, our sector, like every other part of local government and public service suffers from the same threats of transferring undertakings as any other, and the policies applicable to it must be those which are the most relevant and useful to our future. One day you are working for the democratically controlled local authority, the next you are working for a private company. What happens to the continuity of employment rights to which your previous contract entitled you?

There is a range of statutes, case law and precedents and protective trade union measures and procedures that have grown up around this area. It has exercised the minds of trade union legal departments, law makers and barristers not to mention the European Court of Justice.

The political objection to the further fragmentation of youth, community and play work by transferring to new and smaller organisations is fundamental to successful industrial relations at this time. It is not a freelance, privately owned service, it will always depend on state subsidy and on public accountability.

Like many other unpleasant things transfers do happen and have happened to youth, community and play workers. It is likely to happen further with the move to new unitary authorities. Interestingly, one of the lead test cases in this area of legislation is in an area similar to some of the situations within our sector: (*Dr. Sophie Redmond Stichting v Bartol and others (1992) IRLR 366*). This case concerned a grant aided project, supporting drug and alcohol dependants, from which the local authority in Groningen withdrew its previous financial support in favour of another organisation to which contracts had to be transferred, though the new employer did not offer them to all those previously employed.

The law underpinning workers' rights when their contracts are transferred from their existing employer to another has been repeatedly emphasised by the European Court of Justice as stemming from a European Directive which has as its aim the 'safeguarding of employees rights' in the event of transfers. 'The Directive is intended as far as is possible, to safeguard the rights of workers in the event of a change of employer by making it possible for them to work for the new employer under the same conditions agreed with the transferor.' It is accepted that 'the rules applicable in the event of a transfer of an undertaking or a business to another employer are intended to safeguard, in the interests of the employees, the existing employment relationships which are part of the economic entity transferred.' Article 3(1) of the European Directive specifically provides for 'the transfer of the transferor's rights and obligations arising from a contract of employment or from an employment relationship' and from Article 3(2) 'the continued observance by the transferee of the terms and conditions agreed in any collective agreement as well as for the protection of the employees concerned against dismissal by the transferor or by the transferee on the grounds of the transfer alone': Article 4(1).

Recent additions to the legislation that will affect youth, community and play work transfers to another employer deal with whether or not any property is transferred to the transferee by the transferor (e.g. contracting out situations, franchising etc.).

In situations where the employee informs the transferor or transferee that they object to becoming employed by the transferee, the contract of employment does not get automatically transferred. However, despite the apparent sympathy in the European Directives, such an objection would be considered to be a resignation and they will not be treated as having been 'dismissed' by the transferor. This deprives the employee of any right to claim redundancy payment for unfair dismissal unless they can demonstrate a right to terminate their contract without notice because the proposed new conditions in the transferred undertaking would represent a substantial detriment.

Occupational pension schemes do not have to be transferred.

In addition, the duties to consult with recognised trade unions must now be undertaken 'with a view to seeking their agreement to the measures to be taken'. An interesting formulation. This consultation must be assisted by access to relevant information. The transferor and transferee must also both provide the recognised trade union with information about:

- The fact that a transfer is to take place.
- When the transfer will happen.
- Why it is taking place.
- What action will be taken (if any) in relation to employees.
- The social, legal, and economic implications of the transfer for affected employees.
- Details of the planned action the transferor and transferee will take in relation to the employees.

The information is not just required for information's sake, it has purposes. Specifically these are to enable the employees to respond to the employer so that the responses may be reasonably considered and so that the employer can reply to these responses and if they reject them state clear reasons why. If information is not made available employees may seek redress at the Industrial Tribunal.

So, summarising this section so far, a Protection of Employment Agreement needs to be negotiated throughout the service in order to recognise the importance of the service and the joint interest that both managers, employers and staff have in defending it from further erosion. Redundancies can be minimised by regular consultation through LJNCs about future development plans for the services and joint approaches to the employing bodies by management and unions should be developed to assist expansion rather than contraction. Minimum Authorised Establishment levels should be drawn up for each post and service. Where redundancies are proposed, consultation should take place to try to avoid them. Where this avoidance becomes impossible, suitable alternative employment should be sought and found. Grant aid to the voluntary sector should be conditional upon its adherence to standard employment policies and the ability to pay redundancy pay where difficulties arise and on its commitment to achieving professional advice on employment related matters and access to local authority re-deployment procedures. No youth, community and play service, or project in the country can honestly say that it has enough staff at the moment.

Working with and for Connexions and other services: a briefing

CYWU is committed to retaining and extending the JNC Report to all youth work posts. All personal advisers should be paid on JNC terms and conditions. We are committed to retaining the separate professional skill and identity of youth work and the voluntary relationship and value base that goes with it. We want youth workers to advocate for young people and to guide and support them and not to have to police their participation in activities. We also want a properly funded statutory, publicly controlled youth service with an existence and status separate from Connexions and autonomous. We believe that the best possible model involves the constitutional and professional separation of Connexions services and the youth service, separate funding streams for them and separate contracts for staff. This checklist of trade union issues seeks to support branches in maintaining youth work influence over events.

Issues and preparation

Consider CYWU's Conference 2000 Policies—see website.
Consider CYWU's Connexions Conference Report—website www.cywu.org.uk

Planning

No business plan bid should be submitted by any consortium for a Connexions Service without the approval of the trade unions. The Minister responsible for Connexions and the youth service has strongly emphasised to all Connexions services that the unions must be involved at all stages. CYWU and UNISON have regular meetings on Connexions with the minister and the Chief Executive of the Connexions Service National Unit and colleagues.

No planning group should be established without full trade union involvement and negotiations on the bids.

Control

New Connexions services and pilots should be as close to local authority publicly accountable control as possible with genuine partnerships between careers and youth services and the voluntary youth service created.

Union representation

Trade unions (UNISON and CYWU) should be represented on all bodies discussing new services to young people.

Make sure that you know the contact details of the local TUC representative to the Learning and Skills Council. Meet them to discuss youth service issues.

Terms and conditions

Only co-operate if JNC terms and conditions guaranteed for relevant staff.

At the time of writing (January 2002) the Teachers Pension Scheme has refused to recognise personal advisers and educationalists and therefore excluded them from the teacher's pension scheme. This has meant that youth workers who have been transferred over into Connexions services and who are in the teachers' scheme have lost pension entitlements and the union is seeking to resolve this matter.

Transfer of undertakings protection of employment arrangements are short lived, it is vital to negotiate the full package of durable terms and conditions prior to any transfer.

Ensure that full support and supervision and health and safety training are in place before you start work with the new service.

Resourcing

Trade union branches should not give any support to new Connexions services unless there is new money for them. Until there is new money there should be no transfer of staff and no co-operation with the new service. Unless branches hold this line the generic youth service will go into decline.

The youth service must receive more not less funding as a result of local Connexions developments.

Personal advisers

Where these are new posts with a youth work role these should be on JNC terms and conditions.

Youth service staff should boycott all adverts for posts not requiring a qualification and should indicate to the new Connexions services that we will not work with unqualified staff.

Code of ethics

Insist on the adoption within the local youth service and Connexions of CYWU's Code of Professional Ethics, copies in Part Time Workers' Handbook. Refuse to work with colleagues not signatories to this code.

Negotiate purchase of the Part Time Workers' Handbook by all employers of staff working with young people for every worker.

Transfer and secondment of youth service staff

No transfer at all of any youth service staff hours without compensatory repayment into the youth service.

National support

Ensure that national officials with knowledge of legislation and Connexions developments visit you locally.

Training and legal back up

Send members on GFTU, TUC and CYWU Training Courses. Attend national conference 2001. Particular training may be required on the transfer of undertakings protection of employment legislation.

Trade union recruitment

Launch recruitment drive. New services run well if staff are motivated, organised and informed.

Information

Send all local written information to your Union's national office. Part of the difficulty with Connexions is its local variation. We are unlikely to impose national standards unless information is shared.

Further reading and reference

Redundancy. Another excellent short guide from Labour Research Department.

Model Employment Protection Policy: Joint Teacher Association/LEA Model Agreement on the Avoidance of Compulsory Redundancy. Agreed by the five Teachers' Associations, ATL, NASUWT, NUT, PAT, SHA. January 1994.

The Employment Service has an office hours freephone Helpline on questions of redundancy.

There are regional Employment Service Offices that can be contacted for their useful range of free publications on all aspects of employment law, particularly redundancy.

Part 7

Health and Safety

Introduction

Health and safety is a broad area, much neglected in youth, community and play work, and subject to significant new legislation. I have produced a manual and a pocket guide on health and safety with Russell House Publishing and a further book on *Managing Violence and Aggression in Youth and Community Work* with Pepar Publications. This section deals with three areas of particular importance to youth, community and play work which have been subject, in the case of minibus safety, to recent discussion, and in the case of stress and lone working, to very little discussion, despite a high incidence of stress and violence at work.

Model Basic Health and Safety Checklist and Prompt

Are all the Health and Safety (H and S) laws and regulations available to you? ☐

Do you know the name and contact of the CYWU Health and Safety Representative? ☐

Do you know the name and contact of the employer's H and S representative? ☐

Is there an Accident Report Book at work? ☐

Are the H and S Procedures available at work? ☐

Are all staff and volunteers and young people equally trained, informed and aware? ☐

Has your workplace been inspected for risks? ☐

When? . . . .

Is there a thermometer in the Office? ☐

Do you know the legal thresholds of temperature at work? ☐

When was the electrical equipment last inspected? . . . .

How many cubic metres of working space are available to each member of staff? . . . .

Are there hazardous substances on the premises? ☐

Have you been given training in the COSHH regulations? ☐

Is there a fire alarm? ☐

Are Fire Exits clearly identified? ☐

Even for the visually or aurally impaired? □

Are wheelchair users safe in your building? □

How do you evacuate the building? . . . .

Is there a first aid box? □

Is it adequate? □

Where is it? . . . .

Are there enough fire extinguishers and are they of the right type? □

When was the last fire officer's inspection? . . . .

Do you have somewhere to put your clothes and belongings while at work? □

Is there a policy on staffing ratios? □

What is the policy on working alone? □

What is the procedure for dealing with violence at work? □

Are all fixtures and fittings safe? □

Are there enough toilets and wash basins? □

Is there enough ventilation near the photocopier or other equipment? □

Have VDU users been made aware of the new legislation? □

Have VDU users been given eye tests at the employer's expense? □

How often do users take breaks, what does the law say? □

Does the physical working environment need to be improved? □

How is work and lack of support contributing to stress? □

Are the terms of the Food Hygiene and Storage Regulations met? □

Are new staff provided with H and S training on recruitment? □

Are staff trained when new risks become evident? □

What would be considered a serious or imminent danger
at this workplace? . . . .

What protective equipment is available to youth, community
and play workers in situations of risk? . . . .

Do you know the number of Mobile phones, Alarms, Helplines, Solicitor's □
advice lines or are they available somewhere?

What insurance policies exist in case of injury at work? . . . .

Are working hours and rotas legal? □

Is there guidance on hazardous activities? □

Is there guidance on outdoor activities? □

Is there guidance on mini bus driving? □

Have you informed management that you refuse to drive □
mini buses with crew seats or without belts?

Do you take another qualified driver on trips over 150 miles? □

Is all equipment used by user groups safe? □

Does everyone who uses the equipment know how to use it? □

Are there any particular dangers? □

Stress

Elements of work and their effect

Contexts

Organisational function and culture:
> Poor task environment
> Lack of definition of objectives
> Poor problem solving environment
> Poor development environment
> Poor communication
> Non supportive culture

Role in organisation:
> Role ambiguity
> Role conflict
> High responsibility for people

Career development:
> Career uncertainty
> Career stagnation
> Poor status or status incongruity
> Poor pay
> Job insecurity and redundancy
> Low social value to work

Decision latitude/control:
> Low participation in decision making
> Lack of control over work
> Little decision making in work or overload

Interpersonal relationships at work:
> Social or physical isolation
> Poor relationships with superiors
> Interpersonal conflict and violence
> Lack of social support

Home/work interface:
> Conflicting demands of home and work
> Low social or practical support at home
> Dual career problems

Contents

Task design:
> Ill defined work
> High uncertainty in work
> Lack of variety, or short work cycles
> Fragmented or meaningless work
> Under-utilisation of skill
> Continual exposure to client/customer groups

Workload/pace/schedule (quantitative/qualitative):
> Shift working
> Inflexible work schedule
> Unpredictable work hours
> Long or unsocial work hours

These columns are taken from a research report on stress published by the Health and Safety Executive, (HSE Contract research report No. 61/1993, *Stress Research and Stress Management: Putting Theory to Work*). They can be usefully considered in relation to the occupations of youth, community and play work and others within the informal education sector, with a view to remedying what is one of the most destructive aspects of our work, the high stress level. I believe that youth, community and play work, as an occupation, has an especially high concentration of these very commonly identified stress factors. Without denigrating the stress levels that have clearly escalated in other professional groups, there are some features present within them which simply do not exist in youth, community and play work, and which contribute significantly to stress; these include questions of status, legal underpinnings of work, supportive work structures, clearer lines of accountability, and clearer tasks and work objectives.

Some of these commonly recognised contributory factors to occupational stress, are discussed below by reference to youth, community and play work practice. I have been consistently drawn to structural and overtly political commentary. Remedies to the causal factors of stress, consistent with the work itself, are therefore seen as depending upon collective, professional and negotiated organisation. In conclusion, a suggested model statement is provided, for an organisation to begin to demonstrate a commitment to improved work practice. The statement focuses on the factors at work which can contribute to stress and exacerbate those stresses in life, outside work.

Lack of definition of objectives

It is not so much multiple objectives, but the lack of definition of them that is a major contributory factor. This is compounded by the political and professional position of youth, community and play workers. Services require clear statements of purpose, regularly reviewed through staff meetings and an effective communication of new objectives to those working in the field. These objectives need to be translated, through supervision, to plans and targets at unit level.

There is a big 'however' within all this, which relates to incongruity of objectives. Youth, community and play workers, work amidst conflicting and sometimes incoherent objectives. They are normally relating to objectives from:

- the employing organisation
- the management committee of the centre, project or unit they work most with, or for
- the young people
- the adults and
- various sub groupings within the community

including very often the objectives of local ward councillors, or the dominant political group. Often objectives are irreconcilable. The contradictory objectives manifest themselves usually in different individuals with whom the worker must establish trusting and confidential relationships in order to achieve their educational function. The strong commitment to the satisfaction of people that underpins the workers' professional ethos further accentuates the anxiety that can be caused in such chaotic human networks. The simplistic performance indicators imposed by many employers (how many people in the centre last night, how has the crime rate reduced) add incredibly to the stress, not because they are difficult to comply with, but because the message they give to the employee is that the employer is looking for an outcome that is not consistent with their professional training as an educator. As Mark Smith has remarked in *Local Education* (1994), 'The achievements of informal educators are less visible, and those wanting to see the local educators' handiwork, have to look at the changes in the fabric and routines of daily life.' The sort of education in which youth, community and play workers are involved, is part of the participation in the occurrences of the everyday experiences of adults and young people. The work patterns do not reflect those in the predominant education models of didacticism, curriculum planning and task orientation. The process of the educational intervention is methodical and deliberate, while its products and outcomes are far less tangible, and this fact should be appreciated.

There needs to be a reassertion of the educational nature of youth work and community work if we are to minimise the lack of clear definition of objectives that is now so evident. Kerry Young's

The Art of Youth Work does this well for youth work and Val Harris's *Community Work Skills Manual* does this for community work. The National Occupational Standards set out for play work does this in this sector also. The subtle methods of intervention in our work are matters that need greater professional and political recognition. The emphasis of much recent objective-setting has been quantitative, and the balance needs to be tipped politically to the qualitative elements, if the real objectives of the work are to be supported and clarified.

Poor problem solving environment

A more positive culture should be developed within the service around the key procedures advocated in this book. Regular supervision is a good thing. Negotiation through an LJNC with proper communication channels back to those working in the field is a good thing. Regular staff meetings are good things. The use of grievance, collective or individual, when the problem is unresolved by other means is a good thing. Monitoring and evaluation of work, and even appraisal, are good things when based on clear objectives and an appreciation of the education content of the work.

There needs to be a cultural shift, to appreciate the value of organised dissent and disagreement, conducted professionally through clear procedures. If the commitment of the youth, community and play work to countering inequality and social injustice is to be fully developed, then support for workers through supervision, and in negotiating job descriptions through, and often against, the various power structures that impinge upon their work, whether in local government, local business, administrative structures, or community hierarchies, needs to be more readily forthcoming.

Poor development environment

This has two aspects in relation to youth, community and play work. There are the directly contractual matters, and also the pressing social ones. It should be recognised that it is painful in the extreme to continually work in neighbourhoods, where opportunity and environment are in decline, and where the quality of life is run down, rather than enhanced, week by week. Community work and youth work, play valuable reforming roles in improving communal living and educational opportunity, but the persistence of poverty, especially in those areas where most workers are deployed, should spur both a recognition of the general need to reassert the political education element of our work in organised resistance to injustice, and a more realistic set of goals being established by the profession itself. The work alone will not achieve the kind of structural and political changes that are required. Political objectives with wider aspirations, such as those contained in the *Statement of Purpose for the Youth Service*, however rhetorically laudable, mislead students into greater expectations of the work than are actually professionally achievable. We should become more professionally satisfied with smaller advances through a commitment to the education purpose, and more appreciative of the organisations which we can participate in as professionals, to achieve a wider transformative impact. This is not an argument for low aspiration at work, nor for diluting any social justice commitments, merely to recognise the effective contexts in which progressive ideas can best operate.

Poor communication

Staff meetings. Staff newsletters. Reports from LJNC meetings. Open exchanges in supervision. Clear lines of management. These are vital aspects of communication within a service. It is surprising how much such beneficial channels are under attack, how many local authority youth services no longer provide staff meetings, or in how many the new agreements reached through a LJNC are kept like private property, by senior management. Good communications support corporate identity in the best sense and create a positive feeling of being part of something with a clear direction.

Equally critical is the expectation that face to face workers, both full and part-time, will be encouraged to report what is important about their work and gain recognition for it. Another feature of the new managerialism has been the requirement to communicate only some of the more tangible and numeric elements of the work which fit with assessment criteria within the formal education system. New systems of accountability, largely influenced by many of the more negative aspects of the Coopers and Lybrand Report and mechanistic notions of accountability, often encouraged by totally unaccountable free lance consultants, have had very nerve racking effects. As the TUC itself has highlighted in its 1994 paper to Congress on Human Resource Management, the nature of communication, about work related issues, can either engage or disenfranchise a workforce; it can either respect the role of trade unions or be used to deliberately undermine it. If workers are faced with accountability structures which do not match their professional understanding of the work, they will automatically feel alienated. A tremendous amount of work now has to be done to get the employers themselves more engaged in the actual policy direction of the work and to refocus accountability systems on the complicated educational content of the work.

Non supportive culture

It has to be said that the *JNC Report* in part enshrines the notion that the most senior worker will require the least direct supervision. This is a misunderstanding of the role of supervision. All workers need supervision, even if it is to undertake an autonomous, powerful and decision laden position. Supervision levels do not reflect the competence or seniority of the supervised. Supervision describes the employers commitment to defining objectives, supporting staff, communicating, and problem solving, and their concern for health and safety.

The environment of stress will increase in direct proportion to the lack of supervision.

Role ambiguity

This will be a permanent feature of youth, community and play work which is an occupation built creatively on this ambiguity. The role is perceived ambiguously and differently and at different times by all those with whom the worker comes into contact both from the employing side and the client side. Within a working day the youth and community worker, depending on the intervention they are making at any one time, will be friend, agent of the state, teacher, social worker, licensee, treasurer, advocate, enemy, service provider, service enabler, adviser, counsellor, guide, goad, boss, handy person, organiser. It is precisely the fluidity of role that makes the work so interesting and rewarding, yet it can be the most frustrating and stressful side. This however, only emphasises the urgency of ensuring that everything to do with the employment relationship is as unambiguous as possible. The root of this clarity is the Job Description and the reasonableness of the employer's operational expectations, and it is for this reason, that the Model Job Description in the first section of this book includes explicit reference to the social justice element of the work.

Role conflict

As the educational content of the youth, community and play work has been diminished in the contemporary enterprise and 'contract' culture and as the political basis of the main local authority employers has become less identified with democratically controlled welfare statism, so have the potential conflicts grown between employers and workers, who are working with alienated, disenfranchised and hard pressed communities. Becoming an arms length service provider on the basis of a neutralised curriculum that actually does not lead to the provision of a relevant service has led to increasing conflict of roles. The tensions that intense poverty have created in relation to youth workers' attitudes towards crime and substance abuse, for example, are building in major stress factors: if I am expected to stop crime and there is a 30 per cent youth unemployment rate in my neighbourhood what is my role? There is integral role conflict within the job of youth work or community work. The role has perceived elements of education, social welfare, surrogate political activism, and leisure service delivery. The reality that behind each manifestation of role lies a consistent transformative and educational direction needs endorsement in supervision and assessment.

Career uncertainty

Once again, underlying causes only recommend a political and organisational alternative. Where are the career stages within a service? Where are the funds for in service training and sabbaticals? Where incidentally, are the jobs? Isn't it best to train for a more generic set of skills? Career uncertainty leads to the necessity for the Protection of Employment Agreement and to the urgent need to ensure some form of labour market planning nationally. Currently there are not enough students and not enough jobs in youth and community and play work, but there are too many jobs for the number of students being qualified. There needs to be a plan. Consideration also needs to be given now to the welcome development of higher degrees and research qualifications in youth, community and play work. At last adequate opportunities are beginning to appear for quality academic and other research, but this is coinciding with great imbalances in the supply and demand for officer posts.

Career stagnation

The access to re-deployment for the purpose of creative job change and perhaps interchange between neighbouring authorities on a consortium basis, needs to be considered, as does the culture. What is a career? Before the serious cuts, there was high mobility amongst full-time workers within the profession, but not so now. What is the dominant professional attitude towards a career? Is one only a success if one reaches officer level? An appreciation of the values of those who commit themselves early in their career to remaining throughout their working life primarily in face to face work, needs to be put on a par with the values of those who plan to become lecturers or senior officers. The indiscriminate use of freelance trainers and consultants, often with little knowledge of our work, instead of using or developing the talents of existing staff, is a further contributory factor in some areas to the stagnation of careers. Many workers in face to face work still after thirty years or more, testify to the availability of good non managerial and managerial supervision in retaining their freshness and enthusiasm.

Poor status or status incongruity

This is a vital area that should be considered. Within the *JNC Report* it is recognised that youth, community and play workers will liaise with a variety of agencies in the development of their work. This in my view, is a significant understatement of the role and professional status that workers have and the stress that is caused by the misunderstanding of this is significant. Not only are youth, community and play workers expected to liaise with other agencies, this work is an essential professional component of community development, and recognised at least by the Association of Metropolitan Authorities. Staff are trained not just to work with other agencies, but to form them, to understand their social and political dynamics, their inter-relationship and their purpose. Very often youth, community and play workers are instrumental in creating the other agencies: very often they are absolutely instrumental in bringing these agencies together. Youth, community and play workers are frequently the first point of contact for government, local government and elected member approaches to a particular problem within a neighbourhood. Yet in all of their inter-agency involvement, undertaken in true community work style in an enabling and empowering fashion, they are usually the least well paid and most junior members of staff excepting perhaps the local parish clergy! Other professionals in the teams have strong community identities—community doctors, clergy, teachers, social workers, housing officers, all have more easily articulated status and identity than the community worker.

Valuing, rewarding, praising, promoting, creating positive images—these are underestimated elements of personnel management and service level marketing.

Low participation in decision making

A participatory service requires highly participatory styles of management. The actual decision makers within a structure need to be engaged in the decisions taken by the forum, the LJNC, to which workers have direct democratic access. It is also important to have professional access to personnel records, and information concerning the service. Lots of responsibility and no power is a negative thing. To make the political analogy, perhaps it is possible to recognise that stress in workers is a symptom of precisely those oppressive practices and unjust social formations that youth, community and play work itself is theoretically established to relieve.

'But what about management's right to manage' the old guard may say. This model of participatory management incorporates the rights of all levels of the service to be involved and to know. Also, why consult, if you are unprepared to listen and take on board. Management is, after all, merely a function of divided labour.

The regular opportunity to participate in policy formation for the whole service should be afforded to all staff.

Lack of control over work

The inevitability of the unexpected, the multiple roles and functions, the chaotic influx of community demands, that sinking rather than swimming feeling! Control might mean being able to take a raw material and through craft and skill, fashion it into a finished functional or aesthetic object. This is a very rewarding and distinctively human process, there is fulfilment in production, the process of design, execution and creation. This sort of productive experience is not common within informal education practice which capitalises upon the accidental and does not require a frame of testing and examination to check its results and outputs. It is what is on the track and why, rather than what is coming off at the end that is usually of professional interest. Very often, the products of a youth, community and play workers' labours in terms of the emotional and intellectual and behavioural advantage to a person, is never seen by the worker themselves. Physical environments can improve, the posters can be on the wall, the furniture in good repair, the books balancing, but the quality of the educational contact is less tangible and rightly so. Control is further removed when assessment of the work relies on criteria other than those at its core. Less should be done by more workers, and supervision should support its being done well. High levels of uncertainty are integral to informal education practice, which relies on experiment as much as design, and which cannot chose a neatly defined curriculum. Pacing, and workload questions, must be consistently discussed in supervision. This is also why supervision should be freed as much as possible from, as it were, the administrative, in order that creative discussion can take place on the content of work and its planning.

Shift working and unpredictability of time

The intensity and number of extreme stress factors mentioned above, are worsened in youth, community and play work by the nature of the working day. Here we should be concerned to appreciate through supervision the need to deploy working time sensibly. The sessional working week, as defined by the *JNC Report*, appreciates the erratic nature of the work and the unsocial hours. The contribution of this to ill health and psychosomatic stress disorders is not to be underestimated. The fact that many workers are on twenty four hour call out, as key holders or emergency contacts, and that work cannot be planned to accommodate very neat working days, is also something that should be taken more into account. The only good reason for time recording sheets is to enable unhealthy patterns of work to be scrutinised and prevented through supervision. Long days, frequent unsocial hours, irregular and considerable travel, all take their toll. A culture should be developed of looking at the hours that officers and workers spend, with a view to assisting them in improved time management and health care. A supervisor's commitment to complete confidentiality should enable these sessions to consider where appropriate the other feature of stress, which is the inter-relationship between work and life outside. Naturally enough the stress that can be caused by a personal conflict with one's supervisor, means that any staff development system should include a right to chose an alternative supervisor. Do we work to live or live to work?

A rounded approach to stress

Many of the policies and procedures advocated in this book are essential to providing the baseline of clarity of expectation which so significantly relieves stress. Stress does require separate and special attention within the context of a health and safety risk assessment. This is quite consistent with official thinking within this area. It contrasts sharply however, with most practice within youth, community and play work. Stress symptoms are more often registered in youth, community and play work as an expression of individual and professional deficiencies, as a failure to cope with demanding workloads, and an inability to work independently. 'Oh, so and so's burnt out, I've sent them off for a holiday.' 'Take a break and recharge your batteries.' 'They shouldn't really be in a JNC 3 post.' 'You'll never see them if the trouble starts.' 'Not another doctor's note.'

Despite the recognition within youth, community and play work that people are complex constructions of nature, nurture, environment, opportunity, economic circumstances, peer group pressures and the like, when a youth, community or play worker is looking stressed, it is frequently seen as their individual fault. Our commitment as a service to the development of self and identity in a non oppressive environment runs very thin when the ailing colleague is deemed a victim of poor time management, and an inability to cope. Systemic problems are turned into personal and pathological ones. The term 'burn out', heard more frequently in my job these days, calls to mind those bits of magnesium that fizzled in white hot flames in school chemistry. Regrettably, this is just the effect that stress can have. The ability of occupational stress to trigger latent psychological and physical disorders is also something the youth, community and play service should not ignore. Certainly the commercial sector has not. The highest standards of stress management are needed in youth, community and play work, because attention to it is that most human thing, to care for the psychological and physical well being of a colleague.

Such management should be based on the holistic approach now common in other areas of health and safety assessment and risk reduction. *The Health and Safety at Work Act (1974)* is concerned with both psychological and physical well being. It defines 'personal injury' as 'any decrease and any impairment of a person's physical or mental conditions.' The Act initiated an approach to health and safety which was about problem solving within systems. This approach has been carried over into the *Management of Health and Safety at Work Regulations 1992* (Regulation 3). It is also a way of working made very overt in the *Control of Substances Hazardous to Health 1988 Regulations* (COSSH) and their subsequent amendment (1990). COSSH requires a proactive method of both assessing risks and assessing the previous strategies designed to minimise them. COSSH requires:

- Identification of hazards.
- Assessment of associated risk.
- Implementation of appropriate control strategies.
- Monitoring of effectiveness of control strategies.
- Re-assessment of risk.
- Review of information needs, and training needs of workers.

This cycle of prevention and assessment provides the model that should be applied to stress management in youth, community and play work, adapted to account for the more subtle hazards of stress, and become a regular feature of supervision. The problem would be relieved also if there was a common statement within youth, community and play Staff Handbooks, that the department recognises stress as an integral feature of work and not a problem residing within somehow inferior individuals.

Finally, it is to be hoped that dealing with occupational stress will become a recognised part of health and safety welfare in youth, community and play work, and to this end here are some general statements that could perhaps be worked on locally for inclusion in employment policies. Youth, community and play work practice will be significantly enhanced if stress is recognised as being serious and systemic in our work. It will be tackled best if it is appreciated that stress involves both the individual and their whole environment, and that stress is a health and safety hazard. If these points are taken on board, the control of stress by a simple, but holistic approach, should lead to fewer fizzling strands of valuable magnesium.

Model Statement on Stress

1. This organisation recognises occupational stress as a serious potential health and safety problem that must be monitored systematically and minimised. It is recognised that stress is not an individual illness that can be cured by counselling, but that it is a complex phenomena that can cause illness in individuals both psychological and physical. It is recognised also that various categories of staff may be subject to various forms of different stress risk; detached workers, community centre workers, youth workers, play workers, street workers, lesbian workers, gay workers, disabled workers, women workers and men workers may all face different stress factors depending on context. It will be the intention over time, through monitoring, to analyse common patterns and devise reduction strategies.

2. Stress is recognised as resulting from a variety of factors in the working environment that may include the following:
    *   lack of status and reward
    *   ambiguity and conflict in role
    *   unsocial working hours
    *   long hours
    *   conflicting work demands
    *   uncertainties in career development and expectation
    *   high levels of responsibility for people
    *   poor communication
    *   the lack of mechanisms for solving problems
    *   lack of appreciation
    *   isolation at work
    *   low levels of participation in decision making
    *   poor working relationships
    *   continual exposure to individuals and community groups with various and sometimes conflicting demands.

    It is further recognised that stress manifests itself as a result of some or all of these factors, at various levels of intensity, in different individuals, at different stages of their career or life.

3. It is therefore a requirement of regular monthly supervision, in the assessment of general matters relating to health and safety, that consideration will be given to factors likely to cause stress. The potential hazards involved shall be assessed and strategies for remedy will be planned and reviewed at subsequent meetings. Persistent contributory factors will be reported to the Health and Safety Officer and this organisation does not expect workers to be subject to factors which are consistently aggravating stress. Every effort will be made to ensure that users are informed of the appropriate standards of behaviour procedures and equal opportunities policies, and workers will not be expected to work within potentially violent, unnecessarily conflictual, or unresolved situations.

4. It is recognised that clear management expectations, realistic work plans, an ability to seek supervisory support, in service, training and the regular identification of problems are helpful devices in stress reduction and staff and the employing organisation have a responsibility to make them effective. Clear purpose in all of the varied duties and responsibilities of youth, community and play workers is essential, and this will be reviewed regularly through supervision. The identification of critical success and failure factors will be integral to stress monitoring through supervision.

5. It is the intention of this general statement to create an environment in which all staff feel able to:
    *   Identify contributory factors towards their experience of stress.
    *   Agree strategies of intervention to reduce it.
    *   Become informed of ways of reducing identified problems in future.
    *   Monitor and evaluate these strategies.
    *   Obtain management support for stress reduction within an overall concern for the health and safety and well being of staff.

Minibus safety

This has been the most regular standing item on CYWU's safety agenda for many years. In 1993, the Union passed a comprehensive policy which instructed members:

- Not to drive buses with crew seats, or without seatbelts.
- To always ensure rigorous testing of buses prior to journeys.
- To always drive longer journeys accompanied by qualified co-drivers.

After some appalling tragedies in the 1990s, minibus safety became a matter of considerable political and social debate and new policy making. The youth service and education generally have heightened their awareness on the issues. Transport managers have begun to work closely with youth service drivers. Youth workers have been undergoing new minibus driving tests, although tests without comprehensive training are not a great deal of help. Some authorities have ensured that all of their buses are fully equipped with belts and safety equipment.

While there have been many positive developments, the shrinking resource background has not necessarily improved the general safety picture and voluntary sector organisations especially, have not had new money to improve their vehicles. Indeed, most buses used within youth, community and play work are not part of managed fleets. This puts additional pressures on the drivers who are, in the main, full and part-time youth workers. This is the reason for providing what may seem, to veteran drivers, a very basic guide. There is no intention to duplicate the very expert advice promoted by the Royal Society for the Prevention of Accidents (ROSPA) or the Community Transport Association (CTA). This section should be read in conjunction with the advice of the transport experts and my aim is not at the experienced user, but the recently qualified full or part-time worker entering their first post in a voluntary sector organisation with its own dilapidated minibus which is not part of a fleet. No matter how frequently you will be called upon to drive a minibus, the full range of considerations mentioned here and the expert advice referred to should be taken into account. Youth, community and play workers are not drivers by profession; instead they drive as a small but significant part of their professional duties. In this sense they should rely on the expert support of transport professionals in ensuring that what they do and what they drive is completely safe and well understood. Youth workers are not mechanics or long distance lorry drivers. Under no circumstances whatsoever just jump into a bus and drive away. Use the following checklist prior to any trip, short or long, build time into your schedule to work through the checklist before any trip.

Model Pre-departure Checklist

Do not drive a mini bus anywhere unless:

- You have been fully instructed and tested in safe minibus driving.
- You have third party, professional confirmation in writing that the minibus is fully roadworthy and safe to drive. You should have evidence of regular care and maintenance of the bus you drive and all the necessary documents. In addition you should be able to undertake a routine vehicle inspection: tyres, battery, lights etc.
- You have passed the locally recognised test within the service. Please note that a *European Directive* requires new drivers to take a test before they can drive a minibus with more than eight passengers, other than one used purely for social or voluntary purposes. (Details of the types of licenses you require are available from Community Transport Association. Send a stamped addressed A4 envelope. See also further reading section below.)
- You are aware of all of the lines of reporting responsibilities for insurance, health and safety and accident reporting and the contact points for each.
- You are sure that the minibus you will be driving is completely safe and checked with all of its documentation up to date. If in doubt, refuse to drive and refer to your union for health and safety advice. You should have available to you a comprehensive physical checklist of all aspects of the vehicle. How do you check tyres, how do you check brakes?

- The minibus has forward facing passenger seats throughout and is fitted with three point diagonal seat belts throughout. Please note that all road safety experts and organisations advise that buses with sideways facing crew seats are only intended as utility vehicles designed for small scale ferrying around of people, for example, building sites. They are not intended for motorway and long distance driving. Do not use them. In addition, lap only seat belts are not recommended.
- You have on your person a list of the names and addresses of all those you are transporting during the trip and have left a similar list at work with another person. Such details should normally include parental consent forms etc.
- The minibus is appropriate for the user group. Do not wrestle wheelchairs into a vehicle with no proper lift or spacing. There should be one seat for every passenger.
- You have a route plan and have informed someone at base of this.
- You have been trained in accident and emergency procedures.
- All luggage is firmly secured preferably on a roof rack, if not in a trailer.
- There is ample space between the rear of the bus and the passengers.
- You have applied a risk assessment to the whole journey from preparation to conclusion. The structural model of the risk assessment is as outlined in the section on stress above (see page 145–146), the following ingredients should be considered:
  - identify hazards
  - decide who might be harmed and how
  - evaluate degree of risk and adequacy of existing precautions
  - identify further action to control the risk
  - record findings
  - review assessment
  - report risks
  (Note the Community Transport Association can provide guidance on risk assessment.)
- Driving times and hours are reasonable and there is a qualified co-driver for journeys totalling six hours or more.
- You have checked that the minibus complies with the statutory requirement to have an approved fire extinguisher and a first aid kit on board at all times.
- Drivers taking groups in a minibus abroad will also need to ensure that they are fully trained in all of the regulations relating to travel abroad.

This checklist is minimal and basic. In general, a driver should ensure that a minibus and the trip being undertaken are subjected to a full risk assessment. What will be potential loopholes, hazards, problems? Drivers should also be aware that they have rights under health and safety regulations to refuse to drive unless they are fully confident that all health and safety guidelines are met.

Some of the key contents of the checklist are further elaborated below and drivers will need to be aware of local practice.

Seatbelts

A major problem in minibuses is that seatbelts are only usually provided on the driver's and one passenger seat. To provide seatbelts to existing front facing mini bus seats is a costly business. Also, where seat belts are added to some buses it is not possible to add them to safe anchorage points, but only to link them to the seat frame itself. This is not the safest option. Another problem is that often, lap only seat belts are fitted, rather than the familiar car type seat belts which anchor at three points and cross the lap and shoulder. An antiquated aspect of legislation permits three children under 14 to sit on each double seat.

This risky background of manufacturers' practice and legislation at best means that youth and community and play workers will have to adopt a strategic approach to their employing organisations on improving minibus safety. However, safety can never cost too much and unless drivers take a firmer stance on refusing to drive unsafe vehicles they will continue to jeopardise the lives of user groups. Immediate action should be taken to ensure that no youth, community or play worker is expected to drive a minibus unless:

- Diagonal seatbelts are anchored to the frame of the vehicle with proper anchorage points, rather than to the seats.
- Any modifications to fit diagonal seat belts should fully comply with the *Construction and Use Regulations*.
- One seat with a three-point diagonal seatbelt is available for every passenger.
- Any lap belted seat in the front is left vacant.

The vehicle

In addition to the routine safety checks and roadworthiness criteria, of which you should have written evidence from the log book and service report, a driver should bear in mind how inappropriate for carrying passengers is the design of many minibuses. This is because often they are based on commercial van frames designed for carrying loads, rather than people and their luggage. One feature of this is the closeness of the back seats to the rear doors. Drivers should ensure that there is an adequate space between rear doors and the rear-most passengers, even if this means leaving some rear seats empty. This is known as a crush area and would act as a buffer if there was an intrusion in an accident from the rear. You could consider using the rear seats as luggage carriers, or removing the rear seats completely and using the space for luggage.

On youth and community trips you will usually have luggage. Ensure that this does not obstruct passengers and that it is firmly secured. Unsecured items of luggage in a crash or emergency braking situation become lethal flying weapons. Most road traffic experts recommend separate luggage compartments in the form of a roof rack, luggage bins, or a trailer.

Seats in the minibus should all face forward. There should be ample room for entry and exit, especially bearing emergencies in mind. Gangways to all doors should be clear and not obstructed by luggage or passengers. If it takes you five minutes to haul a wheelchair on to a vehicle without a lift, how long will it take you to haul it off in a crash?

ROSPA is advocating that future safeguards on minibuses should include automatic cut off devices for fuel tanks and electrical circuits and anti burst fuel tanks. It is important to enquire about manufacturers' policies in relation to these when purchasing a new bus.

Responsible enough to drive?

Youth, community and play workers are educators, not chauffeurs or mechanics. Driving is a means to an educational end, and very often the discussion with the young people or adults in the mini bus is an integral part of the group building and educational experience. Very often the driver's real work begins when in preparation for the journey or, paradoxically, when it has ended. Youth, community and play workers are always on duty on a journey, a duty which is circumscribed legally. As the Children's Legal Centre's document *Working with Young People: legal responsibility and liability* indicates 'Anyone employed to work with children or young people is under a legal duty of care'. This duty has been defined in case law as acting as a careful parent would. A working definition of this has been 'The body, organisation, authority, or employer should take such precautions for the safety of the children in their care as would any reasonable caring parent.' If you do not do this, and as a result of your negligence an injury, accident, or loss takes place, you and your employer could be taken to court in civil law. So, it is essential not only to be fully competent and proficient to drive, but also to be fully aware of the indemnity and liability insurance cover applying to your activities.

A driver should be trained and tested to drive. Each trip should be properly assessed in terms of the likely total workload associated with it. The chances are that the worker will be up early to panic about attendances, equipment packed, safety of the bus, payments and so on. They will then deal with the high spirits of the passengers and the worries of parents. After that they will have a long drive and on arrival at the destination may well be up until 4.00 am on the social education programme! As an integral part of the risk assessment, it is therefore vital that the total working time in relation to the journey and the sojourn is taken into account and also the likely times when driving will occur. Obviously there will be times during a day when a driver is less alert for driving. All accident research demonstrates that a driver who has been awake for more than seven hours and then drives for more than two hours is in far greater risk of crashing. Similarly, if drivers drive during 'normal sleep times' they increase their risk of accident. If a journey itself will take more than six hours, a second driver should be provided. ROSPA itself recommends that non-professional drivers should not be allowed to drive for more than a total of six hours, even with regular breaks. They say that drivers should have a rest and refreshment break at least every two hours.

If your task is to drive with a co-driver then you will need to concentrate on this. Passengers with special needs, or requiring special attention and supervision should be provided with escorts. Make sure you are appropriately staffed and that problems unrelated to the task of driving are capable of being solved by other colleagues.

Lone working and safe working environments

All working environments in which youth, community and play workers are expected to operate should be subject to risk assessment. There are particular problems facing women workers, disabled workers, lesbian and gay project workers, and black workers. The incidence of violence and harassment against staff is increasing all the time and regrettably CYWU's hospitalisation benefits have been used more than they should. As far as subjective evidence can determine, this is not as a result of malfunctioning relationships with youth and community service clients, but as a result of the general dangers evident in some neighbourhoods.

It is my view that all youth, community and play workers should be provided with a mobile phone and some form of basic protective device and alarm. All workplaces should have an accessible telephone line and alarms in buildings should be connected to local police stations. Procedures for late night call out in emergency should also be clear. Essential car user allowances should be a matter of course to workers operating in rural areas and inner city areas. The employer has a contractual responsibility to care for the workers' health and safety and those aspects of health and safety legislation which impact on this area of work are considered above along with the legal rights that can be invoked if a member of staff feels in jeopardy. If you are worried: don't do it, just say no.

Each employing organisation should negotiate with its staff and place in the Staff Handbook a set of clear expectations, and guidance on risk assessment. This should incorporate clear details of the Authorised Establishment for each post and the anticipated minimum staff levels for each organised activity. In attending to this detail the publication by the Sufficiency Working Group, *Planning for a Sufficient Youth Service,* may be helpful. This draws also on previous studies of actual staffing requirements for each youth work activity, in particular the analysis of the National Advisory Council for the Youth Service, in its publication *Resourcing the Youth Service* which can still be of great value when planning staffing allocations. With financial pressures on units, professional staff have been forced to become supervisors of activities and policemen and women rather than educators. A fresh look at this whole area is required and should be an integral part of management and staff discussions locally. To prescribe at this stage a hard and fast national formula would be pointless. Employers should be encouraged to plan sufficient allocation of resources and to ensure that staff are working in environments where they can educate without fear of harm to themselves or their clients.

Further reading and reference

Given the scope of Health and Safety legislation, and the variety of issues in youth, community and play work, it is worth having a comprehensive guide available. In addition to subscribing to Labour Research Publications and those of the Health and Safety Executive, consider purchasing copies of:

More, W. and Nicholls, D. (1997). *Managing Violence and Aggression: A Model for Youth and Community Centres of Legal Compliance Safe Working Practices and Good Personal Safety Habits for Staff.* Pepar Publications.

Nicholls, D. (1997). *Health and Safety in Youth and Community Work: A Pocket Guide.* Russell House Publishing.

Nicholls, D. (1997). *Health and Safety in Youth and Community Work: A Manual.* Russell House Publishing.

Pearson, P. (2001). *Keeping Well at Work.* Trade Union Congress.

Smith, I. et al. (1989). *Health and Safety, The New Legal Framework.* Butterworths.

See also More, W. (1993). *Ensuring Staff Safety.* Pepar Publications.

Stress

Unfortunately some of the best resources I have come across are phenomenally expensive, or available only in North America, or to the members of various trade unions. There is nothing that I am aware of that has been written in Britain of any use in remedying the problem specifically for youth, community and play workers, but one article from overseas well worth getting through the local article lending scheme is by Bryan, W.L. (1980), *Burn Out in the Public Interest Community*, The Northern Rockies Action Group Inc. This looks at the effects of stress on community workers in Canadian Community Projects. *Stress in the Public Sector, Police, Social Workers and Teachers*, March 1988, by the Health Education Authority is still useful. So too are Booker, O. (1999), *Averting Aggression*, Russell House Publishing, and Thompson, N. et al. (1999), *Stress Matters: A Personal Guide*.

A study of a local authority Youth Service by a University department of Psychology described the part-time staff as displaying symptoms identical to 'psychotic outpatients' at the height of some of their difficulties at work. A *Sunday Times* survey showed youth workers to be in the top 5 of stressful occupations along with nurses, doctors, ambulence drivers and policemen. Local Authority Occupational Health Departments have frequently found unacceptable levels of stress with over 50% absentee rates due to stress at any one time. The problems remain acute in our sector and a priority to be addressed.

Many of the trade union guides to stress, concentrate on basic alterations to the system, particularly those in non educational areas; few advocate as here a more positive role for supervision. Some unions have established stress helplines for despairing remedies, but I have always felt that this encourages the individual pathology approach. Countless management orientated works focus on coping, curing and counselling the victims of stress, so that behaviour is modified rather than the system. This book asks for a more balanced approach in youth, community and play work, which has as its starting point the use of self and others, and which recognises the dialectical interaction between an individual and their experiences and contexts and relationships. In this sense some of the more sympathetic works on supervision need to be considered again. A good starting point is the still relevant document produced by the National Youth Bureau, Feek, W. (1982), *Who Takes The Strain? The Choices for Staff Support*.

Minibuses

The Community Transport Association produces an excellent and comprehensive publications list including: *Your Minibus: is it legal?*, *Starting Up, Identifying Hazards, Minibus Safety, Charter, Driver Assessment and Training Pack, Code of Practice* etc.

ROSPA provide a range of information sheets including:
Minibus Fact Sheet
Seatbelts
Inspection
Safety
Seatbelts for Minibuses and Coaches.

Community Action Driver Information Pack (1990). (Free from Nottingham Community Action.)

Youth Clubs and the Law: Applying for a Minibus Permit (1989). In *Youth Clubs*, No. 55: p45.

Dring, A. *An Introduction to Basic Minibus Driving and Essential Minibus Driving.* Royal Society for the Prevention of Accidents (ROSPA).

Minibus Safety. Community and Youth Workers' Union.

Important News for Drivers of Minibuses (1994). Free fact sheet. Department of Transport, DVLA.

Towing Trailers (1994). Fact Sheet. Department of Transport, DVLA.

Minimum Test Vehicles (1994). Fact Sheet. Department of Transport, DVLA.

Safety on School Journeys. Free Leaflet. National Union of Teachers.

Part 8

Equal Opportunities

Statements and policies on action for equality

Given the value base of youth, and community and play work and their stated national aims, the sector should pioneer and exemplify the best possible practice, regardless of the limitations of the law and especially where legislation is silent concerning, for example, lesbian and gay workers. In many ways the youth, community and play sector has been ahead of others. The *Guidelines to Endorsement of Initial Training* and *RAMPs*, themselves the creation of the field through peer discussion and formulation, stipulate that institutions must demonstrate that recruitment and selection, access and course content will display a strong commitment to equal opportunities. The self centred learning and subject matter of most of the courses emphasises a range of issues pertinent to equal opportunities. Recruitment and selection to post, is undertaken in most employing organisations with relatively stringent equal opportunities guidelines. Work is performed within usually detailed equal opportunities policies. As the main union in the field, CYWU itself has an elaborate equal opportunities policy and mode of operation, so that the value base of its work has ensured that progressive positive action has occurred in many places throughout the service. At least 50 per cent of qualification students are women, and all previous research has shown that a relatively high percentage of students and workers in the field are black and Asian, compared with other sectors of education. The broadening of access to qualification and now the development of *RAMPs* have all strengthened the field. As part of the political education component of the work many staff on JNC contracts are themselves involved in the attainment of opportunities for young people and communities. However, things are by no means perfect.

Assuming that many aspects of the political and professional work on equal opportunities are familiar, and that the many sources of support and information are widely known, or accessible, this section concentrates briefly on some legal and technical questions that should, perhaps, enter the discussion more frequently.

An initial note, however, on access to qualification. Youth, community and play work has been exemplary in its determination to offer a range of routes to qualification while maintaining high, peer assessed standards. There are a variety of different routes to qualification whether full-time college courses, apprenticeship schemes, distance learning, part-time courses, accreditation schemes, or the individual recognition route. The *JNC Report* allows for the consideration of individuals' qualification and experience, which may not be through one of the established routes. Personal experience and qualification are assessed against the criteria set out in the *JNC Report*. This has proved particularly useful in validating the cases of overseas nationals doing excellent voluntary work with their communities in Britain when they have often got equivalent qualifications from their country of origin. Details of this can be obtained from the National Youth Agency, Education and Training Standards Committee.

Some have said that the existence of a qualified profession through JNC and pay and conditions linked to this is in some way against equal opportunities. This sets access above standards in a false way and denies the reality that the existence of the JNC has significantly assisted black and women workers in their entry into the profession. It also fails to appreciate the principles of equal opportunities legislation. The law recognises that someone with a higher qualification deserves more than someone doing the same job with a lesser qualification.

In a case called *Angestelitenbetriebsrat der Wiener Gebietskrankenkasse*, the European Court of Justice rules that psychotherapists with a degree in psychology, most of whom are women, did not do the 'same work' within the meaning of Article 119 (now Article 141) of the Treaty of Rome, as higher paid and predominantly male doctors employed as psychotherapists. Although the two groups of employees performed seemingly identical tasks, they had each received different professional training and, because of the different scope of the qualifications resulting from that training, were called on to perform different tasks.

In another similar case the House of Lords decided in the case of *Strathclyde Regional Council v Wallace and ors* that where the 'material factor' which the employer seeks to rely on is not caused by direct or indirect sex discrimination, then the defence can succeed. This is of course provided that the employer can identify the factors which they allege cause a difference in pay, for example the requirement for a different qualification.

JNC is at root one of the most Equal Opportunities based national collective bargaining agreements and its joint requires on courses for open access and equality of opportunity consideration in recruitment and selection, combine harmoniously with standards.

JNC Advisory Statement on Equal Opportunities in Employment booklet

The Employers' Side and the Staff Side of the JNC are joint signatories to a Advisory Statement on Equal Opportunities in Employment. This covers the following broad areas, see Appendix 3 for the detailed contents:

- Adoption and implementation of an equal opportunities policy.
- Positive measures.
- Recruitment and selection.
- Training.
- Harassment.
- Analysis monitoring and review.
- Outside financial help.
- Assistance for employees with disabilities.
- Legislation and codes of practice.
- Publications and useful organisations.

This statement, together with the local employers' policies on these matters should be readily available throughout the service. The Employers' Side and the Staff Side are both able to give their joint or separate advice on matters covered by it. The document has many limitations as far as youth, community and play work practice is concerned and is best treated as a foundation, a set of minimum recommendations and headings to some of the areas that should be incorporated into local practice. All organisations employing youth, community and play workers should have a comprehensive policy on action for equality.

It is absolutely vital that a local equal opportunities policy explicitly rejects discriminatory practice on any grounds, as they may apply to lesbians and gay men and people with disabilities, and that the current deficiencies in the law are effectively compensated for in local procedure and commitment. There are also hidden prejudices concerning age within youth, community and play work that must be challenged at all stages within a procedure and policy.

Four overlooked elements

In reviewing the nature and application of local equal opportunities policies, it is important to consider four elements often overlooked in planning and budgeting. These are:
1. Career breaks and extended leave.
2. Job sharing.
3. Workers with disabilities.
4. Recruitment and selection
   - testing
   - complaining
   - observing.

1. Career breaks and extended leave

In addition to the customary leave entitlements outlined in the Model Contract and Statement of Particulars in Part 2, it is important that any employment system which embraces equal opportunities, should recognise the particular characteristics of women's employment and the social and cultural needs of those staff with family and dependants in other countries. It should also really be integral to any strategies of staff development that the need for paid sabbaticals, temporary secondments and the like is fully recognised, alongside opportunities for in service training. Staff who leave work to bring up children, visit relatives in other countries or to care for dependent relatives or partners should be able to maintain contact with their employer and return to work with status, pay and prospects fully intact. A fully developed action for equality scheme will outline criteria for:
- Retainer scheme for those on career breaks.
- Length of service qualifying for a retainer.
- Acceptable reasons for requesting career break.
- Guidelines for application and selection for career breaks.
- Terms and conditions while on career break.
- Terms of reference for return to work.
- Recognition that career breaks count as continuous service.
- Complaints and appeals structure within the system.

  In recognition of those colleagues who will have to journey to other countries for education or family reasons, or reasons directly related to their professional development within youth, community and play work, extended leave options are essential within comprehensive equal opportunities rights. Consideration would have to be given to outlining details for:
- Reasons for extended leave.
- Application and selection procedures.
- Complaints and appeals mechanisms.
- Ability to take all of one year's leave at one time.
- Ability to extend leave year by agreement according to agreed criteria.
- Ability to carry leave over from one stipulated year to the next.
- Ability to take leave in certain circumstances at less than the normal required notice.
- Ability to take parts of the following year's leave in the current leave year.

2. Job sharing

Job sharing is where two or more people share the hours of one full-time post and receive a wage or salary and other benefits pro rata to the hours each works. This is different of course from part-time working. The purpose of job sharing is to open up employment opportunities. It has many advantages to both the employer and staff. It should be an opportunity advertised as available for new posts, and should also be an opportunity available to transform existing posts. Job share applicants should be accorded equal treatment at interview.

If a candidate on being offered the post decides that they would prefer to job share it, then the following could be considered:

A) Try to recruit a job share partner from remaining suitable candidates. Approach them in order of merit.

B) If this is not possible the successful applicant should be offered a contract either 1) for the post on a *temporary job share* basis or 2) for the post on a *temporary full-time contract* with a positive commitment by the employer to seek a job sharer.

If one of, say, two job sharers leaves, the first opportunity to take up the vacant hours should be offered to the remaining job share partner. If this is not accepted, the vacancy for a job share partner should be advertised using the established system. If there are no applications, then the remaining sharer could be redeployed provided that the once job-shared post can be filled by a full-timer. If no suitable alternative position is available the remaining job sharer should be considered supernumerary until a suitable alternative is found, using where appropriate the redeployment policy.

3. Workers with disabilities and the Disability Discrimination Act 1995

A good action for equality policy within an employing organisation will contain positive statements about the employment of people with disabilities and will operate a 'guarantee interview scheme' which grants interviews to registered disabled people and those who declare themselves as disabled who meet the essential criteria for the job. It should also specifically agree to include them whether or not they meet the desired criteria. Naturally job advertisements should all carry the approved logo 'Positive About Disabled People'. The policy will also be explicitly party to the 'Sheltered Placement Scheme' which provides funds from the Employment Service to meet part of the costs of employing disabled people unable to undertake the full range of duties normally required for a job. Youth, community and play service departments should actively encourage the employment of people with disabilities.

The Disabled Persons (Employment) Acts 1944 and 1958 required that three percent of employees be registered disabled. Most employers come far below this. Overall only 0.9 percent of the entire British workforce in employment are disabled and disabled workers capable of working are three times more likely to be unemployed than able bodied workers. The figure is not yet known for the youth, community and play service, but on the basis of CYWU data, is considerably less than this generally meagre percentage. For those workers now working in youth, community and play organisations constituted as limited companies, it is noteworthy that one of the requirements of the *Companies Act 1985* is that Directors' Annual Reports must contain a statement describing the policies they applied to the recruitment and career development of disabled people. This applies to companies with over 250 employees, but is a useful device for all organisations to consider, whatever their size.

There are 6.25 million disabled workers in Britain. It is vital therefore that positive measures are taken in advertising, interviewing techniques, policy statements and involvement in the service to redress this imbalance. Codes of practice on the employment of people with disabilities have proliferated since 1948, but there is consistent refusal to legislate positively for disabled people. The Employment Service publishes a comprehensive code which has no legal force but the Royal Association for Disability arid Rehabilitation (RADAR), the Disability Alliance, and the Trade Union Disability Alliance have more extensive and meaningful models and advisory notes, as do the TUC, the GFTU and the National League of the Blind and Disabled, a trade union which is now part of the Iron and Steel Trades Confederation.

Though the attitudinal barriers to the involvement of disabled youth, community and play workers in the service should be minimal, the physical barriers are still immense. Some youth, community and play work college courses are completely inaccessible to students in wheelchairs or with visual impairments. With the Albemarle basis of so many youth and community premises, and their appalling state of disrepair, working environments are less than congenial. Even assistance available through the Employment Service is infrequently accessed and the voluntary sector, particularly in community centres, has not taken advantage of the grants that do exist. Grants to employees and employers have been rationalised into a scheme known as 'Accesses to Work'. Applicants under this scheme can be awarded up to £21,000 over five years and financial support can cover:

- Alterations to premises or a working environment so that an employee with a disability can work there.
- A communicator for people who are deaf or have a hearing impairment.
- A part-time reader or assistance at work for someone who is blind.
- A support worker if someone needs practical help either at work or getting to work.
- Equipment (or adaptions to existing equipment) to suit individual needs.
- Adaptations to a car, or taxi fares or other transport costs if someone cannot use public transport.

This consolidated scheme is run by the Placing, Assessment and Counselling Teams (PACTs) based in local job centres. Perhaps it is time also that local youth services became aware of the work of colleagues within the PACTs in order to make young people and community groups themselves more aware. Local youth, community and play services are ideally placed to establish effective networks with those non profit and other agencies specifically designed to support various disability groupings and to give general assistance to the campaign for improved legislation and rights.

In 1995 the *Disability Discrimination Act* (DDA) came into force; this was the first time that legislation outlawed discrimination on the grounds of disability. However the trade unions are still campaigning to improve the Act particularly as it still allows discrimination for so called 'justifiable reasons' and because the Act unfortunately only covers workplaces with more than 15 employees and only covers direct discrimination. The DDA was strengthened in April 2000 by the formation of the Disability Rights Commission (DRC). The DRC can conduct formal investigations and enforce action to address any unlawful discrimination and can support individuals in cases to Employment Tribunals in a similar way to the Equal Opportunities Commission and the Commission for Racial Equality. Protection under the DDA starts from the first day of employment.

To qualify for rights under the Act a person's disability has to meet all of the specified requirements; their disability must be 'a physical or mental impairment which has substantial and long term adverse effect on a person's ability to carry out normal day to day activities'. All of these words are still subject to refinement and agreement in the courts as to how they apply in individual circumstances but some patterns of description have been established in case law.

Under the DDA employers have a legal obligation to make reasonable adjustments in order to avoid putting their disabled staff at a substantial disadvantage. The Employers' Forum on Disability (EFD) promotes good practice on the employment of disabled people and has useful action plans and checklists.

4. Recruitment and selection

Testing

Testing is frequently a value laden and subjective process. Where general aptitude testing, or psychometric testing is used for youth, community and play work, it is better to beware and to negotiate it away. Any form of testing within a recruitment system should relate to the essential and desirable requirements of the job description and to the main duties of the post in question. It helps for the 'examiners' to know the desired outcome in advance. There should be joint agreement locally on the use of testing, as it can be discriminatory. The Equal Opportunities Commission have a particularly good booklet on this matter which can be used to consider general problems, *Avoiding sex bias in selection—testing guidance for employees.*

Complaining

All recruitment and selection systems and steps should be subject to monitoring and all should make it clear that a complaints procedure exists at all stages within them. Applicants can complain about any aspect of the procedure knowing that the complaint will be dealt with by a senior officer. In order to remedy and root out the cause of complaints, it should be agreed that any complaint, and the response to it, should be recorded at the LJNC meetings. Also, the presence of a staff side observer at all stages of the process, particularly in a situation of reorganisation, is desirable and a way of avoiding problems. The documentation circulated to candidates should outline the following:

- The employer's commitment to action for equality should include an invitation to the candidate to complain about any aspect of the recruitment and selection process they have been involved in with the potential employer.
- Any complaints should be directed to the most senior officer appropriate, (chair of management committee or director of personnel).
- A written acknowledgement should be sent together with a commitment to investigate the complaint within a two week period and informing the complainant of the outcome of the investigation.
- A thorough investigation should take place and the complainant will be invited to make further contact as appropriate with the designated investigating officer.

Observing

It is highly desirable that observers from both sides of the LJNC are present at all stages of the interview process. Their function should not be to participate in the decision making but effectively to moderate the proceedings. They should assess the practice against the underlying policy and procedure agreed by the employer. Does what happens match up with what should happen?

The nature of illegal discrimination

There are two types of discrimination described in the law: 'direct' and 'indirect' discrimination. It is the policy of progressive movements and trade unions to get as many categories of worker included in these descriptions as relevant. Currently it is unlawful to discriminate on grounds of sex, marriage, or race including colour, nationality and ethnic or national origin. Direct discrimination means that it is illegal to treat a person less favourably on any of these grounds than others would be in the same or similar circumstances.

Indirect discrimination means that it is unlawful to apply a requirement or condition which, although applied equally to men, women or racial groups, is such that a considerably smaller proportion of one of these groups can comply with it, or that negatively and disproportionately affects one of the groups. Any employment action then, whether appointing, advertising, making redundant etc. could have an indirectly discriminatory implication. Indirect discrimination is no less severe in legal terms.

Further reading and reference

See Appendices for Select Bibliography and details of Addresses.

This section in itself could be a book. Various catalogues of published resources on equal opportunities are in fact of book length. The field is enormous. Most youth, community and play workers will already have access to a variety of materials, so here is a highly concentrated choice:

Equal Opportunities: a Trade Union Response. A clear concise paper available from the General Federation of Trade Unions, Educational Trust.

Equal Opportunities Commission, publishes a range of publications, particularly *Negotiating for Equality* and a *Model Equal Opportunity Policy*.
RADAR Directory for Disabled People.
Ramdin, R. *The Making of the Black Working Class in Britain*.
Vogel, L. *Marxism and the Oppression of Women*.

And materials from:
- British Council of Disabled People (BOCDP)
- Centre for Accessible Environments (CAE)
- Employers' Forum on Disability (EFD)
- National Aids Helpline
- Royal Association for Disability and Rehabilitation (RADAR)
- Royal National Institute for Deaf People (RNID)
- Royal National Institute for the Blind (RNIB)
- Trade Union Congress
- Trade Union Disability Alliance (TUDA)

Part 9

Financial Problems

How to avoid them

Let me start with a piece of advice for which all youth, community and play workers in future generations will be indebted to me.

The golden rules

Record immediately in the books available for that purpose, every item of income and expenditure for which you are responsible:

- Follow all employers financial regulations to the letter.
- Record in writing to your line manager, any suspicion, problem or concern that you have about the operation of the finances in the centre, or project where you work.
- Never ever under any circumstances mix personal and work expenditure, even if you repay immediately, or if your failure to make a temporary loan to the organisation is a matter of life and death.
- Never sign a document that makes you in any way legally responsible for a financial transaction at work unless you have your employer's written approval for this beforehand and are fully indemnified for this action by those benefiting from it.

There you are, and that came free! It sounds of course extremely common sensical, but in the frantic and varied working day of a youth worker, community worker or play worker with so many competing demands, working at such a variety of different levels and with so much emotional stress often, it is not that simple.

Youth workers and community workers have always had responsibilities for finance and administration built into their conditions of service and indeed their grading structures. Many are now responsible for huge budgets amounting, in an increasing number of instances, to a third of a million pounds. As workers become autonomous cost centre managers, and central budgets are devolved to Community Education Councils and units, staff are pressed to take on more and more complicated financial responsibilities. There has been a contradiction in devolving to the community. Volunteers for treasurerships have not been exactly queuing up, and the burden falls to the paid staff. Unit resource planning, area fund raising from Europe and Government, allocation of authority resources, these are all common and complex responsibilities performed by workers. In fact youth and community workers are quite exceptional at their level of salary within education for the extent of their legal and financial responsibilities. Many neighbourhoods benefit by millions of pounds over time because of the involvement of local community workers in attracting resources. Within projects workers on JNC contracts must know basic accountancy and auditing, how to apply for substantial European and British grant aid, deal with day to day cash management, VAT, PAYE, Corporation Tax and rating regulations, and a host of finance related matters.

Despite this high level of responsibility there is minimal preparation on the qualification courses for this area of work and there is very little in service training and expert back up. As a consequence, staff can be caught painfully between the unclear and possibly dubious practices of a local treasurer, the different expectations of the local authority in relation to the financial management of the centre, the different expectations still of the centre's accountant, who will be full of the strictures of the Institute of Chartered Accountants, and the menacing and often unclear pronouncements of the local authority's audit department. They have a habit of marching in at the strangest of times just when one of those little plastic bank bags full of Mars bar money has gone missing.

There are a number of basic things which can be introduced to help all concerned. Roles and responsibilities should be crystal clear, mutually agreed and recorded in writing. Training and support from experts should be ever present and available. Staff should not be expected to take on positions of liability without full indemnity protection and the awareness of their employer. Lay treasurers, however hard to come by, should manage a project's accounts. Accountants should monitor and check them and help prepare the annual report. The role of youth, community and play workers should be to advise and professionally review all of these functions. Finances should be reviewed at least monthly. There should be a designated local authority officer available to support staff and a similar voluntary sector contact.

The role given to workers in the scheme below, makes them responsible for ensuring that a financial duty is carried out, but it does not oblige them to undertake the task themselves. Their role is to advise and to ensure that structures are present, not to take on the roles in the first instance and not to be held legally accountable for the funds. Where this is inevitable or desirable, the full boundaries must be clarified in writing. The elected treasurer of the project is made legally responsible for the actual accounts. It is implied by the scheme that professionally the worker is present not to operate the financial routine in detail, but to ensure that those constitutionally and legally responsible for it are enabled to undertake it. This is part of community development. The reality of much of the enforced financial responsibility which workers have had to bear is that diminished budgets have been devolved to the community without the requisite training for community activists to manage it. As a result the responsibility is foisted on the worker. Clear lines must be drawn for the effective operation of a system. In taking on financial responsibilities the staff concerned must be supported, inducted and trained in what they do, how financial systems operate and where funds can be obtained and how a project's financial profile can be enhanced. The model scheme offers a macro view of financial management that concentrates on responsibilities rather than the fluid and vast area of rules and regulations pertaining to different aspects of financial management. These areas are effectively covered by many of the resources mentioned at the end.

Model Financial Scheme

Introduction

1. This Scheme recognises that the prime function of all youth, community and play work staff is the informal education of users. In carrying out that prime function it is recognised that staff will undertake a combination of face to face work duties, plant and personnel management, promotion of service delivery, training, supervision, and finance and administration. It is therefore the intention of this Scheme to introduce financial measures and lines of accountability which are straightforward and clear in order that the prime function of each post may be executed.

2. An officer within the youth, community and play service (hereinafter referred to as the Officer) has been designated to be the main point of contact for any queries concerning the operation of this Scheme or matters which arise not covered here. It is also to the Officer that any youth, community or play worker will immediately report should they become aware of any financial management contrary to this scheme.

3. Further it is recognised that from time to time youth, community and play staff may be seconded to projects within the voluntary sector which may have their own accounting procedures. It is not expected that staff seconded by the Authority will be involved in the financial management of voluntary sector centres unless otherwise authorised through supervision. Staff shall in these circumstances primarily act as advisers. The Authority shall provide annual training in Government and charitable fund raising opportunities and regulations.

4. It is assumed that for the purposes of this Scheme that the officer accountable for the management of a centre or project's finances is the elected treasurer of the organisation, hereinafter called the Treasurer. The management board of the centre is hereinafter referred to as the Committee. Where it is agreed with the Authority that an officer takes responsibility for a project or centre's accounts, full training and support will be available from the Authority, and the situation will be reviewed as requested through regular supervisory meetings.

5. Under no circumstances will an officer of the Authority or any worker enter into any agreement for equipment, services, goods, hire purchase, lease, mortgage, or like agreements or act as signatory thereto.

6. Under no circumstances will an officer of the Authority or any worker enter into any agreement that makes them potentially liable for loss or damage or bankruptcy unless the express permission, supported by the line manager, of the Head of Department has been obtained. In such circumstances, the Authority shall ensure that full indemnity cover is arranged to protect the officer or worker and the Authority.

7. Only in circumstances agreed jointly by the Authority and the Committee shall a worker or other officer be expected to be signatory to any account.

Bank accounts

1. Current and deposit accounts in the name of the Committee shall be opened and maintained at a bank of their choice. No other bank accounts in respect of any activities associated with the centre or its sub-groups shall be opened without the prior approval of the Committee. The Authority shall provide where requested details of the best use of investments, but shall not be liable for the losses of the Committee.

2. All monies received on behalf of the Authority or the Committee shall be paid in for credit to the Committee's current bank account not less frequently than twice a week where the average daily income from all sources exceeds £50 and, otherwise, once a week but so that the total of such monies remaining on the premises overnight shall not exceed £150 or such other limits as the chair of the Committee may from time to time authorise in writing. A safe shall be used at all times by the Committee.

3. All payments on behalf of the Committee, other than those made from a petty cash account of an approved amount authorised by the Committee, shall be made by a cheque drawn on the current account. No income shall be used for immediate cash payment. All income shall be recorded and banked.

4. All cheques drawn on the current bank account and all documents authorising transfers between the deposit and current bank accounts shall bear the signatures of two approved and responsible officers.

Annual accounts

The Treasurer shall present to each annual meeting of the Committee:
- An account of receipts collected and payments made during the preceding financial year.
- A balance sheet as at the preceding 31st March.
- A statement of the results of 'trading' activities.
- A copy of the auditor's report on those accounts.

Current accounts

The Treasurer shall present to each meeting of the Committee a summary of the receipts and payments from 1st April to a convenient date immediately before the meeting, supported by bank statements, the receipt and payment cash book and the petty cash account book. The Committee shall receive the accounts and records and shall make such enquiries into these accounts as they deem necessary. The fact of presentation and a brief summary of the accounts together with a note of sums due to and from the Committee shall be recorded in the minutes of that meeting. The Youth, Community and Play Worker may be called upon to advise on financial matters and management as appropriate.

Form of accounts

The accounts, books and records referred to in the foregoing clause, shall be based upon the forms set out in Appendix (A) attached to this scheme. *(An appendix should be provided locally as appropriate.)*

Financial duties of officers

1. The youth, community and play worker

The Youth, Community and Play Worker (the Worker) shall operate financial systems as agreed by the Authority and Committee and recorded in supervision meetings. Support and training in this role shall be given and an officer designated within the department (the Officer) to whom routine queries may be addressed. In general the Worker with senior responsibility within a centre will:

a) Ensure the operation of safe and efficient arrangements for the custody and control of property and monies belonging to the Authority and the Committee and other such bodies that may support the centre, or other such monies as may be generated by the centre's activities.

b) Ensure that the Committee establishes procedures and responsibilities for collecting and recording all monies due to the Authority and the centre.

c) Ensure that the Committee makes satisfactory arrangements to bank all monies collected in accordance with this Scheme.

d) Ensure that checking and certification of each invoice takes place before presentation to the Treasurer for payment. Further ensure that the Committee has suitable arrangements for verifying receipt of the goods or performance of the service, and ensure that the goods or services agree with the order.

e) Ensure the operation of a petty cash imprest account of amounts determined by the Committee and ensure that the cash balance is held in the safe at all times.

f) Ensure that the Committee has made someone responsible for the safe keys at all times and make secure arrangements for their custody in their absence.

g) Ensure that the Committee maintains all records necessary to control the income received by and properly belonging to the Authority and the centre including inventories of equipment, vehicle journey records and such other records as may be required by the Authority and the Committee.

h) Perform such other financial duties as may from time to time be assigned to them by the Committee within the conditions of appointment determined by the Authority.

2. The treasurer

The Treasurer shall undertake such duties as the Committee may from time to time require and shall be recognised as the main elected officer responsible for the accounting, audit and other legal requirements of the centre finances. In the event of the duties below not being carried out for a period of one calendar month, it shall be the duty of the Committee to make such other arrangements as are appropriate to perform the duties of the Treasurer. The duties shall include:

a) Operating safe and efficient arrangements for custody and control of property and monies belonging to the Authority and the centre.

b) Verifying that all income due to the Authority and the centre has been brought to account and banked.

c) Paying all monies due to creditors by cheque, standing order or direct debit on production of adequately documented, certified invoices.

d) Preparation and presentation of statements of account to each meeting of the Committee.

e) Presentation of accounts and all supporting documents and information to the auditor for examination.

f) Publication of clear charts of financial functions and responsibilities.

Expenditure and other items

All payments made on behalf of the centre, other than minor items met from the petty cash account, shall be subject to:

1. The issue of an order for the goods or services.
2. Certification after verification of:
    a) receipt of goods or performance of service
    b) compliance with order
    c) accuracy of arithmetic, extensions and totals
3. Verification by the Treasurer that the foregoing checks have been made and that the expenditure is within the total of any approved estimate.
4. Verification by the Treasurer that the amount of any subsidy or other approved contribution or of any expenditure to be borne by the Committee has not been exceeded. Any excess shall be reported to the next meeting of the Committee.
5. a) Expenditure in excess of £200 shall not be incurred without the prior approval of the Committee.
    b) Expenditure in excess of £100 but less than £200 shall not be incurred without the prior approval of the Chairman and the Treasurer of the Committee.
    c) Nothing in this article shall preclude the expenditure on any one occasion by the Worker of an amount not exceeding £100 or such lesser sum as may be agreed by the Committee without approval.

Income

The income to be accounted for shall include:
- Membership subscriptions.
- Attendance fees.
- Games fees.
- Government or European or other grants.
- Income from Credit Unions.
- Donations.
- Profits on sales.
- Coffee bar sales.
- Craft and other sales.

- Lettings income.
- Fund raising event income.
- Members' contributions.
- Bank deposit interest.
- Other sundry income.
- Monies for international and other residential work.

These and any other forms of income shall be recorded on the date of receipt in both the ledger and the bank paying in book.

General

1. The Committee or any officer of the centre may at any reasonable time seek the advice and aid of the Authority on any matter relating to the insurance, finances or accounts of the centre.

2. In the event of any irregularity affecting income, expenditure, cash, stores or any of the resources of the Authority or the Committee coming to their notice, members, officers, voluntary helpers or servants of the Committee or the centre shall immediately inform the Authority via the Worker who shall, similarly, immediately inform the appropriate audit division in accordance with the Authority's financial regulations.

3. The Authority undertakes to provide detailed guidance notes on:
   - Travel and subsistence claims.
   - Accountancy procedures and bookkeeping.
   - Corporation tax.
   - Pay as you earn.
   - Authority income.
   - Lettings.
   - Performing Rights Society.
   - Insurances.
   - Cash in transit procedures and insurance.
   - Grant aid.
   - Fundraising.
   - Orders, tenders and invoices.
   - Hire of other resources.
   - Retention of records.
   - Audit procedures.

4. The Authority undertakes to review this Scheme annually through the LJNC.

Part 10

Being Managed

The changing management practices

In youth, community and play work, many local authority employers are remote from management, many managers think they are employers and many management committees mismanage. Often theoretical management models have replaced practical management support at the individual level. Management is a good thing and should not be mistaken for the right to arbitrarily impose instructions. The right to manage is earned, to the extent that it incorporates consultation, negotiation, planning and support.

Another dilemma in this area of work is the proliferation of management levels each requiring a set of different approaches. Full-timers on JNC contracts manage part-time staff, part-time staff manage volunteers and other part-time workers and Officers on Soulbury contracts manage them all. Different approaches may be required for each category managed. All too frequently new management directions are generated by freelance consultants recruited outside normal equal opportunities procedures and who do not necessarily project employer-led initiatives. Reasonably objective inspection by Her Majesties Inspectors has been replaced by subjective freelance judgement linked to the price tag on the contract. As cuts take effect, sometimes management grades disappear and staff at the sharp end are left to sink, or swim without professional support. Some local authorities have gone so far as to say that if staff on JNC Level 3 contracts are getting paid so much why do they need managers above them! Additionally, as a result of cuts to in service training budgets, staff development policies endorsed by the NYA have not exactly proliferated in the last few years and those previously established have been forced to decay.

In this environment the notion should be re-established that employers must set clear policy directions in order that managers *can* manage, and *must* manage through clear lines of accountability, staff development policies and regular supervision. This should be done within a coherent framework of industrial relations whereby full recognition is given to the place of collective bargaining and the role of representative trade unions.

However, it will not be that simple. A number of very subtle management techniques have entered youth, community and play work. Usually inappropriately culled from industry and using 'buzz words' familiar in the new human resources 'management-speak', these techniques have begun to stifle informal education practice, de-skill and de-professionalise staff.

In summary, the independent engagement with clients previously supported and qualitatively assessed by monthly supervision and in service training, has been replaced with direct interference in the daily routine by quantitative assessment techniques. Some freelance trainers and managers have argued that, unless the service becomes more accountable in the wake of the *Coopers and Lybrand* report, the obsession with performance indicators and competence, in the terms of the current, but ephemeral, political interest, will not prove its worth. Inappropriate appraisal and monitoring techniques have been introduced in many places. It has been like judging the quality of Shakespeare by weighing one of his books on a meat hook. Not only has this trend proved stunningly ineffective, but it has soured the professionalism of workers.

Further still, as can be seen from the current penchant for a youth, community and play work NVQ, the deprioritisation of resourcing for peer-led endorsement, and support for Regional Accreditation and Moderation Panels within the National Youth Agency in England, the whole question of a qualified workforce, is for the first time being put in question. This occurs at a time when, as a result of market forces holding sway in the colleges, there have never been so many students in training.

Many new management techniques and training forms, like NVQs themselves, originate in private, manufacturing industry and always rest uneasily within education and service sectors and consequently get only partly translated. In youth, community and play work, it is the part translation that is the problem. The service has begun to speak a new language, a patois, part stock exchange, part conperson's dialect. An obsession with quality and mechanistic monitoring techniques have spawned in inverse proportion to the provision of the service. Fewer workers are left to deliver face to face work and the amount which they are expected to achieve and the volume of work they are expected to undertake increases as a consequence. In lean times, management is regrettably often about getting more for less.

The problems of assessing and developing the quality of the service have been compounded also by the break up of the specialist HM Youth Service Inspectorate and the introduction of the off-the-shelf Ofsted Framework for the Inspection of the Youth Service. This framework is welcome in that it begins to provide an objective set of criteria, but the criteria themselves are highly charged politically. They are highly charged because the framework consciously dismisses the idea of judging a service against the underlying resource base that would constitute an adequate or sufficient service in the circumstances. In addition it emphasises many of the quantitative, non educational aspects of the work.

Let me put the political changes more crudely still. If a community worker were approached by the local community to mobilise resistance to keep the local colliery open as an objective, rather than do an oral history or photography project with those involved in trying to save the colliery, their work would not fit easily into the appraisal techniques being used today. How would such a worker record the three hour secret meeting with the colliery manager? How would they justify visiting the jailed picket?

Alternatively, the youth worker working with a terminally ill young person for four hours a week is going to reduce their face to face work, because only one young person will benefit.

Both examples are real ones. Both were part of one worker's working life. Again the diversity of roles for skilled professional workers is something not easily appraised using many of the new methods.

Rather than introducing appropriate forms of social and educational appreciation for youth, community and play work, the unelected who have determined such matters, have seen the work as more like an uncontrollable person requiring a straightjacket. Though the sector has not been blighted by the nonsense of a national curriculum, nevertheless the unelected have moved on to alter the nature of the work by other means. The full story of this will have to be told elsewhere, but instead some observations follow on what is a significantly neglected aspect of the management relationship: what happens when a worker first enters the profession. Experience of the first year of work often sets the tone for the whole working career.

The probationary year

As far as the Government is concerned there is no longer a requirement to complete a probationary year in order to receive a Department for Education number confirming your status on a national register as a fully qualified worker. However, there is a section of the *JNC Report* on the probationary year. Given the history of the probationary year, there remains some inadvertent and less innocent ignorance within employing organisations of the exact purpose of a probationary year for a full-time worker on a JNC contract. Some have perpetuated the illusion for example, that a worker is not fully qualified after their college course until they have successfully completed the probationary year. This is not so. The points below should help to develop a clearer view of probation and support for workers in their first year after college.

What is probation?

Literally a trial by ordeal! Within youth, community and play work, it should not be so daunting. In a set of guidelines drawn up by the Council for Education and Training in Youth and Community Work (CETYCW—now known as the Education and Training Standards Sub Committee (ETS) of the National Youth Agency (NYA)) and in the *JNC Report*, the probationary year is depicted as enabling new entrants to make a significant contribution to the service within a year of completing training.

Probation is:

- An aid to the transition from initial training to full-time work in the service.
- To provide induction and in service training during the first year of work.
- To provide professional or non managerial supervision.
- To provide assessment at the end of the first year's work.

In other words, the probationary year is the first year for a newly qualified worker during which the employer should make necessary arrangement, for supporting them in all matters relating to good practice.

The probationary year is not:

- A form of qualification. Once a worker has their college certificate or diploma, or that element of their course which has been endorsed by the ETS and JNC for professional recognition, they are fully and finally qualified.
- An elaborate initiation into a secret society during which managers make subjective, unsubstantiated judgements as to a newly qualified workers' suitability for admission.

The use of the word probation and the way in which some employers use the probationary year clouds the issue. The threat of failing the probationary year is an unnecessary threat. All there should be is a first year of induction support, with particular mechanisms established for those entering full-time work within the service for the first time. Once a worker has qualified through whatever route they have taken, they are qualified; technically they can be immediately employed in any JNC level post. The first year in work should be viewed as a creative opportunity, with the onus on the employer to support the member of staff; it is not a test. The mechanism for getting rid of a member of staff not considered capable is the Disciplinary Procedure, not the failing of probation.

During the first year of work staff will undergo an employment probation which considers such matters as timekeeping, compliance with regulations and normally will last for around three months.

All new employees to any new post should receive induction training. This is particularly important in the first year of employment after training. The quality of induction is the employer's responsibility, it should involve the employer informing new staff of the rules, relevant contacts, procedures and systems which enable staff to operate their job descriptions.

In addition, all staff should receive regular supervision and have the option of non managerial supervision.

Three, possibly four support meetings, clearly distinguished into these categories, should be arranged for all new staff.

Small employing organisations within the voluntary sector will have extreme difficulty in complying with these professional requirements simply because of resourcing and staffing levels, and the high percentage of volunteers often involved. It is particularly important therefore to ensure that professional resourcing for first year induction support should be made available through the partnership with the local authority sector, or as part of a consortium with the voluntary sector. Resourcing for this support should be integral to service level agreements.

The first year of induction support should be an important feature of staff development. The absence of a nationally endorsed staff development policy in any employing organisation will considerably weaken its capacity to claim good employment practice. The *Guidelines for the Endorsement of Staff Development Policies* define such a policy as 'an agreed procedure for the joint and continuing identification of the training needs of each individual member of staff, and the systematic provision of training to meet them and the enhancement and enrichment of each individual member of staff through personal development, through job description, through job development and through organisational development.' A return to the importance of this is required.

Further reading and reference

See also Select Bibliography and List of Addresses in Appendices.

The following articles all appeared in *Rapport* available from CYWU:

Nicholls, D. (1991). New Role and Organisation for the Youth Service. August.

Williamson, Dr. H. (1994). 'Quality' Realities of the Youth Services. March.

CYWU (1994). The Future of Education and Training in Youth and Community Work and the Irrelevance of NVQs. November.

The Information team of the National Youth Agency provide an excellent reading list of material relating to Staff Development.

Ainley, P. (1993). *Class and Skill, Changing Divisions of Knowledge and Labour.* Cassells.

Association of Community Workers (1994). *Community Work Skills Manual.* Contains many useful sections relating to this chapter. There is an especially helpful section on supervision.

Fisher, Dr. J. (1994). ALM, Management Techniques. *Federation News,* 44:3, September. Available from CYWU Branch Secretaries and the General Federation of Trade Unions.

Maree, G. (1993). *We're Counting on Equality: Monitoring Equal opportunities at Work in Relation to Sex, Race, Disability, Sexuality, HIV/AIDS and Age.* HEE.

National Youth Agency (1993). *Report of the Working Party to Define the Core Elements of Youth and Community Work Training.* Useful for focusing on the nature of the work.

NCVO (1994). *Equality in Action.* NCVO.

NCVO (1994). *Planning for the Future.* NCVO.

Nicholls, D. et al. (1994). *Planning for a Sufficient Youth Service.* CYWU.

Smith, M. (1994). *Local Education.* Open University Press.

Tash, J.M. (1967) (2nd Edn. 1984). *Supervision in Youth Work.* YMCA

TUC (1994). *Human Resource Management.* London: TUC Publications.

Wandsworth Volunteer Bureau. *Key Elements of Good Practice in Working with Volunteers.*

Weaver, J. (1993). *How Much Did I Change the World Today: Evaluating Development Education; a Handbook.* The Development Education Project.

Part 11

Appendices

Appendix 1 Landmarks in the history of the struggle for part-time youth, community and play workers

1961

JNC established.
Bessey Report on part-time workers' training.

1973

The Community and Youth Service Association (CYSA—CYWU's predecessor organisation), the National Union of Teachers (NUT) and the National Association of Youth and Community Education Officers (NAYCEO) jointly undertake a survey into the disparities of treatment and employment conditions of part-time workers throughout the country.

1976

Standing Committee on Part-time Workers Issues formed in CYSA. (Moved by N. Pirie—Liverpool.)

1977

CYSA concerned that part-time workers did not get full union benefits in membership and resolved to change this.

1978

CYSA again reveals broad disparity in treatment of part-time workers throughout the country and seeks harmonisation linked to JNC rates.
Realities of Training. Major report on the training of adults who volunteer to work with young people.

1979

Conference calls for CYSA to negotiate parity for part-time workers through JNC. (Avon Branch moved.)

1981

Part-time workers' employment and role the subject of a special CYSA Conference.
CYSA forms Women's Caucus.

1982

P. Coughlin surveys terms and conditions. First major survey since 1973. Eight per cent of CYSA's membership are part-time workers.

1983

Conference forces Salaries and Tenure Committee (S and T) to do more work on negotiating under JNC. (Coventry Branch moved.)
Further survey on part-time workers conditions.
CYSA becomes CYWU.

1985

Part-time Workers' Caucus established.
Day Conference on and for part-time workers.
Starting From Strengths document on training produced. Student based learning.
Amalgamation Working Party seeks new deal for the Union to give all members equal benefits and services.
Black workers organise in CYWU.

1986

April: new S and T elected, all members particularly associated with the struggle for part-time workers within the Union.
May: S and T formulates strategy for national negotiations.
First inclusion of claim for part-time workers in JNC Claim.
Nov: JNC employers' first response to part-time claim.
JNC Working Party on Part-time Workers established.

1987

Jan: JNC Working Party on Part-time Workers meets. Reviews whole ground.
Feb: Working Party meets again.
Sept: Major article to agitate amongst CYWU membership on part-time issues in *Rapport*.
Strategy paper from General Secretary to NEC.
National CYWU campaign for part-time workers launched.

1988

March: CYWU negotiates equal benefits and services for all members.
April: Breakthrough. JNC scope extended to include part-time workers. Minimum conditions agreement made.
November: Major CYWU research on breaches of national agreement, costs of pro rata payment throughout the country and continued disparity in rates (N. Kyle, J. Lyford, P. Connor.)

1989

JNC Staff Side paper on part-time workers, continues pressing for parity.
March: CYWU releases further survey results.
Sheffield part-time workers surveyed for profile of qualification and work. (P. Connor et al.)
CYWU negotiates improved benefits and services for all members.
Sept: First JNC notification to employers that part-time workers must receive pay increases in line with *JNC Report*.
JNC Staff Side Equal Pay Working Party meets to prepare equal pay case.
CYWU and Unions win establishment of new JNC Working Party on part-time workers.

1990

Jan: JNC Working Party meets.

Feb: *Rapport* launches parity fight.
JNC Joint Secretarial Survey on part-time workers.
Feb: CYWU and NAYCEO sign Joint Charter on part-time workers.
May: CYWU negotiates precedent setting full parity deal for part-timers in Walsall.
June: JNC Working Party meets.
Value the Workers, Value the Service article in *Rapport*.
JNC survey and recommendations begin to emerge.
European Commission makes radical proposals on part-time workers parity this year.
Sept: JNC Circular on sickness and maternity pay and leave.
Oct: Lancashire CYWU submits paper to employers.
JNC Working Party meets.
CYWU Fights important tribunal on continuity of service and aggregated contracts.
Dec: JNC Working Party meets.
Consultation on endorsing RAMPs published.

1991

Feb: *Kowalski v Freie Hansesstadt* case sets precedent on equal treatment and parity.
JNC Secretaries visit Ealing and Wiltshire to examine work of part-time workers.
CYWU Policy Statement produced.
March: JNC Working Party meets.
JNC Circular agrees qualified worker working part-time over six sessions must receive parity.
Paper to Staff Side on European legislation. (D. Abse.)
CYWU prepares legal challenge.
Cuts in service and redundancies begin to bite.
May: CYWU negotiates new deal for part-time workers in Bexley.
Aug: CYWU battles against redundancies of part-time workers in Rochdale.

1992

Jan: CYWU launches petition for statutory base for youth service.
CYWU National Policy Statement published.
RAMPs for endorsement of part-time worker training begin to be established.
March: Somerset County Council Policy for the employment and deployment of part-time workers.
May: CYWU promotes awareness of part-time workers' rights.
CYWU members around the country play leading role in establishing RAMPs.

1993

CYWU lobby of Parliament.
Report of the Working Party to Define the Core Elements of Youth and Community Work Training advocates professionalism and high quality of qualification of all part-time workers.
TUC passes comprehensive motion of equality. (UNISON, IRSF, Soc. Radiographers.)
Oct: JNC survey of part-time workers' pay.
Nov: CYWU opposes experimentation of NVQs among part-time workers.

1994

RAMPs develop, first part-time workers' national certificates issued.
March: House of Lords judgement declares equality of treatment for part-timers required.
June: McNair and Now—JNC Claim prioritises parity again.
Sept: *Warren v Wylie and Wylie* case permits worker under eight hours to claim unfair dismissal.
Planning a Sufficient Youth Service published. Advocates staffing formula and *improved funding*.
The Future of Education and Training in Youth and Community Work published. Advocates education rather than behavioural assessment at work through NVQs.
Coventry and Hereford and Worcestershire commence new negotiations on part-time workers in the light of CYWU campaign.

First *History of Part-time Workers' Struggle in Youth and Community Work* is published.
Comprehensive guide to part-time workers' parity produced.
JNC Claim reiterates parity demand and unions press ahead.
Working Party established which culminates in full review of part-time workers agreements under JNC by ACAS.

1995

A new national Part-time Workers' Agreement under JNC.

1996

CYWU negotiates with all employers to implement the new national Part-time Workers Agreement.

1997

New local agreements complete in many employing organisations in England.

1998

CYWU presses national employers for review of implementation of National Agreement.
CYWU forms Part-time Workers' Issues Committee.

1999

New *JNC Report* published containing first comprehensive set of terms and conditions for part-time workers.

2000

JNC Staff Side presses employers to reduce the threshold for part-time workers' pay scales.
CYWU raises campaign to review local employers' implementation of the National Agreement.

Appendix 2 Matters dealt with in the *JNC Report*

List of approved qualification courses.
Conditions of service for full-time staff.
Conditions of service for part-time staff.
Scope of the JNC (i.e. it applies to all posts in the field even in voluntary sector).
Constitution of the JNC.
Equal opportunities.
Written particulars of terms of employment.
Qualifications.
Working time.
Sickness scheme.
Maternity scheme.
In service training.
Pension provision.
Leave.
Probation.
Periods of notice.
Grievance procedure.
Disciplinary procedure.
Official conduct.
Workers temporarily undertaking additional duties.
Grading structure.
Salary Ranges.

Choice of scale from ranges.
Appointment or promotion.
London area payments.
Additions for longer training or higher qualifications.
Payment of increments.
Compensation for residential duties.
Irregular working patterns.
Safeguarding and unqualified workers.
Appeals.
Interpretations.
Part-time workers.
Extract from *Trade Union Relations and Employment Rights Act 1993*.
Qualifications.
Notes on probation.
Grievance procedure.
Disciplinary procedure.
Grading criteria matrix.
Determination of the Authorised Establishment.
Guidance on the application of the trainee scale.
Salary scales and allowances.
Appeals against salary grading.

Appendix 3 Matters covered by the JNC Advisory Statement on Equal Opportunities in Employment booklet

Adoption and implementation of an equal opportunities policy

Introduction, reasons for adopting an equal opportunities policy, organisational/economic, social, image, legal. Implementing an equal opportunities policy. Control of the equal opportunities policy. Funding and resources. Making the policy known. Obligations on employees.

Positive measures

Positive action. Training bodies. Section 37, *Race Relations Act 1976*. Section 47, *Sex Discrimination Act 1975* (as amended). Positive action for women. Positive action to promote racial equality. Measures for other groups. Special provisions for people with disabilities. Induction. Health and safety. Integration into the workforce. Access and facilities. Adaptions and aids. Travel to work. Training. Existing employees who become disabled. Other special measures. Special provisions relating to sexuality.

Recruitment and selection

Policy. Job descriptions. Employee specifications. Application forms. Advertising policy. Internal versus external advertising. Format of advertisements. Methods of advertising. Use of outside agencies. Recruitment literature and job information. Selection. Shortlisting. Interviews. Tests. Record keeping. Complaints procedure. Health screening.

Training

Introduction. General considerations. Special programmes to tackle discrimination in the workplace. Training to improve employment practice.

Harassment

Procedures for dealing with harassment.

Analysis, monitoring and review

Introduction. Information requirements. Sources of information. Existing records. Questionnaire to existing employees. Information provided by job applicants. Information on the selection procedure. Other information. Review and targeting.

Outside financial help

The EEC Social Fund.

Assistance for employees with disabilities

Access and facilities. Adaptions and aids. Travel to work. Trial periods. General.

Legislation and codes of practice

Sex and race discrimination. Legislation, exceptions, genuine occupational qualifications, types of discrimination, positive action, making a claim, Commissions, *Race Relations Act—Section 71*. People with disabilities and the law. Code of practice on the employment of people with disabilities. Disabled persons register. The quota system. Records. Sexuality.

Appendix 4 Useful addresses

JNC Employer's Side
Layden House,
76–86 Turnmill Street,
London EC1M 5QU

JNC Staff Side
NUT, Salaries,
Hamilton House,
Mabledon Place,
London WC1H 9BD
Tel: 02073 886191

CYWU
302 The Argent Centre,
60 Frederick Street,
Hockley,
Birmingham B1 3HS
Tel: 01212 443344

Labour Research Department
78 Blackfriars Road,
London SE1 8HF

National Youth Agency
16–23 Albion Street,
Leicester LE1 6GD
Tel: 0116 285 3700

Centre for Organisational Health and
    Development
Department of Psychology,
University of Nottingham,
Nottingham NG7 2RD

Community Transport Association
High Bank,
Halton Street,
Hyde SK14 2NY

Royal Society for the Prevention of Accidents
Cannon House,
The Priory,
Queensway,
Birmingham B4 6BS

National Union of Teachers (NUT)
Hamilton House,
Mabledon Place,
London WC1H 9BD
Tel: 02073 886191

General Federation of Trade Unions Educational
Trust
Central House,
Upper Woburn Place,
London WC1H OHY

Equal Opportunities Commission
Overseas House,
Quay Street,
Manchester M3 3HN
Tel: 0161 833 9244

Commission for Racial Equality
Elliot House,
10–12 Allington Street,
London SW1E 5EH
Tel: 02078 287022

Trade Union Congress
Congress House,
Great Russell Street,
London CIB 3LS
Tel: 02076 364030
E-mail: info@tuc.org.uk
Website: www.tuc.org.uk

National Aids Helpline
Tel: 0800 567123
    0800 282445 Asian languages
    0800 282446 Cantonese
    0800 282477 Arabic
    0800 521361 Minicom service

The British Council of Disabled People (BCDP)
Litchurch Plaza,
Litchurch Lane,
Derby DE24 8AA
E-mail: general@bocdp.org.uk
Website: www.bcodp.org.uk

The Centre for Accessible Environments (CAE)
Nutmeg House,
60 Gainsford Street,
London SE1 2NY
E-mail: info@cae.org.uk
Website: www.cae.drc-gb.org

The Employers' Forum on Disability (EFD)
Nutmeg House,
60 Gainsford Street,
London SE1 2NY
Website: www.employers-forum.co.uk

The Royal Association for Disability and Rehabilitation (RADAR)
12 City Forum,
250 City Road,
London EC1V 8AF
E-mail: radar@radar.org.uk
Website: www.radar.org.uk

The Royal National Institute for the Blind (RNIB)
224 Great Portland Street,
London W1N 6AA
E-mail: helpline@rnib.org.uk
Website: www.rnib.org.uk
Textphone users call via Typetalk 0800 515152

The Royal National Institute for Deaf People (RNID)
19–23 Featherstone Street,
London EC1Y 8SL
E-mail: helpline@rnid.org.uk
Website: www.rnid.org.uk
Textphone: 08088 089000

The Trade Union Disability Alliance (TUDA)
36 Foxes Way,
Warwick CV34 6AY
Tel: 01926 402 195

NCVO Publications
Regent's Wharf,
8 All Saints Street,
London N1 9RL

Employment Services
Freephone helpline: 0800 848489
                     01324 583322
                     01612 281892
                     10214 564411
                     01923 210700

Appendix 5   **ACAS contact numbers and addresses**

ACAS can be used for the following:
- Free 24 hour, confidential phone advice.
- Booklets on a wide range of employment related matters.
- Free training.
- Arbitration, advice or conciliation in disputes.

Northern Region

Westgate House, Westgate Road, Newcastle-upon-Tyne NE1 1TJ.
Tel: 0191 261 2191

Commerce House, St. Albans Place, Leeds LS2 8HH.
Tel: 0113 431371

London, Eastern and Southern Regions

Clifton House, 83–117 Euston Road, London NW1 2RB.
Tel: 0207 388 5100

38 King Street, Thetford, Norfolk IP24 2AU.

Suites 3–5 Business Centre, 1–7 Commercial Road, Paddock Wood, Kent TN12 6EN.

South and West Region

Westminster House, Fleet Road, Fleet, Hants GU13 8PD.
Tel: 01252 811868

Regent House, 27a Regent Street, Clifton, Bristol BS8 4HR.
Tel: 0117 9744066

Midlands Region

Warwick House, 6 Highfield Road, Birmingham B15 3ED.
Tel: 0121 456 5856

Nottingham Office: Anderson House, Clinton Avenue, Nottingham NG5 1AW.
Tel: 01602 693355

North West Region

Boulton House, 17–21 Chorlton Street, Manchester M1 3HY.
Tel: 0161 228 3222

Cressington House, 249 St. Mary's Road, Garston, Liverpool L19 ONF.
Tel: 0151 427 8881

Bradshawgate House, 1 Oak Street, Accrington, Lancs BB5 1EQ.
Tel: 01254 871996

Scotland

Franborough House, 123–157 Bothwell Street, Glasgow G2 7JR.
Tel: 0141 204 2677

Wales

3 Purbeck House, Lambourne Crescent, Llanishen, Cardiff CF4 5GJ.
Tel: 02090 761126

Head Office

Brandon House, 180 Borough High Street, London SE1 1LW.

Appendix 6A **Memorandum of Understanding between the JNC and the Government**

Qualifying training for youth and community work
Professional endorsement and recognition

Scope

1. This is a memorandum of understanding between both sides of the Joint Negotiating Committee for Youth and Community Workers and the Department for Education on the subject of relative responsibilities and arrangements for the professional endorsement and recognition of qualifying training for youth and community work. It is concerned only with initial training leading to the status of qualified youth and community workers.

2. The parties to this agreement recognise that the Joint Negotiating Committee (JNC) has a legitimate concern with the standards of any training leading to professional recognition, since such recognition constitutes an entitlement to the provisions of pay and conditions of service for qualified workers laid down in the *Report* of the JNC.

3. Recognition, however, is the culmination of a process of academic and professional scrutiny and evaluation. The first stage, of initial academic validation, is internal to the institution offering the course. The second stage entails a full professional assessment of the academic and practical content of the course and its relevance to the objectives of youth and community work, and of the ability of the providing institution to realise its intentions within the resources available to it. This function, which we here term 'professional endorsement' is necessarily a centralised one, to be undertaken by a single body with the necessary authority and competence.

4. Recognition of courses as conferring qualified status requires a consensus between the representatives of youth and community workers and their employers: the two sides of the JNC. However, the JNC's concern is with the general principles governing recognition, and the broad categories of eligible qualifications, rather than with individual courses.

Future arrangements

5. Subject to formal agreement by the parties it is proposed as follows.

6. The Department for Education will ask the body known as the National Youth Agency (NYA) to undertake the professional endorsement of initial training courses leading to qualified youth and community worker status.

7. The NYA Executive Board will establish an Education and Training Standards Sub-Committee which will have delegated responsibility to grant professional endorsement to courses leading to a professional qualification in youth and community work. The Education and Training Standards Sub-Committee will also be concerned with the *endorsement of in-service training for full-time and part-time staff* and the accreditation of local authority and voluntary organisations' staff development policies, as set out in the Statement of Functions of the NYA.

8. The Education and Training Standards (ETS) Sub-Committee will be constituted by the NYA Executive Board in accordance with its memorandum and articles of association. The NYA Executive Board will appoint from its members a Chair of the Sub-Committee. Two places on the Sub-Committee will be reserved for JNC representation.

Relationship with the JNC

9. The JNC, in conjunction with the NYA, will agree the broad policy guidelines and general principles on which professional endorsement should be based. The NYA through its ETS Sub-

Committee will interpret and apply those guidelines and principles to courses and individuals and will notify the JNC which can then make appropriate amendments to its report.

10. The ETS Sub-Committee will have responsibility for the maintenance of standards by a continuity of surveillance, and for the continued monitoring of courses as well as their initial endorsements; it will assess courses and cases of individual recognition against the agreed criteria.

11. It is the intention of the JNC that decisions of the ETS Sub-Committee which are reached by the process outlined in paragraphs 9 and 10 will be accepted at a meeting of the JNC. These arrangements will be open to review at the request of either Panel of the JNC, or the DFE, or NYA through DFE.

Resources

12. The NYA and its ETS Sub-Committee will need the assurance of continuing Government support to provide the professional and supporting staff to undertake the professional endorsement function, in line with the arrangements set out in the statement of functions of the NYA.

Department for Education May 1994

Appendix 6B **Memorandum of Understanding in Wales**

Qualifying training for youth and community work
Professional endorsement and recognition
Scope

1. This is a memorandum of understanding between both sides of the Joint Negotiating Committee for Youth and Community Workers and the Welsh Office on the subject of relative responsibilities and arrangements for the professional endorsement and recognition of qualifying training for youth and community work. It is concerned only with initial training leading to the status of qualified youth and community worker.

2. The parties of this agreement recognise that the Joint Negotiating Committee (JNC) has a legitimate concern with the standards of any training leading to professional recognition, since such recognition constitutes an entitlement to the provision of pay and conditions of service for qualified workers laid down in the report of the JNC.

3. Recognition, however, is the culmination of a process of academic and professional scrutiny and evaluation. The first stage, of initial academic validation, is internal to the institution offering the course. The second entails a full professional assessment of the academic and practical content of the course and its relevance to the objectives of youth and community work, and of the ability of the providing institution to realise its intentions within the resources available to it. This function, which we here term 'professional endorsement' is necessarily a centralised one, to be undertaken by a single body with the necessary authority and competence.

4. Recognition of courses as conferring qualified status requires a consensus between the representatives of youth and community workers and their employers: the two sides of the JNC. However, JNC's concern is with the general principles governing recognition, and the broad categories of eligible qualifications, rather than with individual courses.

Future arrangements

5. Subject to formal agreement by the parties it is proposed as follows.

6. The Welsh Office will ask the body known as the Wales Youth Agency (WYA) to undertake the professional endorsement of initial training course leading to qualified youth and community worker status.

7. The WYA Management Board will establish an Education and Training Standards Committee which will have delegated responsibility to grant professional endorsement to courses leading to a professional qualification in youth and community work. The Education and Training Standards Committee will also be concerned with **the endorsement of in-service training for full-time and part-time staff** and the accreditation of local authority and voluntary organisations' staff development policies, as set out in the Statement of Functions of the WYA.

8. The Education and Training Standards Committee will be constituted by the WYA Management Board in accordance with its constitution (memorandum and articles of association). The WYA Management Board will appoint a Chair of the Committee. Two places on the Committee will be reserved for JNC representation.

Relationships with the JNC

9. The JNC, in conjunction with the WYA will agree the broad policy guidelines and general principles on which professional endorsement should be based. The WYA through its ETS Committee will interpret and apply those guidelines and principles to courses and individuals and will notify the JNC which can then make appropriate amendments to its report.

10. The ETS Committee will have responsibility for the maintenance of standards by a continuity of surveillance, and for the continued monitoring of courses as well as their initial endorsement; it will assess courses and cases of individual recognition against the agreed criteria.

11. It is the intention of the JNC that decisions of the ETS Committee which are reached by the process outlined in paragraphs 9 and 10 will be accepted at a meeting of the JNC. These arrangements will be open to review at the request of either Panel of the JNC, or the DFE, or WYA through DFE.

Resources

12. The WYA and its ETS Committee will need the assurance of continuing Government support to provide the professional and supporting staff to undertake the professional endorsement function, in line with the arrangements set out in the statement of functions of the WYA.

Appendix 7 Key publications on development and training for part-time youth, community and play workers

This list does not include many of the local training course outlines and induction materials that pioneered this area. I have selected the main national documents and asterisked those that seem to me particularly decisive in the development of training. The National Youth Agency has comprehensive holdings of materials, both local and national, relating to the history of training of part-time workers.

Anderson, C.J. (1975). *Participants in Part-time Youth Work Training*. NYB.

Bessey, G.S. (1961). *The Training of Part-time Youth Leaders and Assistants*. Ministry of Education: HMSO.

Bolger, S. and Cattermole, F. (1981). *The Loughborough Conference on the Training of Part-time Youth Workers in the National Voluntary Youth Organisations*. NCVYS.

Bolger, S. and Scott, D. (1984). *Starting from Strengths*. The Report of the Panel to Promote the Continuing Development of Training for Part-time and Voluntary Youth and Community and Play Workers. NYB.

Bradford and Ilkley College (1985). *Models of Part-time Youth Work Training. Eleven Profiles from the Yorkshire and Humberside Region*. Bradford and Ilkley College.

Bunt, S. (1989). *Appraisal for the Part-time Youth Worker*. Kent County Council.

Butters, S. et al. (1978). *Realities of the Training of Adults Who Volunteer to Work with Young People in the Youth and Community Service*. NYB.

CETYCW (1990). *Guidelines for the National Endorsement and Regional Accreditation and Moderation of Qualifying Training for Part-time and Volunteer Youth and Community and Play Workers*. CETYCW.

Chelms, S. et al. (1978). *Courses Advisory Panel Report: A Review of the Work of Tutors Involved in Training Part-time Youth Workers*. London Training Group.

Harper, B. (1983). *Better than Bessey? A Review of the Training Provision for Part-time and Voluntary Youth Workers in the Statutory Sector in England and Wales*. NYB.

Her Majesty's Inspectors (1986). *Report on Inspection of Part-time and Volunteer Youth Leader Training*. Rotherham.

Her Majesty's Inspectors (1989). *Report on Part-time Youth Work Supported by the LEA in the Cynon Valley District of Mid Glamorgan*. Welsh Office.

Her Majesty's Inspectors (1992). *The Training of Part-time and Youth Workers: A Report by the HMI*. DES.

Her Majesty's Inspectors (1989). *Report on the West Glamorgan Local Education Authority Stage 1 Course for Part-time Youth Workers*. Welsh Office.

Jackson, M. (1990). *Qualification, Regional Moderation and National Validation: A Consultative Document*. CETYCW.

Jardine, M. (1986). *From Strength to Strength: A Practical Resource for Unit Training*. NYB and NIAYC

JNC (1995). *Part-time Workers' Agreement*. JNC

JNC (1996). Circulars 101,101A,102,103, 104.

JNC (1999). Circular 121: *Access of part-time workers to in service training*.

JNC (2000). *Consultation on the Development of Occupational Standards for Youth Work*. PAULO: National Training Organisation

Kendra, N.S. (1985). The Demythologisation of Part-time Youth Work Training. *Youth and Policy*.

Lakeman, N. (1974). *For the Part-time Youth Worker*. NAYC.

Ministry of Education (1966). *Second Report on the Training of Part-time Youth Leaders and Assistants*. HMSO.

National Association of Youth Service Officers (1962). *The Recruitment, Training and Employment of Part-time Youth Leaders*.

National Youth Agency (1994). *Guidelines to Endorsement of Regional Accreditation and Moderation Schemes*. NYA.

National Youth Agency (2000). *National Occupational Standards for Youth Work*. NYA.

Norton, E., Ireland, D., Davies, B. and Nicholls D. (1994). *The Future of Education and Qualification in Youth Work, and Community Work and the Irrelevance of NVQs*. CYWU.

Ntuk-Idem, M.J. (1977). *An Evaluation of Basic Training for Part-time Youth Leaders*. Surrey County Council.

Pickles, M.B.R. (1974). *The Training of Part-time Youth and Community Workers*. NYB.

Redmin, W. (1987). *Knowing what you know: The Report of Phase 1 of the Portfolio Project: A DES Experimental Project*. Consortium of National Councils of YMCAs.

Scott, D. (1987). *Strengths and Competences of Voluntary and Part-time Youth and Community Workers: A Feasibility Study*. CETYCW.

Appendix 8 **Select bibliography**

See also further reading chapters at the end of each Part of this book.

Most of the information relating to part time workers can be found on the pages of *Rapport*, the national journal of the Community and Youth Workers' Union (CYWU). File copies are kept at the National Youth Agency, at the headquarters of CYWU and in many College libraries.

The next main sources of information concerning part-time youth, community and play workers are the records of the *Joint Negotiating Committee for Youth and Community Workers (JNC)*; these are kept by both the Employer's Side and the Staff Side Secretaries of the JNC. In addition the National Youth Agency holds comprehensive items on the question of training and qualification for part-time workers.

CYWU holds many model agreements, but it is hoped that much of the best practice has been outlined in this publication.

Abse, D. (1991). *Rights of Part-time Youth and Community Workers, in Relation to New European Legislation and European Court of Justice Rulings, and their Interpretations of Equal Pay/Equal Treatment Legislation*. Report to JNC Staff Side.

ACAS (2000). *Code of Practice on Disciplinary and Grievance Procedures*.

Adirondack, S. (1998). *Just About Managing? Effective Management for Voluntary Organisations and Community Groups* (3rd Edn.). London Voluntary Service Council.

Adler, S., Laney, J. and Packer, M. (1993). *Managing Women*. Open University Press.

Bartol, K. and Martin, D. (1995). *Management*. London: McGraw Hill.

Batsleer, J., Cornforth, C. and Paton, R. (1992). *Issues in Voluntary and Non Profit Management*. Addison Wesley.

Billis, D. and Harris, M. (Eds) (1996). *Voluntary Agencies: Challenges of Organisation and Management*. Macmillan.

Bloxham, S. (1993). Managerialism in Youth and Community Work. In *Youth and Policy*, Summer; No. 41.

Bolger, S. (1984). *Starting from Strengths*. NYB.

Bradford, S. and Day, M. (1991). *Youth Service Management*. Youth Work Press.

Callow, F. (1988). Part-time Youth Workers. *Rapport*.

Cattermole, F., Airs, M. and Grisbrook, D. (1987). *Managing Youth Services*. Longman.

Clarke, J., Cochrane, A. and McLaughlin, E. (1994). *Managing Social Policy*. Sage.

Connor, P. (1989). *Survey of Part-time Youth Workers (in Sheffield)*. Sheffield Polytechnic.

Coughlin, P. (1982). Part-time Survey. *Rapport*. Articles relating to the struggle for part-time workers.

Coulshed, V., Mullender, A. and Malahleka, B. (1992). *Management in Social Work* (2nd Edn.). Macmillan.

Cox, T. (1993). *Stress Research and Stress Management: Putting Theory to Work*. Nottingham: Health and Safety Executive.

CYWU (1986). *Salaries and Tenure Committee Minutes*, 19th May. (Atkins, S., Coughlin, P., Dibben, R., Gale, M., Lyford, J., Nevill, M. and Nicholls, D.) Prepares Part-time Parity Claim and Questionnaire.

CYWU (1989). *Report on the Survey Used to Construct a Profile of Part-time Youth and Community workers*. With Dickinson, A., Davies, N., Egan, L., Jacobs, M., Jones. A., Johnson, P., Keech, P., Lambert, P., Coughlin, P. and Wisher, S.

CYWU (1990). *Discussion Paper to JCC Sub Committee of Part-time Workers*. Lancashire CYWU.

CYWU (1992). *Youth Work and Community Work into the Twenty First Century*. Policy Statement.

CYWU (1993). *Against NVQs*. Leaflet to a Conference.

CYWU (1994). *The Future of Education and Training in Youth and Community Work and the Irrelevance of NVQs*. CYWU Policies.

Daniel, S. (1997). *Confidentiality and Young People*. Centre for Social Action.

Dawson, S. (1996). *Analysing Organisations* (3rd Edn.). Macmillan.

Ewing, K.D. (Ed.) (2001). *Employment Rights at Work*. Reviewing the Employment Relations Act 1999.

Flanagan, H. and Spurgon, P. (1996). *Public Sector Managerial Effectiveness*. Open University.

Fontana, D. (1989). *Managing Stress*. Routledge.

Forbes, D., Hayes, R. and Reason, J. (1998). *Voluntary But Not Amateur* (5th Edn.). London Voluntary Services Council.

Gann, N. (1996). *Managing Change in Voluntary Organisations*.

Gawlinski, G. and Graessle, L. (1988). *Planning Together*. Bedford Square Press.

Green, R. (1994). *The Ethical Manager*. Prentice Hall, Macmillan.

Grimwood, C. and Popplestone, R. (1993). *Women, Management and Care*. Macmillan.

Griseri, P. (1998). *Managing Values, Ethical Change in Organisations*. Macmillan.

Handy, C.B. (1986). *Understanding Schools and Organisations*. Penguin.

Handy, C.B. (1988). *Understanding Voluntary Organisations*. Penguin.

Handy, C.B. (1993). *Understanding Organisations*. Penguin.

Handy, C.B. (1997). *The Hungry Spirit*. Penguin.

HMI (1991). *Efficient and Effective Management of Youth Work*. DES (Ref 167/91/NS).

Holloway, C. and Otto, S. (1989). *Getting Organised*. Bedford Square Press.

Holmes, J. (1980). *Professionalisation: A Misleading Myth*. National Youth Bureau.

Hughes, O.E. (1994). *Public Management and Administration: An Introduction*. Macmillan.

Income Data Services, (1990). Part-time and Temporary Workers. *Employment Law Supplement*, 59.

Isaacs, A. (1993). Part-time Caucus Report. *Rapport*.

Jackson, M. et al. (1993). *Report of the Working Party to Define the Distinctive Elements of Youth and Community Work Training*. NYA.

JNC (1985). *Minutes of the JNC Staff Side Meeting*, 5th December. CYWU record strong intention to achieve parity under JNC.

JNC (1986). *JNC Staff Side Pay Claim*. First inclusion of substantial demand for part-time workers. (Staff Side Secretary at this time McFarlane, D.)

JNC (1986). *Minutes of the meeting of the JNC for youth and community centre wardens held on Monday 17th November*. Agrees to jointly examine the part time claim through a working party.

JNC (1986). *Minutes of the meeting of the JNC for youth and community centre wardens held on Tuesday 24th June*. Employers' first response to this claim.

JNC (1987). *Notes of the meeting of the JGSR (P/T) Working Party*, 13th February.

JNC (1987). *Notes of the meeting of the JGSR (P/T) Working Party*, Tuesday 6th January at the Education Department Leopold Street, Sheffield. (Employers Side: Stevens, M., Widdison, I., Cattermole, F., Fagg, V., Bowler, R. Staff Side: Coughlin, P., Lyford, J., Findlay, J., McFarlane, D., McGrane F.) Covered all aspects of parity.

JNC (1987). *Paper by the Joint Secretaries*. Part-time Workers, 25th February. (Debates definition of trained part timer. Defines as one who has completed locally recognised scheme. One obstacle is the lack of CETYCW endorsed local qualification courses.)

JNC (1988). *Joint Education Services Circular No. 5*, 7th April. (Part-timers brought within the scope of the JNC for the first time.)

JNC (1989). *Joint Education Services Circular No. 21*, 21st September. (First notification of part time workers pay increase.)

JNC (1989). *Notes of a Meeting of the Equal Pay Working Party of the Staff Panel of the JNC for Youth and Community Workers*, 16th May. (Nicholls, D., Robertson, H., Freeman, M. and McKee, A.)

JNC (1989). *Notes of decisions taken by the Staff Panel's Working Party at its meetings on 4th December*. (Corry, R., Tanton, M., Nicholls, D., Groom, P., Moore, B., Robertson, H., Fawcett, B., Freedman, M., McKee, A.) (Initiated visits to examine work in detail.)

JNC (1989). *Part-time Youth and Community Workers*. A Staff Panel Paper.

JNC (1989). *Staff Panel Circular No. 1*, 23rd February. (1988 Pay Increases.)

JNC (1990). *Education Employers' Bulletin No. 84*, 16th January.

JNC (1990). *Education Employers' Bulletin No. EEB/108*, 20th June.

JNC (1990). *JNC Survey Questionnaire*.

JNC (1990). *Joint Education Services Circular No. 36*, 28th September. (See in particular, Annex 1, Sickness and Maternity Pay and Leave.)

JNC (1990). *Joint Secretarial Questionnaire on Part-time Workers*.

JNC (1990). *Minutes of the first meeting of the JNC's Working Party on Part-time Youth and Community Workers*, 29th January. (Employers' Side: Edwards, M., Airs, M., Kingston, M., Hestor, M., Cattermole, F., Widdison, I., Main, K., Fagg, V., Walker, M. and Duncan, A. Staff Side: Nicholls, D., Corry, R., Robertson, H., Groom, P., Forde, D., Freedman, M. and Barrett, S.)

JNC (1990). *Minutes of the fourth meeting of the JNC's Working Party on Part-time Youth and Community Workers*, 10th December. (Employers' Side: Main, K., Widdison, I., Walker, M., Duncan, A., Fagg, K.V. Staff Side: Fawcett, B., McNea, C., Robertson, H., Sinnott, S., Freedman, M., McKee, A.)

JNC (1990). *Minutes of the second meeting of the JNC's Working Party on Part-time Youth and Community Workers*, 18th June.

JNC (1990). *Minutes of the third meeting of the JNC's Working Party on Part-time Youth and Community Workers*, 12th October. (Employers' Side: Airs, M., Main, K., Widdison, I., Walker, M., Duncan, A., Edge, M. Staff Side: Nicholls, D., Moore, B., Robertson, H., Corry, R., Tanton, M., Sinnott, S., Freedman, M., McKee, A.)

JNC (1990). *Notes for the Meeting of the Employers' Side of the Part-time Working Party*, 18th June.

JNC (1991). *Annex III* to the Circular immediately above *Report of the JNC Working Party, Part-time Youth and Community Workers*.

JNC (1991). *Annex V, Summary of the Views of the Employers' Side of the Working Party on Part-timers*.

JNC (1991). *Annex VI, Summary of the Views of the Staff Side of the Working Party on Part-timers*.

JNC (1991). *Annex VII, Recommendations in respect of pro rata pay and conditions for certain workers*.

JNC (1991). *Annex VIII, Recommendations in respect of hourly/sessionally paid part-time workers*.

JNC (1991). *Joint Education Services Circular No. 41*, 21st March. (Introduces further improvements for JNC qualified staff working part time.)

JNC (1991). *Minutes of the fifth meeting of the JNC's Working Party on Part-time Youth and Community Workers*, 12th March. (Employers Side: Main, K., Walker, M., Duncan, A., Fagg, K.V. Staff Side: Fawcett, B., McNea, C., Corry, R., Tanton, M., Freedman, M., McKee A.)

JNC (1993). *Survey of Part-time Workers' Pay*, October. CYWU.

JNC (1994). *Minutes of the working parties to discuss Staff Side claim for part-time workers.*

JNC (1999). New *JNC Report* incorporating part-time workers.

JNC. Circulars 101, 101A,102, 103 104.

JNC. *Joint Secretaries' Report to the JNC's Joint Working Party on Part-time Staff on visits to Wiltshire County Council and London Borough of Ealing.* Walker, M. and Freedman, M.

JNC. *Report of the ACAS Review of the JNC* in respect of part-time workers.

Keegan, G. (1989). Survey Results. *Rapport*, March.

Keegan, G. Survey undertaken by CYWU into local authority costs of paying pro rata rates. *Rapport.*

Keegan, G. Survey undertaken by CYWU into local authority pay rates for part-time youth and community workers. *Rapport.*

Keegan, G. Ten Local Authorities in breach of the JNC National Agreement. *Rapport.*

Kyle, N. (1988). *JNC Staff Panel Papers*, November.

Lawton, A. and Rose, A. (1994). *Organisation and Management in the Public Sector.* Pitman.

Lyford, J. Part-time Workers' Rights. *Rapport.*

Lyford, J. Part-time Workers: Towards One National Strategy at National and Local Level. *Rapport.*

Millar, G. (1995). Beyond Managerialism: An Exploration of the Occupational Culture of Youth and Community Work. In *Youth and Policy*, Autumn; 50.

Morgan, G. (1997). *Images of Organisation* (2nd Edn.). Sage.

Mullins, L.J. (1996). *Management and Organisational Behaviour* (4th Edn.). Pitman.

National Youth Agency. *Guidelines to the Endorsement of Regional Accreditation and Moderation Panels.*

Newton, T. (1996). *Managing Stress: Emotion and Power at Work.* Sage.

Nicholls, D. (1985). Class First For CYWU. *Rapport*, February.

Nicholls, D. (1985). Union Authority on Pay, Local Authority at Stake. *Rapport*, December.

Nicholls, D. (1986). CYWU Must put on the Pressure. *Rapport*, December.

Nicholls, D. (1987). Are You Serious? *Rapport*, May.

Nicholls, D. (1987). Branches to Build on Improved Offer. *Rapport*, June.

Nicholls, D. (1987). Community Workers Unionised: The Missing Link. *Talking Point*, No. 86, September. Association of Community Workers. .

Nicholls, D. (1987). Part-time Workers: Keep Up the Pressure. *Rapport*, September.

Nicholls, D. (1988). 1988 JNC Pay Claim. *Rapport*, September.

Nicholls, D. (1988). Part-time Workers Come Under the JNC Report. *Rapport*, April.

Nicholls, D. (1988). *Report to National Executive Committee.*

Nicholls, D. (1988). Single Status Workforce. *Rapport*, July.

Nicholls, D. (1989). Pay Claim Settled. *Rapport*, October.

Nicholls, D. (1989). Salaries and Tenure: a personal view of last year's work. *Rapport*, March.

Nicholls, D. (1990). CYWU Walsall Branch Wins Major gain for Part-time Workers. *Rapport*, May.

Nicholls, D. (1990). Part-time Workers' Charter with NAYCEO. *Rapport*, February.

Nicholls, D. (1990). Part-time Workers' Parity Fight: National Battle Begins in Earnest. *Rapport*, February.

Nicholls, D. (1990). Pride and Prejudice. *Young People Now*, No. 19.

Nicholls, D. (1990). Value the Workers, Value the Service. *Rapport*, June.

Nicholls, D. (1991). CYWU Wins Good Deal for Part-time Workers in Bexley. *Rapport*, May.

Nicholls, D. (1992). Part-time Worker's Rights. *Rapport*, May.

Nicholls, D. (1992). Valuing Part-time Workers. *Youth Clubs*, No. 69.

Nicholls, D. (1993). *CYWU Branch Support Pack*, July.

Nicholls, D. (1993). RAMPs, Less Bumpy Than Expected. Rapport, February.

Nicholls, D. (1994). Rebuild Community Work. *Talking Point*, No. 150, February. Association of Community Workers.

Nicholls, D. (1995). Victory for Part-time Workers. *Rapport*, April.

Nicholls, D. (1997). *Health and Safety in Youth and Community Work.* Lyme Regis: Russell House Publishing.

Nicholls, D. with Ireland, D., Norton, R., Davies, B., Adams, J., Thornhill, P., Weedon, M., Hutton, E., Beddoe, J., George, H., Griffiths, G. (1994). *The Future of Youth and Community Work Training.* CYWU.

Nicholls, D., with McCready, L. (1994). Part-time Workers' Rights. *Rapport*, July.

Nicholls, D., with McCready, L. (1994). Pay and Parity the Key. *Rapport*, July.

Nicholls, D., with Parker, B., Bell, A., Singh, J., Allen R. et al., (1994). *A Sufficient Youth Service.* CYWU.

Ofsted (1995). *Inspecting Youth Work, Inspecting Adult Education: A Framework.* Updated 1997.

Ofsted (1997). *Quality Assurance in Local Authority Adult and Youth Services.*

Pedler, M., Burgoyne, J. and Boydell, T. (1997). *A Manager's Guide to Self Development.* McGraw Hill.

Pearson, P. (2001). *Keeping Well at Work.* A TUC Guide. Trades Union Congress.

Pollitt, C. (1993). *Managerialism and the Public Services.* Basil Blackwell.

Ranson, S. and Stewart, J. (1994). *Management of the Public Domain.* Macmillan.

Rideout, Prof. R. (1994). *Briefing Note to CYWU Training Event.*

Rose, A. and Lawton, A. (1999). *Public Services Management.* Pearson Education.

Schafer, W. (1996). *Stress Management for Wellness.* Harcout Brace.

Smith, M. (1984). *Organise!* Booklet. NAYC Publication.

Somerset County Council (1992). *Policy for the Employment and Deployment of Part-time Youth Workers.*

Startks, M. (1991). *Not for Profit, Not for Sale: The Challenge of Public Sector Management.* Policy Journals.

Stead, D. (1992). *Facing Facts: The Future Delivery of Local Youth Services.* National Youth Agency.

Stewart, A. (1994). *Empowering People.* Pitman.

Tash, J.M. (1967) (2nd Edn. 1984). *Supervision in Youth Work.* YMCA.

Torrington, D., and Weightman, J. (1994). *Effective Management: People and Organisations.* Prentice Hall.

Trington, D. (1991). *In Search of Management Culture, Chaos and Control in Managerial Work.* Routledge.

Walsall MBC (1990). *Report to Committee on Part-time Youth and Community Workers.*

Winter, R. (1991). *Outline of a General Theory of Professional Competence.* The Anglia/Essex Asset Programme.

Wright, P. and Taylor, D. (1994). *Improving Leadership Performance.* Prentice Hall.

Young, K. (1992). Please Check Your Change. In *Young People Now*, February: pp. 38–39.

Appendix 9 **List of abbreviations**

This list contains past and current abbreviations that students and new workers may encounter. Organisations marked with an asterisk are still in existence and further details of them can be obtained on the CYWU website.

ACAS*	Advisory, Conciliation and Arbitration Service
ACU*	Active Communities Unit—Home Office Section
ACW*	Association of Community Workers
ALA	Association of London Authorities
ALBSU*	Adult Literacy and Basic Skills Unit
ALC*	Association of Labour Councillors
AMAZE*	Association of Christian Youth and Childrens' Workers
APL	Assessment/Accreditation of Prior Learning
APYCO*	Association of Principal Youth and Community Officers
ARA*	Anti Racist Alliance
ARQ	Alternative Routes to Qualification
BAC*	British Association for Counselling
BASSAC*	British Association of Settlements and Social Action Centres
BASW*	British Association of Social Workers
BCLA	Boys' Cub Leaders Association
BUM	Business Unit Manager
BYC*	British Youth Council
CA	Community Association
	Children Act
CAB*	Citizens' Advice Bureau
CATS	Credit Accumulation and Transfer Scheme
CDF*	Community Development Foundation
CDMF*	Community Dance and Mime Federation
CEDC*	Community Education Development Centre

CEO	Chief Education Officer
CEP	Community Education Project
	Community Enterprise Project
CEVE*	Community Education Validation and Endorsement (Scottish ETS)
CHAR*	Campaign for Single Homeless People
CHE*	Campaign for Homosexual Equality
CIPFA*	Chartered Institute of Public Finance and Accountants
CLS*	Community Learning Scotland
CM*	Community Matters
Cmnd	Command Paper
CNAA*	Council for National Academic Awards
Connexions*	Youth Support Services built on expanded former private careers companies.
CPAG*	Child Poverty Action Group
CPF*	Community Projects Foundation
CRE*	Commission for Racial Equality
CSNU*	Connexions Service National Unit
CVS	Council for Voluntary Service
CWVYS*	Council for Wales Voluntary Youth Services
CYWU*	Community and Youth Workers' Union
DDA*	Disability Discrimination Act
DETR*	Department of the Environment Transport and the Regions
DfEE	Department for Education and Employment
DfES*	Department for Education and Skills (Renamed DfEE 2001)
DLF*	Disabled Living Foundation
DoER	Department of Environment and the Regions
EAT	Employment Appeal Tribunal
EIEIO	Endorsement of Informal Education Interim Officers' Group
EO*	Employers Organisation
EOC*	Equal Opportunities Commission
E&T	Education and Training Committee (CYWU)
ET	Employment Tribunal
ETS*	Education and Training Standards sub committee of NYA and WYA
EWO*	Education Welfare Officer
EYCDC*	Early Years and Child Development Centre
FCWTG*	Federation of Community Work Training Groups
FEU*	Further Education Unit
FTA	Failure to Agree
GEST	Grant for Education Support and Training (DfEE)
GFTU*	General Federation of Trade Unions
GLA*	Greater London Authority
GLC	Greater London Council
GLCC	Greater London County Council
HAPA*	Handicapped Adventure Playground Association
HMI	Her Majesty's Inspectorate (See Ofsted)
IT	Industrial Tribunal
IWA*	Indian Workers' Association
JCC	Joint Consultative Committee
JNC*	Joint Negotiating Committee for Youth and Community Workers
JNCTP*	Joint National Council for Training in Play
LACSAB*	Local Authorities Conditions of Service Advisory Board
LEA	Local Education Authority
LGA*	Local Government Association
LGMB	Local Government Management Board (formerly LACSAB)
LSC*	Learning and Skills Council

LVSC*	London Voluntary Services Council
M1	Y&C Training Scheme (Northants, Beds, Bucks etc.)
MDC	Metropolitan District Councils
NABC*	National Association of Boys' Clubs
NACAB*	National Association of Citizens' Advice Bureau
NACRO*	National Association for the Care and Rehabilitation of Offenders
NAJJ*	National Association of Juvenile Justice Workers
NAPO*	National Association of Probation Officers
NATFHE*	University and College Lecturers' Union
NAYCEO*	National Association of Youth and Community Education Officers
NAYLO	National Association of Youth Leaders and Organisers—1963, CYWU
NAYT*	National Association of Youth Theatres
NCB*	National Children's Bureau
NCH*	National Childrens' Homes
NCN*	National Coalition for Neighbourhoods
NCVO*	National Council for Voluntary Organisations
NCVYS*	National Council for Voluntary Youth Services
NEWI	North East Wales Institute (Cartrefle Y&C Training Course)
NFDYW*	National Federation of Detached Youth Workers
NIACE*	National Institute of Adult and Continuing Education
NOGLYW	National Organisation for Gay and Lesbian Youth Workers
NPFA*	National Playing Fields Association
NSPCC*	National Society for the Prevention of Cruelty to Children
NTO	National Training Organisation
NUT*	National Union of Teachers
NVQ	National Vocational Qualification
NYA*	National Youth Agency
NYB	National Youth Bureau, Forerunner of the NYA
PAULO	Not an acronym, but a name for the short-lived NTO in our sector
PHAB*	Physically Handicapped and Able Bodied
RAC	Regional Advisory Council for further education
SACES*	Scottish Association of Community Education Staff
SCCD*	Standing Conference for Community Development
SCEC	Scottish Community Education Council
SEU	Social Exclusion Unit
SPRITO*	Sport and Recreation Industry Lead Body
SSC	Sector Skills Council
S&T	Salaries and Tenure Committee (CYWU)
SWAT	South Wales Apprenticeship Training (Y&C Apprenticeship scheme)
TAG*	Training Agencies Group
TC	Trades Council
TEC	Training and Enterprise Council
TUC*	Trades Union Congress
TUDA*	Trade Union Disability Alliance
VLFE	Validating Learning from Experience
WAFTYCW	Welsh Association for Full Time Youth and Community Workers
WAY*	Wales Youth Agency
WAYC*	Wales Association of Youth Clubs
YEC	Youth Exchange Centre
YMCA*	Young Mens Christian Association
YOT	Youth Offender Team
YSU*	Youth Service Unit (DfES Department)
YWCA*	Young Womens' Christian Association